50 0356237 5

330.156
BLA

UWE, BRISTOL
WITHDRAWN
LIBRARY SERVICES

UWE
University of the West of England
BRISTOL

BOLLAND LIBRARY

Please ensure that this book is returned by the end of the loan period for which it is issued.

UWE, BRISTOL B1085A.10.94
Printing & Stationery Services

AF795563

Michal Kalecki (1899–1970)

Pioneers in Economics

Series Editor: Mark Blaug

Professor Emeritus, University of London
Consultant Professor, University of Buckingham
Visiting Professor, University of Exeter

This important series presents critical appraisals of influential economists from the 17th century to the present day. It focuses in particular on those economists who were influential in their own time and whose work has had an impact – often inadequately recognized – on the evolution and development of economic thought. The series will be indispensable for a clear understanding of the origin and development of economic ideas and the role played by the leading protagonists of the past.

A full list of published titles in this series is printed at the end of this volume.

Michal Kalecki (1899–1970)

UWE, BRISTOL

19 JUN 1995

Library Services

Edited by

Mark Blaug

Professor Emeritus,
University of London

An Elgar Reference Collection

© Mark Blaug 1992. For copyright of individual articles please refer to the Acknowledgements.

All rights reserved. No part of this publication may be reproduced, stored in a retrieval system, or transmitted in any form or by any means, electronic, mechanical, photocopying, recording, or otherwise without the prior permission of the publisher.

Published by
Edward Elgar Publishing Limited
Gower House
Croft Road
Aldershot
Hants GU11 3HR
England

Edward Elgar Publishing Company
Old Post Road
Brookfield
Vermont 05036
USA

A CIP catalogue record for this book is available from the British Library

A CIP catalogue record for this book is available from the US Library of Congress

ISBN 1 85278 503 9

Printed in Great Britain by Galliard (Printers) Ltd, Great Yarmouth

Contents

Acknowledgements

The editor and publishers wish to thank the following who have kindly given permission for the use of copyright material.

Academic Press Ltd. for articles: A. Asimakopulos (1985), 'Kalečki and Keynes on Finance, Investment and Saving', *Cambridge Journal of Economics*, **7** (3/4), 221–33; D.M. Nuti (1986), 'Michal Kalecki's Contribution to the Theory and Practice of Socialist Planning', *Cambridge Journal of Economics*, **10**, 333–53.

Australian Economic Papers for article: Ferdinando Targetti and Bogulslawa Kinda-Hass (1982), 'Kalecki's Review of Keynes' General Theory', *Australian Economic Papers*, **21** (38), 244–60.

Basil Blackwell Ltd. for articles: Joan Robinson (1977), 'Michal Kalecki on the Economics of Capitalism', *Oxford Bulletin of Economics and Statistics*, **39**, 7–17; G.D.N. Worswick (1977), 'Kalecki at Oxford, 1940–44', *Oxford Bulletin of Economics and Statistics*, **39**, 19–29; Sidney Dell (1977), 'Kalecki at the United Nations, 1946–54', *Oxford Bulletin of Economics and Statistics*, **39**, 31–45; Wlodzimierz Brus (1977), 'Kalecki's Economics of Socialism', *Oxford Bulletin of Economics and Statistics*, **39**, 57–67; Edward Lipiński (1977), 'Michal Kalecki', *Oxford Bulletin of Economics and Statistics*, **39**, 69–77; Éprime Eshag (1977), 'Kalecki's Political Economy: A Comparison with Keynes', *Oxford Bulletin of Economics and Statistics*, **39**, 79–85; Robert W. Dimand (1991), 'Keynes, Kalecki, Ricardian Equivalence, and the Real Balance Effect', *Bulletin of Economic Research*, **43** (3), 289–92.

M.E. Sharpe, Inc. for articles: Peter J. Reynolds (1983), 'Kalecki's Degree of Monopoly', *Journal of Post Keynesian Economics*, **V** (3), 493–503; Claudio Sardoni (1984), 'Some Ties of Kalecki to the 1926 "Sraffian Manifesto"', *Journal of Post Keynesian Economics*, **VI** (3), 458–65; E. Ray Canterbery (1984), 'Galbraith, Sraffa, Kalecki and Supra-Surplus Capitalism', *Journal of Post Keynesian Economics*, **VII** (1), 77–90; Liliana Basile and Neri Salvadori (1984–85), 'Kalecki's Pricing Theory', *Journal of Post Keynesian Economics*, **VII** (2), 249–62; Peter Kriesler (1988), 'Kalecki's Pricing Theory Revisited', *Journal of Post Keynesian Economics*, **11** (1), 108–30.

Every effort has been made to trace all the copyright holders but if any have been inadvertently overlooked the publishers will be pleased to make the necessary arrangement at the first opportunity.

In addition the publishers wish to thank the library of the London School of Economics and Political Science and The Alfred Marshall Library, Cambridge University for their assistance in obtaining these articles.

Introduction

If you want to make an impact on contemporary economics, you must be in the right place at the right time and also you must publish in the right language. Michal Kalecki violated all three conditions: he discovered many of the basic elements of the Keynesian system three years before Keynes published his *General Theory* (1936), and he went beyond Keynes in embedding those elements in a model that incorporated the phenomena of imperfect competition, but he published these ideas in Polish while sitting in Warsaw. In 1935, when he finally published simultaneously in French and English, his ideas were expressed in abstruse algebra and were therefore ignored for a new reason. By the time of the appearance of his first books in English, *Essays in the Theory of Economic Fluctuations* (Allen & Unwin, Russell, 1939) and *Studies in Economic Dynamics* (Allen & Unwin, 1943), the Keynesian steamroller was in full swing and Kalecki was misunderstood as saying more or less the same thing as Keynes. It is only in recent years that the full measure of his economic ideas has been appreciated. Some post Keynesians, such as Robinson have even gone so far as to rank Kalecki above Keynes as a point of departure for the reconstruction of macroeconomics in the 1980s. This is a minority view. Nevertheless, Kalecki's reputation has continued to wax even as that of Keynes has waned.

Kalecki was born in 1889 in Lodz, Poland. He studied engineering at Warsaw Polytechnic and at Gdansk Polytechnic but never took his degree. In his twenties, he worked as a freelance economic journalist and from 1929 to 1937 as an analyst at the Polish Research Institute for Business Cycles and Prices. In 1940, having visited Britain several times in the preceding years, he joined the Oxford Institute of Statistics to work on wartime rationing schemes and to pursue his theoretical work on business cycles. In 1954 he published *Theory of Economics Dynamics* (Allen & Unwin, 1954; 2nd edn, 1965), followed in 1966 by the English translation of his first Polish book, *Studies in the Theory of Business Cycles: 1933–1939* (Basil Blackwell, 1966) and in 1969 by the translation of another Polish book, *Introduction to the Theory of Growth in a Socialist Economy* (Basil Blackwell, 1969). He returned to Poland in 1955 to serve as economic adviser to the Polish government and later as Polish representative to the United Nations; he was a leading contributor to the Polish Planning Commission's Perspective Plan, 1961–75, which however was made obsolete as soon as it appeared by Gomulka's fall from power. He died in 1970. Two posthumous collections of papers, *Selected Essays on the Dynamics of the Capitalist Economy: 1933–1970* (Cambridge University Press, 1971) and *Selected Essays on the Economic Growth of the Socialist and the Mixed Economy* (Cambridge University Press, 1972, are testaments to his productive life.

Perhaps the most interesting feature of Kalecki's economics is the way in which he starts from Marx and works out a Keynesian model of a long-run equilibrium growth by attributing all savings to capitalists, savings being simply a proportion of profits, and by assuming that firms set prices by marking-up average costs, the level of the mark-up being determined by the strength of their monopoly power. In so doing, he integrated business cycles and economic growth into one framework, even providing along the way a coherent argument for believing that capitalist governments would never in fact be able to sustain full employment levels of income for any length of time. Early versions of this theory were set out in equations and were often criticized for being tautological, that is, true by the definition of terms. Later, however, Kalecki put flesh on the mathematical skeleton by various theoretical arguments, supplemented by empirical results. The fact remains, however, that the model is available in four or five successive versions and much depends, therefore, on which version a friend or critic is discussing. This fact, in addition to all the other reasons previously mentioned, has reduced the impact which Kalecki might otherwise have had. Nevertheless, the continued influence of Kalecki, particularly on post Keynesian writers at the University of Cambridge in England, is amply demonstrated by J. Robinson and J. Eatwell's textbook, *Introduction to Modern Economics* (McGraw-Hill, 1973), large parts of which are pure Kalecki.

Note

Several paragraphs in this Introduction were borrowed from my *Great Economists Since Keynes* (Wheatsheaf Books, 1985).

[1]

MICHAL KALECKI ON THE ECONOMICS OF CAPITALISM

By JOAN ROBINSON*

1.

In the natural sciences it is common enough for the same discovery to come almost simultaneously from two independent sources. The general development of a subject throws up a new problem and two equally original minds find the same answer, which turns out to be validated by further work. In the history of economic thought, there is one notable example of this phenomenon, the discovery of the theory of employment by Maynard Keynes and Michal Kalecki. In the social sciences, experiments are not made in laboratories but thrown up by history. The problem to which they were both searching for an answer was the breakdown of the market economy in the great slump of the 1930's.

The orthodox economists were still reiterating the old doctrine of a natural tendency to equilibrium under the free play of market forces and enunciating the proposition that the central problem of economic analysis is the allocation of scarce means between alternative uses, as though the whole nation was a single peasant farmer deciding what to grow to feed his family. (This doctrine, in a garbled form, has been revived and, even today, is taught in the leading American textbooks.) It was not possible, in 1932, to deny that millions of workers were unemployed or that, in USA, national income had fallen to half its value of three years before, but these phenomena were attributed to 'frictions' that held up the working of market forces, to the folly of trade unions in preventing wages from falling further, or to a scarcity of gold that was constricting the monetary system.

Unshakable faith in equilibrium was derived from a conception that ran deep into the heart of orthodox theory—the notion that the growth of wealth for society as a whole, like that of a single family, depends on saving. 'Saving is a form of spending'; whatever an individual does not spend on consumption (giving employment in producing commodities for sale) is devoted to investment (giving employment in creating additional productive capacity in the form of capital equipment and stocks). The simple and obvious point, that occurred independently to Keynes and to Kalecki, is that in a modern capitalist economy, accumulation is not controlled by household saving but by the investments of profit-seeking firms. In the situation of the slump, investment was low because prospects of profit were weak and uncertain. Because investment was low, employment was low and incomes were low. Because incomes were low, expenditure was low. Therefore business was working below capacity and there was little demand for new investment goods (capital equipment and stocks).

Government expenditure on public works would create jobs and raise incomes. The wages, and later, profits would be spent, so that incomes and employment would increase. Each increase would lead to further spending. The total increase

* The lecturer is an Emeritus Professor of Economics in the University of Cambridge, England.

in income would be related by a 'multiplier' to the original outlay, while savings would be increased by as much as the original government expenditure.

To accept this point of view meant to admit that there is an inherent defect in the *laissez faire* system, that the concept of a natural tendency to equilibrium is mis-conceived, and that household saving is a consequence rather than a cause of capital accumulation. Since this went to the heart of orthodox doctrine, a stout resistance was put up. The Keynesian argument was still in dispute when war broke out in 1939. After the war, government policy in the capitalist world could not return to the prescription of complete *laissez faire*, but academic teaching (especially in USA) resisted every attempt to reconsider the orthodox position. Keynes' version of the new theory was emasculated and wrapped up again in equilibrium and Kalecki's version was simply ignored.

2.

In England the argument started, in 1929, with a debate about the case for Government loan expenditure on public works as a means of reducing unemployment. On the academic plane, Keynes was still working on his *Treatise on Money*. As soon as it was published, a great storm of argument broke out in Cambridge. By 1933 it was clear that what Keynes was looking for was not a theory of 'money' but a theory of the determination of output as a whole. In the summer of 1934 the main lines of the *General Theory of Employment, Interest and Money* had become clear, but the book was not published until 1936. I had been writing some essays drawing a number of riders from the main theory,[1] holding them back to be published when the *General Theory* was out. One of these appeared in the *Economic Journal* in June 1936.

Soon afterwards I received a letter, evidently from a foreigner visiting England, who said that he was interested in my article as it was close to some work of his own. I thought this very strange. Who could claim to be doing work that was close to this—the first fruits of the Keynesian revolution? When Michal Kalecki turned up, I was still more astonished. He cared little for party manners or small talk and plunged directly into the subject. He was perfectly familiar with our brand new ideas and he had invented for himself some of Keynes' fanciful concepts, such as the device of burying bank notes in bottles and setting off a boom in mining them.[2] As we talked, I felt like a character in a Pirandello play, I could not tell whether it was I who was speaking or he. But he could challenge a weak point in Keynes' formulation and quickly subdued my feeble attempt to defend it.

He told me that he had taken a year's leave from the institute where he was working in Warsaw to write the *General Theory*. In Stockholm someone gave him Keynes' book. He began to read it—it was the book that he intended to write. He thought that perhaps further on there would be something different. No, all the way it was his book. He said: 'I confess, I was ill. Three days I lay in bed.

[1] Some of these are republished in *Collected Economic Papers*, Vol. IV, Basil Blackwell, Oxford.

[2] *General Theory*, p. 129.

Then I thought—Keynes is more known than I am. These ideas will get across much quicker with him and then we can get on to the interesting question, which is their application. Then I got up.'

Kalecki did not make any public claim to his independent discovery of the *General Theory*. I made it my business to blow his trumpet for him but I was often met with scepticism. In USA, only Laurence Klein recognized (in the *Keynesian Revolution*, 1947) that Kalecki's system of analysis was as complete as Keynes' and in some respects superior to it.

At the end of his life, Michal told me that he felt he had done right not to make any claim to rivalry with Keynes. It would only have led to a tiresome kind of argument. Perhaps scepticism about my claim for him was due to the difficulty of believing that anyone was capable of taking this high line in our degenerate age.

The only reference Kalecki ever made to the question is in the preface to a selection of essays, published, alas, posthumously[3]: 'The first part includes three papers published in 1933, 1934 and 1935 in Polish before Keynes' *General Theory* appeared, and containing, I believe, its essentials'.

These papers establish, without any doubt, the fact of Kalecki's independent discovery of what is now known as Keynes' theory. Moreover, it was not only in Polish that he had publication priority over Keynes. He read a paper to the Econometric Society, in October 1933, on 'A Macro-dynamic Theory of Business Cycles'[4] which contains the basic elements of the theory of saving, investment and employment. At the same date I published a piece on 'The Theory of Money and the Analysis of Output'[5] which was a kind of interim report on how far the Keynesians had got by that time and it is now evident that Kalecki had got much further.

When Kalecki came to Cambridge in 1936, we told Keynes about him, but he was not much impressed. His own ideas were in full spate (he was thinking about rewriting the *General Theory* in a completely different way) and he had no patience with anyone else's. He picked on a phrase in the *Econometrica* paper that seemed to him too 'monetarist', though in fact it contained a point of view which he later came to himself. Keynes did not sympathize with Kalecki's political presuppositions and by background and temperament they could not have been further apart. I commented on this once, saying 'oil and vinegar would not mix'. Some critic objected that they are mixed every day, but they need constant stirring. Neither of these two characters was easy to stir. However, Keynes took the trouble to get a research project set up to provide Kalecki with a job. (This was just before the war and nothing much came of it.)

Although Michal behaved in public with a kind of scholarly dignity which is nowadays all too rare, he was naturally disappointed at lack of recognition. He said to me once: 'in the economics profession, no one notices the difference between good work and rubbish'. (I have been disappointed by this myself.)

[3] *Selected Essays on the Dynamics of the Capitalist Economy, 1933–70*. Cambridge University Press, 1971.

[4] *Econometrica*, No. 3, 1935.

[5] Reprinted in *Collected Economic Papers*, Vol. I.

3.

The important question is not about priority, but about the content of the theories. In several respects, Kalecki's version is more robust than Keynes'.

Theory of Prices. (Keynes' treatment of the prices of particular commodities was rather vague.) Orthodox teaching was that of Pigou—under competitive conditions, each firm produces such an output that marginal cost equals price, provided that price exceeds average prime cost. This can be illustrated by a diagram. In the short-period case, with given plant, Pigou's U-shaped curves can be reduced to a reversed L, with constant average prime cost (APC) up to capacity output.

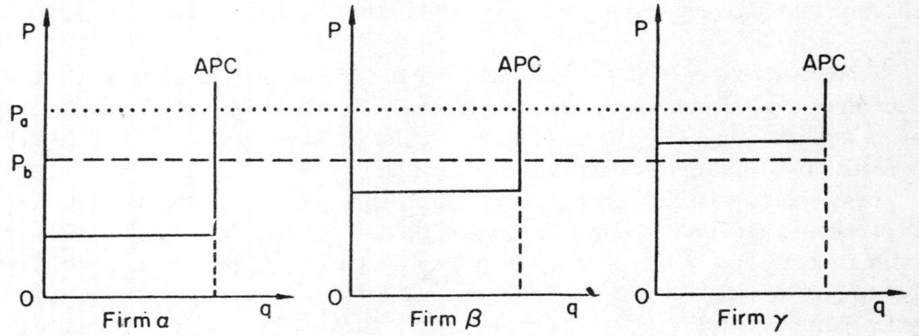

When the price of the commodity being produced is OP_a all three firms are producing it. When it is at OP_b, the two low cost plants continue to produce and the high cost plant (firm γ) has been put into moth balls.

This theory requires that any plant that is working at all is working to capacity, but in the slump, obviously nearly all plants were working part time, and yet prices did not fall to equality with prime cost. Profit margins held up, even when marginal cost was no greater than average prime cost. The 'marginal revenue' concept was brought in to explain this phenomenon, but Keynes did not use it. (He introduced the idea of 'user cost', (the loss of value of equipment due to using it rather than leaving it idle) to reconcile competition with the evident fact that a profit margin entered into supply price even in a deep slump. This theory does not correspond to business behaviour. His elaboration of it did not take root and it has faded out in the post-Keynesian tradition.)

Kalecki opened up a more promising line. He divided the price system into two parts. In the trade in raw materials, supply and demand rules. In manufacturing industry, prices are set by the producer; the profit margin that he is able to enjoy (the excess of price over average prime costs) depends upon the 'degree of monopoly' in the market where he sells.

The expression degree of monopoly has been misunderstood. Kalecki has been accused of reducing it to circularity by defining the degree of monopoly as the ratio of the gross margins to prices. What it means is the absence of price competition (there are other forms of competition in salesmanship, product differentiation etc.).

The weaker is price competition in any market, the greater is the freedom of firms to set prices in excess of costs. The ratio of margins to prices is a symptom of the degree of monopoly.

Kalecki at first advanced his theory in strictly short-period terms and he argued that the overall degree of monopoly in industry as a whole is all that is needed to account for the shares of wages and gross profits. I objected that there must be some long-period element in the relation of prices to costs. The ratio of overheads to prime costs, which varies between industries for technical reasons, must have some influence on the gross profits that they require. Kalecki met this by suggesting that firms with high overheads act in tacit agreement to 'protect their profits'. This was an admission of long-period influences on the formation of prices but it was not well integrated into the short-period analysis.

The old 'full cost' doctrine went to the other extreme. It appeared to hold that prices of manufactures are determined solely by average cost, which would imply that prices fall when demand increases because overheads are spread over a larger output. This argument was put forward in ideological terms to defend businessmen from the implication that they behave monopolistically. The modern theory of administered prices is closer to Kalecki's view, for it means that producers set prices in advance of knowing sales, but it admits a long-period element into the process in the sense that firms are assumed to take account of average costs for a standard output. The realized net profit varies with the relation of actual to standard output.

The latest views advanced, for instance by Adrian Wood[6] and A. S. Eichner,[7] is that large firms set prices in such a way as to abstract from the market as much net profit as they need to finance the investment that they plan to carry out (taking account of the retention ratio and the gearing ratio that they maintain).

Such theories can never be quite convincing for motivation in business is multidimensional and cannot be squeezed into a simple formula; moreover in modern conditions a market does not exist independently of the commodities which innovating firms choose to offer for sale. The question of the formation of profit margins still needs more investigation.

Unfortunately, it will never be possible to get a knock-down answer, for investigation is concerned with *ex post* results, not with *ex ante* decisions. But in any case, it was the principle of the 'degree of monopoly', that is the absence of price-competition, that opened up the question.

The importance of the determination of profit margins as an influence in the level of real wages, which Kalecki stressed, is now generally recognized, and so is the influence upon industrial prices of the fluctuations in the markets for raw materials, governed by supply and demand. (As OPEC reminds us, the degree of monopoly has to be brought into the theory of that kind of market as well.)

The importance of Kalecki's line of argument was in integrating the analysis of prices with the analysis of effective demand. Before Keynes, they were kept in two separate boxes; in America now the division between micro and macro theory

[6] *A Theory of Profits*, C.U.P., 1975.
[7] *The Megacorp and Oligopoly*, C.U.P., 1976.

is more complete than ever; but no progress can be made with either until they are united in a truly general theory.

Savings and Investment. A powerful simplification that Kalecki introduced into the theory of distribution is the assumption that earned income is generally spent week by week as it is received, while expenditure out of unearned income (rent, interest and dividends) does not immediately react to a change in receipts (moreover, changes in profits are not immediately passed on in dividends).

He was then able to sum up the whole theory of effective demand as follows:

> We may consider first the determinants of profits in a closed economy in which both government expenditure and taxation are negligible. Gross national product will thus be equal to the sum of gross investment (in fixed capital and inventories) and consumption. The value of gross national product will be divided between workers and capitalists, virtually nothing being paid in taxes. The income of workers consists of wages and salaries. The income of capitalists or gross profits includes depreciation and undistributed profits, dividends and withdrawals from unincorporated business, rent and interest. We thus have the following balance sheet of the gross national product, in which we distinguish between capitalists' consumption and workers' consumption:
>
> | | |
> |---|---|
> | Gross profits | Gross investment |
> | Wages and salaries | Capitalists' consumption |
> | | Workers' consumption |
> | Gross national product | Gross national product |
>
> If we make the additional assumption that workers do not save, then the workers' consumption is equal to their income. It follows directly then:
>
> Gross profits = Gross investment + capitalists' consumption.
>
> What is the significance of this equation? Does it mean that profits in a given period determine capitalists' consumption and investment, or the reverse of this? The answer to this question depends on which of these items is directly subject to the decisions of capitalists. Now, it is clear that capitalists may decide to consume and to invest more in a given period than in the preceding one, but they cannot decide to earn more. It is, therefore, their investment and consumption decisions which determine profits, and not vice versa.[8]

Nowadays, so much stress is laid upon retained profits as the source of finance for investment that we are in danger of slipping back into a new kind of Say's Law, and forgetting that saving cannot take place without investment to generate an excess of income over consumption. Last year's retained profits may be financing this year's investment, and this year's retentions may be going to finance investment

[8] *Selected Essays, op. cit.* p. 78 *et seq.*

next year, but the profits accruing this year are the result of this year's expenditure on investment and capitalists' consumption.

Kalecki's way of setting out the essential principle of effective demand avoids two weak points in the Keynes' formulation. The first is the concept of the 'propensity to consume'. Keynes relies upon a psychological law that men are disposed to increase their consumption as their income increases, but not by as much as the increase in their income. Kalecki separates the 'men' into workers and capitalists and incomes into wages, which will be fully spent as they are received, and profits, of which a proportion will be handed over to rentiers (with a time lag) and partly spent by them. For Keynes, 'men' and their incomes are undifferentiated, while for Kalecki the overall relation of national income to consumption is strongly influenced by its distribution between work and property.

The second point of difference with Keynes concerns the proposition that 'savings equals investment', over which we made very heavy weather in the early stages of the Keynesian revolution. Kalecki simply asserts that a rise in the rate of investment will increase the flow of wages, which will be spent, and if the accompanying rise in profits causes an increase in spending out of dividends, profits will rise by so much the more. Thus there is an increase in retained profits equal to the increased outlay on investment.

After working out the pure model, Kalecki brings back the budget, the foreign balance and intermediate incomes which combine earning and saving. This provides all the essential elements of the theory of effective demand, but it lacks the exposition of the multiplier, which makes the Kahn–Keynes version more persuasive.

The monetary aspect of the theory was much more fully elaborated by Keynes, but Kalecki was the first to emphasize that finance has to be available before investment begins, while saving comes afterwards. This was the point over which Keynes stumbled when we showed him the *Econometrica* article.

Money-wage Rates. Kalecki joined with Keynes in attacking the then prevalent view that cutting wages was the best way to increase employment. Keynes argued that an all-round cut in money-wage rates would reduce prices more or less equally, so that real wages would not fall, but the burden of debt would be increased and investment discouraged. Kalecki argued that if prices did *not* fall, real wages would be cut, and unemployment would increase because of the fall in demand for wage-goods. Kalecki was not very keen on pressing the reverse argument, that rising money-wage rates raise prices and fail to raise real wages. He was very suspicious of those who use the problem of inflation to attack the trade unions. The last essay that he published is an analysis of 'Class Struggle and Distribution of National Income'.[9]

The Short-Period theory of distribution. There are two elements in Kalecki's analysis of profits, the share of gross profit in the product of industry is determined

[9] *Selected Essays, op. cit.*

by the level of gross margin, while the total flow of profits per annum depends upon the total flow of capitalists' expenditure on investment and consumption.

Combining these two theories, we find the very striking proposition that firms, considered as a whole, cannot increase their profits merely by raising prices. Raising profit margins reduces real wages and consequently employment in wage-good industries. The *share* of profit is increased but the total profits remain equal to the flow of capitalists' expenditure. (Kalecki argued that the mere expectation of higher profits will not increase expenditure, for the firms would wait to see if more profits were going to accrue, and, for firms as a whole, they will not.)

This argument is illustrated as follows:

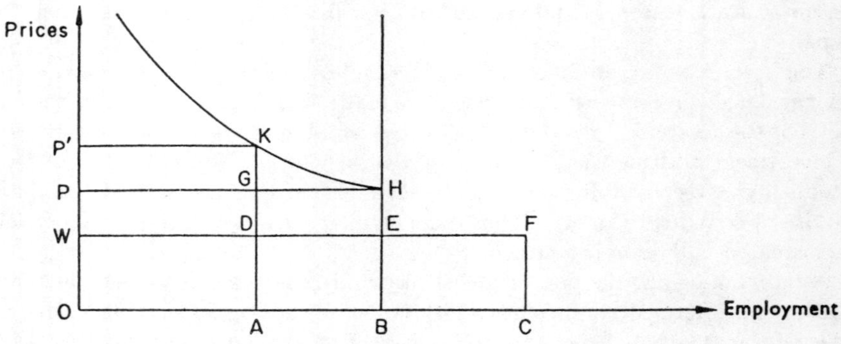

The x axis measures employment and the y axis prices. BC represent employment in the investment sector, and OW·BC its wage bill. Profit on the sale of consumption goods is represented by a rectangular hyperbola subtending an area equal to OW·BC, above the WF line (consumption out of profits is omitted for simplicity).

When the competitive price level, OP, rules, employment in the consumption sector is OB: at the price level OP', employment in that sector is OA and unemployment AB, if employment in the investment sector remains unchanged.

In this way, Kalecki was able to weave the analysis of imperfect competition and of effective demand together and it was this that opened up the way for what goes under the name of post-Keynesian economic theory.

The Trade Cycle. Kalecki provided the first coherent model of the mechanism of a self-repeating trade cycle (Kaldor, Goodwin and many others have built on his foundations). The clue to his analysis is the distinction between investment decisions and actual investment outlay. Today, plans are being laid for investment in the light of expectations held today. If prospects are such that investment plans exceed current investment, then current investment will be higher in the next period; consequently profits will be higher, expectations will be higher, and so the 'self winding up' process of boom is under way. Meanwhile the stock of productive capacity is gradually growing, and when the growth of capacity overtakes the growth of current production, utilization falls, prospects of profit are dimmed and the boom collapses.

As with all such models, the theory of an automatic recovery from a slump was rather weak, and Kalecki later gave up the search for a 'pure' trade cycle and sought for an analysis combining fluctuations in activity with accumulation over the long run.

The Marginal Efficiency of Capital. The distinction between investment and investment decisions enabled Kalecki to clear up the confusion in Keynes' treatment of the inducement to invest. Keynes set up a schedule of the 'marginal efficiency of capital' (comparable with the rate of interest), for various levels of investment, and he argued that it must be a diminishing function of the rate of investment because, *first*, in the short run, a higher rate of investment raises the relative cost of capital goods, and, *secondly*, when it has been completed, a larger stock of capital depresses the prospect of profits.

Here Keynes had lost his grip on his own theory. The inducement to invest is supposed to depend upon *expectations* of future profits. These must be partly subjective, in the minds of individual businessmen, and they must depend largely on the current level of profits, which is influenced by the current level of investment. An increase in the rate of investment today would raise current profits all round and the influence of this in raising expected profits for individual firms would far outweigh any change in costs that it might cause.

Keynes' schedule of m.e.c. collapses future time into the present moment, confusing the forward-looking expectations of profits of individual firms with the profits that will be realized for industry as a whole. Moreover, he projects the argument into the long run and assumes that a larger stock of capital will entail a lower rate of profit, thus relapsing into the 'classical' theory he intended to combat.

Kalecki sorts the analysis out; conditions today influence investment decisions being taken, and they will affect the conditions that prevail in the future when they are being carried out.

Keynes fell into another confusion. He argues that the rate of investment, at any moment, will be such as to equate the marginal efficiency of capital (that is, the expected rate of profit) to the rate of interest. This is a fudge to begin with, because marginal efficiency of capital is related to the rate of interest by an allowance for risk which varies with the state of confidence. Letting that pass, how can it be true that the amount of investment firms plan to make, over the immediate future, is limited only by the cost of borrowing? The amount of finance that a firm can command, as Kalecki pointed out, depends upon its liquidity and its credit standing. The distribution of borrowing power between firms depends upon their existing capital and their past success. The rate of investment is not regulated by *the* rate of interest which is the same for everybody.

Kalecki was free from the remnants of old-fashioned theory which Keynes had failed to throw off. He could see through these confusions at the first glance. His amendments are completely in line with the main argument of the *General Theory*. Kalecki gets Keynes back onto the rails where his 'classical' education had led him astray.

The Political Trade Cycle. The most famous of all Kalecki's insights into the economics of capitalism is contained in a short article published in 1943 on 'Political aspects of full employment.'[10] He predicted that, when governments understand how they can maintain full employment by budgetary policy, they will not really want to do so, because continuous full employment would undermine the power of business leaders to control the workers and to keep down wages. On the other hand, too much unemployment is not popular with the electorate. Thus he predicted that after the war we should experience a political trade cycle with alternating *stop* and *go.*

The final paragraphs of the article make sad reading after 30 years experience of how accurate Kalecki's prediction turned out to be:

> Should a progressive be satisfied with a regime of the 'political business cycle' as described in the preceding section? I think he should oppose it on two grounds: (i) that it does not assure lasting full employment; (ii) that Government intervention is tied down to public investment and does not embrace subsidizing consumption. What the masses now ask for is not the mitigation of slumps but their total abolition. Nor should the resulting fuller utilization of resources be applied to unwanted public investment merely in order to provide work. The Government spending programme should be devoted to public investment only to the extent to which such investment is ***actually needed.*** The rest of Government spending necessary to maintain full employment should be used to subsidize consumption (through family allowances, old age pensions, reduction in indirect taxation, subsidizing of prices of necessities). The opposers of such Government spending say that the Government will then have nothing to show for their money. The reply is that the counterpart of this spending will be the higher standard of living of the masses. Is not this the purpose of all economic activity?
>
> 'Full employment capitalism' will have, of course, to develop new social and political institutions which will reflect the increased power of the working class. If capitalism can adjust itself to full employment a fundamental reform will have been incorporated in it. If not, it will show itself an outmoded system which must be scrapped.
>
> But perhaps the fight for full employment may lead to fascism? Perhaps capitalism will adjust itself to full employment in *this* way? This seems extremely unlikely. Fascism sprang up in Germany against a background of tremendous unemployment and maintained itself in power through securing full employment while capitalist democracy failed to do so. The fight of the progressive forces for full employment is at the same time a way of *preventing* the recurrence of fascism.

Long Run Growth. From the first, Kalecki was trying to broaden the theory of investment to include a theory of accumulation over the long run, but he was never satisfied that he had got to the bottom of it.

[10] *Political Quarterly* No. 4, 1943.

In the preface referred to above he wrote:

> It is interesting to notice that the theory of effective demand, already clearly formulated in the first papers, remains unchanged in all the relevant writings, as do my views on the distribution of national income. However, there is a continuous search for new solutions in the theory of investment decisions, where even the last paper represents—for better or for worse—a novel approach.

I had a running argument with Michal on this subject. He regarded my use of the concept of 'animal spirits' as somehow irrational (though to me it was only a modification of the Marxian imperative: 'Accumulate! Accumulate! That is Moses and the Prophets'). He maintained that new inventions raise prospects of profit and stimulate investment. I pointed out that, according to his own theory, if steady accumulation is maintained, the rate of profit on capital will be constant.

In the end we compromised on the view, set out in this last paper, that inventions raise the prospect of profit for the technically progressive firms that make innovations, not the average realized profit for industry as a whole.

Though Kalecki liked to express his ideas in neat formulae, he was always conscious of the limitations of that style of exposition, and set his arguments against the background of history, politics and institutional change.

In the United States, Keynes' theory was melted down and moulded into a 'neoclassical synthesis', but Kalecki proved indigestible and was simply ignored. Now that disillusionment with the synthesis is setting in, perhaps he will get a hearing at last.

Faculty of Economics,
University of Cambridge,
England.

[2]

KALECKI AT OXFORD, 1940–44

By G. D. N. Worswick*

Introduction

Michal Kalecki joined the staff of the Oxford University Institute of Statistics (as it was then called) at the beginning of 1940. He was at the height of his intellectual powers, and during the next five years he maintained an astonishing flow of original ideas, large and small. In an age of increasing specialization the characteristic of his approach to economic theory was that it was integrated: the best example is the way in which the new ideas of monopolistic competition were tied into his dynamic theory of economic fluctuations. Any classification of his work under different headings thus runs the risk of making artificial distinctions, but if we bear this in mind we can separate the work which Kalecki did for the Institute's official programme, which took the greater part of his time, from the continued development of his theory of the dynamics of a (non-war) capitalist economy which had been most recently published in 1939 in *Essays in the Theory of Economic Fluctuations* and was to lead to *Studies in Economic Dynamics*, published in 1943. This latter work is discussed by Joan Robinson, and I will confine myself to his work on the Institute's programme.

A brief word on the Institute itself must be inserted here before I come to Kalecki's particular contribution. The Institute was started in 1935 with the intention of introducing statistics into social studies in Oxford. From earliest days the research undertaken was predominantly economic and there were informal links with the Oxford Economists' Research Group which brought together dons interested in empirical work, in the wider sense. The best known activities of the research group were the enquiries leading to the Meade/Andrews paper on the rate of interest and the Hall/Hitch paper on pricing behaviour.[1] Among the main projects begun at the Institute itself was a large scale statistical study of the mobility of labour.

The Institute had been launched with a grant from the Rockefeller Foundation and when the war came the Foundation decided it would continue to support a programme of monitoring and studying the British war economy. In the first year of the war there were many changes in personnel at the Institute. Most of the dons in the Economists' Research Group and some of the research staff of the Institute went off to Whitehall in one capacity or another, or, as in the case of Henry Phelps Brown, joined the army. Within a year only Ian Bowen of the original members remained and he was soon to go off to the Ministry of Works, but not before he had made arrangements with Blackwells to launch the three-weekly *Bulletin*. Jacob Marshak, the Director, was in the United States when war broke out and he did not return. To replace him Professor Arthur Bowley, who had

* The lecturer is Director of the National Institute of Economic and Social Research, London.

[1] *Oxford Economic Papers* (old series) Nos. 1 & 2, October 1938 and May 1939.

already retired from the London School of Economics, came out of retirement on a half-time basis to take the directorship. There were a few fairly recent graduates on the junior staff: Philip Andrews, John Buckatzsch, Goronwy Daniel, Alec Ellis, Leonard Nicholson and myself and later on Peter Ady, and Mary Gisborne had already started her life-long association with the Institute. The remaining posts were gradually filled by economists who were in different degrees refugees. Burchardt and Moos had arrived in Oxford before the war and soon they were joined by Mandelbaum, Miss Schulz, Schumacher and Uhlich from Germany, Forcheimer, Halpern and Steindl from Austria, Balogh from Hungary, Goldmann from Czechoslovakia and Frankel and Kalecki from Poland.

War Finance

Kalecki's assignment in the Institute's programme was War Finance. He wrote regular analyses of the financial situation, especially of Budgets. In those days the statistical information on which to base an analysis was minimal. Nevertheless these articles, some of which are reprinted in *Studies in War Economics* (Blackwell 1947), though short, go directly to the main issues. He had a very clear idea of the role of the financial system in a war economy. His picture of things, what we would nowadays call a model, is set out in a paper entitled 'What is Inflation?' which was published in June 1941. If, in an economy in which there are initially unemployed resources, there is a spontaneous expansion of demand, the response on the supply side will to begin with be an increase in output (and employment); but first in one sector and then in another supply will become inelastic.

Kalecki's model of price determination had been published in 1939 in *Essays in the Theory of Economic Fluctuations*.[2] When there is slack in a sector the supply curve is more or less horizontal and price is determined by average prime costs plus some percentage margin to cover overheads and profits. However, if the rise in demand continues to the point where the marginal cost curve begins to rise steeply and to leave behind the curve of average prime costs, then prices (and profits) will rise relative to 'the normal relations between price and prime costs'. It was this phenomenon which Kalecki regarded as both the key to the presence of inflation and its measure. For each sector the excess of average prices over what the 'normal relations' would indicate would be a measure for inflation in that sector, and the same measure, averaged, could be applied to the economy as a whole.

It is characteristic of this approach to inflation that the share of wages in any sector will fall when inflation is encountered, and for the economy as a whole, if we disregard productivity change, inflation will be accompanied by a fall in real wages. If, in this situation workers try to restore the position by pushing up

[2] An earlier version had been published in *Econometrica*, April 1938. A feature of Kalecki's prewar models of (non-war) capitalism was that the upswing of the trade cycle came to an end *before* the steeply rising section of the supply curve. Kalecki's cycle was damped, but kept going by random shocks. This was in contrast to later models, such as Hicks', in which an inherently explosive cycle was kept in bounds by a full employment ceiling and a floor of autonomous investment. Nevertheless, although he does not quote his own (non-war) price theory, Kalecki's war-time inflation theory is a natural extension of the former.

nominal wages they cannot succeed, for as nominal wages are raised so will be prime costs and correspondingly prices. What they will do is set in motion the vicious spiral of prices and wages.

At the time Kalecki placed a fair amount of emphasis on the idea that he had come up with a good *measure* of inflation. However, we do not hear much more of this particular aspect. Inflation could be temporarily postponed by the running down of stocks, and this he called *latent* inflation. If maximum prices were fixed and demand exceeded supply, distribution would become haphazard and this he called *repressed* inflation.

Clearly this model fits very well the transition from a peace-time economy with under-employment to a war economy in which war expenditure first sucks in unemployed resources and then is carried still further so that consumption, initially raised by the multiplier, has to be halted and then made to fall once more. Since in his models workers did no saving, consumption of wage earners would also have to fall by amounts depending on the curtailment of non-wage earners' consumption. The model fits well the move from under-employment to the point where the vicious spiral is set in motion. It does not look ahead to the case where that spiral has been going for some time. For instance, there is no suggestion of the possibility that prices could be rising, and even accelerating, at a time of falling profit margins. In fact the kind of situation we saw in the late sixties and early seventies appears to be explicitly ruled out. 'A rise in the price level due to devaluation of the currency, or an increase in wage rates followed by a rise in prices in an economy with unemployed resources, will not start the type of self-generating spiral process for which the term inflation is generally reserved.'[3] Kalecki was to modify this position a few years later when we wrote the Full Employment book, and we were trying to foresee the working of full employment in peace-time circumstances.

What lay behind Kalecki's model was a conviction that inflation was essentially a question of the distribution of scarce consumer goods and services. His idea of sectoral inflation is interesting in itself, but it led him to a further observation:

> This is very important from the point of view of remedies. It follows clearly that to prevent inflation in general we must deal with 'inflations' in particular groups of commodities, and this may be done only by rationing.[4]

In his famous *Times* articles on 'How to pay for the War',[5] Keynes had argued that to close the inflationary gap between disposable income and available supplies of consumer goods and services, taxation of the rich alone would be insufficient: income tax would have to be extended down the scale to cover wage earners, the majority of whom had hitherto been exempt. To mitigate the damage to incentives Keynes suggested that most of the tax deducted from lower incomes should be set aside in the form of 'deferred pay', allowed to earn interest, and returned after the war as 'postwar credit', the payment of which would be matched by a postwar capital levy. Keynes acknowledged the need for a minimum ration of

[3] *Studies in War Economics*, Blackwell, 1947, p. 82.

[4] *Ibid*, p. 83.

[5] Three articles published in November 1939. These were developed into a small book *How to Pay for the War*, published by Macmillan in 1940.

consumption goods to be made available to all at a low fixed price. But he objected to any extensive rationing: 'The abolition of consumers choice in universal rationing is a typical product of that onslaught, sometimes called bolshevism, on differences between one man and another by which existence is enriched.'[6]

Putting forward a scheme of what he called the general rationing of expenditure in January 1941,[7] Kalecki began by explaining why he thought the Keynes' scheme would not do:

> For the working class the consolation offered by prospective postwar enjoyment of compulsory savings is of a rather shadowy character. As to the well-to-do, on whom in the last version of Mr. Keynes' scheme falls the chief burden of compulsory saving, it is even less efficient than income tax in cutting their consumption: seeing compulsory savings accumulating on blocked account they are more likely to save less on a voluntary basis or to dissave than they would if taxed to the same extent.

Kalecki acknowledged the difficulties of extending specific rationing to cover a wide range of consumers' expenditure and went on, in a few lines, to set out his own proposal:

> The scheme is based on a simple principle. A total maximum expenditure in retail shops is fixed at, say, 25 shillings a week for an adult and 15 shillings for a child under 14.
>
> Expenditure on services is not included in our scheme, because some of them are not scarce (e.g. education, entertainments) while others may, if necessary, be controlled much more simply by direct methods: dwelling space by billeting; travelling by reducing the number of trains and abolishing first-class; gas and electricity by direct rationing; domestic services by fixing the maximum number of servants, etc. etc.
>
> Apart from services, certain categories of goods could be bought coupon free: 1. medicine; 2. newspapers and books; 3. repairs. For people who have lost their chattels as a result of bombing, newly married couples, etc., special allowance should be made. The coupons required for the purchase of meals in restaurants must be only a certain definite proportion of their price since it includes the cost of service.

Kalecki foresaw that any plausible figure for a uniform ration of expenditure would be beyond the reach of the poorest section of the population. He did not like the idea of their simply selling surplus expenditure coupons to the rich, and instead proposed that they should be allowed to sell any unused coupons to the government at their equivalent value. In this way they could close half of the gap between the expenditure ration and that part of it which they could originally afford.

Kalecki's models are nearly always very abstract and he never liked cluttering them up with detail. But his objectives were usually concrete and this applied

[6] *Ibid.*, p. 63.
[7] *Studies in War Economics*, p. 138.

particularly to his war economics. He was a problem solver and his outstanding gift was his inventiveness. Although not a practical man in the ordinary sense of the term—we used to say that he got his ideas about British society from his Cambridge landlady—he was usually able to put his finger on the points where a general scheme might break down. I have mentioned already his proposal for dealing with the sale of unused coupons by the poor. On this occasion he went a good deal further in trying to anticipate various practical objections. What would happen if coupons were destroyed by bombing? How could the expenditure ration be kept in line with available supplies and thus a secondary 'inflation' of coupons be avoided? He even went into problems of do-it-yourself, whereby people bought components and assembled them rather than buying them in shops. I remember some hilarious discussions (hilarious for us, he took such things very seriously) on the ingredients of cakes.

I thought at the time, and I still think, that the paper on General Rationing was the most important single thing which Kalecki did in war economics. It is natural to ask what influence it had on actual policy. Of direct influence there is little, if any, evidence. The war broke out in September 1939 and petrol rationing was introduced at once. The specific rationing of food—bacon, butter, meat and sugar—was introduced at the end of the year. On the other hand clothing and footwear rationing did not come until mid-1941 and the points rationing of groceries in December of that year. Kalecki's scheme was published in January 1941 so that it was, in principle, in time to influence the way in which rationing was to be extended beyond the basic food stuffs. I have not instituted a search in depth on this question, but I notice that Brian Reddaway in his chapter on rationing in the National Institute *Lessons of the British War Economy*, published in 1951, made no reference to Kalecki or to the scheme.[8] There is just a hint in Hancock and Gowing's official history of the British war economy: 'The attempt to find some universal form of rationing met with failure. The possibility of a total value ration for expenditure was mentioned, but it never developed into a practical issue; for how was 'expenditure' to be defined? If it embraced less than all goods and all services, excess money incomes would spill over into the unrationed field. But how could it embrace them all? The needs of a population of forty odd millions varies so widely that an average expenditure ration for all goods and services must be grossly inadequate for some and over-generous for others. Again, would the ration be a flat one or graded according to income?'[9] From the context it is not clear what was the date of these discussions, but from the quotation it seems that they must have taken place before Kalecki's scheme was published, inasmuch as he does meet several of the objections raised. So of direct influence there was probably very little. Nevertheless I think that Kalecki's exposition may have helped along the cause of rationing in general. I have already quoted Keynes' observation which

[8] Cambridge University Press 1951. Mr. Reddaway did argue against the idea that ration coupons could be related to *value*, rather than to some 'unchanging characteristic of the good'. But this was only in the context of the rationing of clothing. Once the start had been made with specific rationing of food stuffs, it became much less likely that any further extension of rationing would be on a value basis.

[9] W. K. Hancock & M. M. Gowing, *British War Economy*, HMSO, 1949, p. 329.

indicated some distaste for it and it is clear from Hancock and Gowing that some officials at least shared that distaste and could never really understand why rationing was popular.

Liquidity and Long Term Loans

In his collected papers there are only two pieces dealing with international economics and, with one small exception, he wrote nothing in this field in Oxford. But the exception is remarkable.

In 1943 the famous Keynes and White plans for postwar international monetary arrangements were published. The former was for a Clearing Union, while the latter proposed the setting up of a Stabilization Fund for the provision of international liquidity. The Institute *Bulletin* published, as a special supplement, an analysis of the Keynes and White plans which contained three articles. One by Schumacher explained the problem of international liquidity and how it might be helped by the alternative Keynes and White proposals, and another by Balogh dealt with the foreign balance and full employment. In between was a short paper by Schumacher and Kalecki which discusses the following question: suppose that you set up an international clearing union (or fund) with limited reserves and suppose also that some countries choose to run persistent surpluses in their balance of payments on current account. If they simultaneously engage in long term lending of the same order of magnitude no problem will arise, but if they do not, they may simply pile up an increasing share of the world's reserves, with consequent embarrassment for other countries. Keynes, it will be remembered, had already anticipated this prospect and had suggested penalizing not only debtors but also creditors in international trade. The implication of the Kalecki/Schumacher paper was that this might not in fact be enough to deter some countries from being persistent creditors.

They pointed out that there were countries, which we would nowadays call developing countries, which quite properly should borrow long to cover deficits in their trade balances while they develop their economy internally. These they called A countries. Then there were B countries who might be obliged to run deficits for a while for a variety of other reasons, which would aim nevertheless at the restoration of balance. One could, of course, make some kind of international rule that developed surplus countries would be obliged to make long term loans to A and/or B countries. But it was unlikely that such a high degree of international order could be established. Instead they suggested that an International Investment Board should be set up and attached to the Clearing Union. It would be given power to make long term loans to either A or B countries. These loans would be debited to a special investment account but credited to the 'normal account' in the Clearing Union of those countries. There was a refinement of this proposal, whereby A countries might be required to spend part of their loans in B countries, e.g. advanced countries which have had surplus capacity but trade deficits at the same time.

By linking the International Investment Board with the Clearing Union it would be possible to ensure that any tendency of persistent creditors to soak up international liquidity would be offset by appropriate long term lending by the Investment Board because in the nature of things their loans would be quickly spent from their normal accounts and thus restore the stock of international liquidity. This type of arrangement was very much discussed in the 1960s and was known as the 'Link'. The Kalecki/Schumacher article is the first place known to me where this is suggested.

Full Employment

The Economics of Full Employment was published in October 1944,[10] within a few weeks of Beveridge's *Full Employment in a Free Society*.[11] The sub-title of the Oxford Book was 'Six Studies in Applied Economics'. There is no question that each of the six authors pulled his full weight; even so Joan Robinson had the rights of it when she devoted a long review in the *Economic Journal*[12] to the contributions of Kalecki and Balogh, dealing respectively with the domestic and international aspects of full employment, and she was also right in observing that we had not wholly succeeded in integrating the two approaches.

Kalecki's argument was that while the problem of foreign trade might present perhaps the greatest *practical* difficulties on the road to full employment, the assumption of a closed economy was desirable in order to make clear the fundamental *theoretical* problems. It is arguable that this distinction is a false one and that just as the Institute group failed to achieve a proper integration of domestic and international aspects of full employment, so British economists generally have continued to fail in this respect, at some cost to the conduct of economic policy. But I have no time to chase this attractive hare and must return to Kalecki's contribution, which he called 'Three Ways to Full Employment'.

They were:
1. Deficit spending
2. Stimulating private investment
3. Redistribution of income from higher to lower income classes.

Kalecki argued that both 1 and 3 were economically feasible, but that 2 was not.

As to deficit spending, whether achieved by increased public expenditure with given tax rates, or by lower taxes (including increased subsidies) given public expenditure, there were three types of objection. First it would drive up the rate of interest and reduce *pro tanto* private sector investment (the Treasury View) or, to use the modern term, it would result in 'crowding out'. Secondly, it would cause inflation. Thirdly the burden of the National Debt would rise. Most of the arguments in response to these objections are too familiar to be recited here, but two matters call for mention.

By now Kalecki had recognized the possibility of a continuing vicious spiral of money wages and prices which led him to consider a combination of price control and a 'wages policy'. As regards financing the growing interest on the National Debt he proposed either an annual capital tax or else a 'modified' income tax

[10] Blackwell, 1944.
[11] George Allen & Unwin, 1944.
[12] March 1945, p. 77.

designed to mitigate any adverse effect on the inducement to invest. His suggestion was that income tax (or profits tax) should be assessed on gross income, before the deduction of depreciation, and that all investment expenditure, whether for replacement or for expansion, would be deductible from taxable income. He invited the reader to consider an entrepreneur who on the basis of £100 cash invested expects a gross profit of £10 a year. One shilling in the pound of income tax (5 per cent) would reduce expected profits to £9½. But, by investing £100, the entrepreneur would under Kalecki's system get £5 reduction in his income tax, so that the true cost of the investment would be £95 and thus the rate of return would be restored to 10 per cent.

The rationale of the redistribution of income route was the implicit raising of the propensity to consume by shifting income from rich to poor, but that also might have damaging effects on the inducement to invest and once more the 'modified' income tax was invoked.

The reason why the way to full employment by stimulating private investment was closed is of particular interest at a time when economic policy is resting heavily upon a hoped for recovery of industrial investment. 'The tragedy of investment is that it causes crisis because it is useful.'[13] Kalecki returns time and again to this fundamental paradox. On this occasion he argued that on the one hand there is a level of gross investment, call it I_r, which is sufficient 'to expand the capacity of equipment *pari passu* with the increase in working population and productivity of labour, i.e. proportionately to full employment output'. On the other hand, there is a level of gross investment, I_f, which is sufficient to secure full employment. There is no reason why $I_f = I_r$, and in general $I_f > I_r$. If, by lowering the rate of interest far enough, investment is pushed up to I_f, then capacity utilization will begin to fall and it will go on falling so that further reductions in the rate of interest would be needed to keep investment up. (Or alternatively bigger and bigger tax remissions or subsidies would be necessary.) Kalecki acknowledged that in principle lowering interest rates might lead to the 'deepening of capital' but he doubted whether in practice I_r could be sufficiently raised in this manner.

It is interesting that Kalecki never started off from the equality of I_f and I_r, then proceeding to ask what would be the necessary conditions for that equality. Many years later, in the *Economic Journal* for March 1962, he argued that the Harrod/Domar knife-edge was ephemeral, in the sense that 'any deviation from the path determined by it renders the system stationary'. As to his acknowledgement of the possibility of a chronic wage–price spiral, this was a subject more fully dealt with by my own study in *The Economics of Full Employment*, and calls for no comment here.

Military strategists are often charged with trying to win the last war, and the full employment economists (the term Keynesian seems unduly restrictive) were sometimes charged with trying to spend their way out of the great depression. To bring such a charge against Kalecki would have been ludicrous. The last of the many articles he wrote for the BULLETIN was published in December 1944 and carried the title 'Employment in the United Kingdom During and After the

[13] *Essays in the Theory of Economic Fluctuations*, Allen and Unwin, 1939, p. 149.

Transition Period'. On the assumption that the piled up demand for industrial reconstruction and domestic restocking was not dissipated in inflation but was kept under control as long as necessary by rationing and physical controls, the 'transition period' in the United Kingdom might last for more than six years into the early 1950s, by contrast with an estimate for the United States which had lately been made by Steindl of some two to three years. So far as conditional forecasts can ever be tested those projections stood up well.

A year before *The Economics of Full Employment* came out Kalecki had published an article on the 'Political Aspects of Full Employment'.[14] In it he argued that business leaders, sometimes characterized as 'captains of industry', would show little enthusiasm for policies of maintaining full employment, despite the fact that full employment would bring with it higher profits. Given the advances in economic thinking, business leaders might be forced in the event of a slump to tolerate some expansionist measures undertaken by government, but in such cases they would show a preference for measures to stimulate private investment rather than increases in public investment or subsidies to mass consumption. In effect business leaders would go as far as accepting a 'political business cycle' in which full employment might be reached at the top of the boom but there would still be slumps, albeit relatively mild and short-lived. 'Progressives', however, ought not to be satisfied with a political business cycle but should insist on a policy of maintaining full employment. Workers also would benefit from fighting for 'full employment capitalism'. There was no danger that this would lead to fascism; on the contrary, it was a very effective way of preventing the recurrence of fascism. Kalecki thought that for permanent full employment to be possible capitalism would have to adjust itself and accept what would amount to fundamental reforms; if it could not, so much the worse for capitalism.

Kalecki's Influence

None of the writing which I have described is easily accessible. Most of the *Bulletin* articles to which I have referred are reprinted in the Blackwell volume of *Studies in War Economics* published in 1947. *The Economics of Full Employment* is long out of print. During the Second World War undergraduate studies were not entirely extinguished as in the First, but they were very attenuated. Kalecki gave lectures towards the end of his stay, which were appreciated, but there is no large body of Oxford students to constitute a Kalecki generation. The greatest influence he exerted here was upon his colleagues: the tangible evidence of this is to be seen in the two books by Joseph Steindl *Big and Small Business*[15] and *Maturity and*

[14] *Political Quarterly*, October–December 1943. The article was based on a lecture given to the Marshall Society in Cambridge in the spring of 1942.

The theme of the 'political business cycle' has been picked up again lately by Lindbeck and Nordhaus and there is likely to be a renewed interest in Kalecki's paper. A shortened version of it was included in the *Selected Essays in the Dynamics of the Capitalist System*, a collection of some of his papers which was published by the Cambridge University Press in 1971. The interested reader is recommended to go back to the original article in *Political Quarterly* from which the summary in this lecture was made; the *Selected Essays* version includes not much more than half of the original text.

[15] Blackwell, 1949.

Stagnation in American Capitalism,[16] but all his Institute colleagues learned from him: some of them, like Goldmann and later Steindl returned to their own countries, and others stayed to teach in Oxford or at other British universities. I should like to end with a few comments about the impression which he made.

The Oxford Institute gave me my first full time job; my background was that I had taken Finals in mathematics and had had a year of rather hectic study of economics and politics. I came to the Institute by the accident of war *via* the joint recruiting board. I quickly found myself helping, first, Ian Bowen and then Frank Burchardt with the editorial responsibilities of the three-weekly *Bulletin*, which was a good way of seeing what was going on and learning the subject at the same time. I have little doubt now that the mathematician in Kalecki was an attractive force though it did not seem so at the time. Coming to economics very late, with little knowledge of history and virtually none of political and economic institutions, I regarded economics as a very different kind of study from mathematics and for many years I was actively hostile to mathematical economics. What I liked about Kalecki was that he used just that amount of mathematics that was needed and no more; it was only later on that I realized that he had far more in the shop than he ever put in the window. The second thing which appealed to me was the way in which his concepts and analysis seemed to lead naturally to illustrative statistics. By modern econometric standards it was all very primitive: he looked up his own figures, such as there were, and did his calculations on a slide rule. His power of concentrated thought was astonishing. His room in the New Bodleian was originally intended for the practical purpose of book binding and was medium-sized, rather dark, and sparsely furnished. There were bookshelves but they were empty bar a copy of Joan Robinson's *Essays in the Theory of Employment*. If you called on him, as like as not you would find him pacing up and down deep in thought. Many of us seek inspiration by hunting around through the library to see what others have said but he would never take any idea or theorem for granted: almost invariably he would re-work it himself.

Equally he had the power to switch off. I used to find this disconcerting. I had long discussions with him about the wage–price spiral when we were writing the Full Employment book, and would have been happy to go on after hours, but when closing time came he would stop abruptly, and say we should start again where we left off on Monday morning. It was often more than a mere interruption, because, while you could rarely make him change his ground in the course of discussion he might well do so when he had thought the problem through over the week-end. On Monday morning you might find to your consternation that he was now putting forward with great conviction the very arguments he had so passionately opposed on the previous Friday night.

Although his writing was often technical and abstract, behind it there was always a very strong moral purpose. In wartime, austerity was the common lot, but for him it meant that his heart and his intellect could be in harmony. I fear I am making him sound very solemn. He did have an acute sense of humour and in later life accumulated a vast store of jokes, especially political jokes, which his

[16] Blackwell, 1952.

wife Ada would encourage him to relate as a form of relaxation. But he used to warn us: 'Never make jokes about serious matters: they will always come true'. Not that he ever really understood the English. When he came back to Oxford many years later he told me that he was reading *Sinister Street* and I drew his attention to the fact that the Oxford college portrayed there was my own college Magdalen. He was delighted, but I quickly realized that he was not taking in my further observation that things had changed a bit since Compton Mackenzie's day. As an economist I always regretted that Oxford let Kalecki slip at the end of the war, but had he remained he would not have been able to keep his illusions about us, which would have been sad in a way. In those days, for me, he was the best economist in the world: there was no doubt about it. I must admit that at that time my acquaintance with other economists, whether in person or on paper was limited. Since then I have managed to widen my horizons a bit, though not nearly keeping pace with the enormous extension of the frontiers of economics. If one takes a stand in some particular specialism, be it some corner of mathematical economics or econometrics or welfare economics, one can think of names which might stand against his. A few years ago at the British Association I sounded off about the state of economics and I contrasted some of the activities which go on under the umbrella of economics with 'serious economic science'. I did not offer a definition of that term. When I think about it now, I realize I must have had at the back of my mind a model of a 'serious economist'—Michal Kalecki. I thought him the best when I knew him in the war, and I still think so.

*National Institute of Economic
and Social Research,
London.*

[3]

KALECKI AT THE UNITED NATIONS, 1946–54*

By SIDNEY DELL

Introduction

This paper discusses Kalecki's work at the United Nations during the period in which he worked there, namely from 1946 to 1954.

It is hardly necessary to say that Kalecki's creativity and brilliance, and above all his deep understanding of the economic and social forces required for growth and development, had a profound influence on most of those with whom he came into contact, whether on the staff or in the councils of the UN. Yet international organizations, like national civil services, are not always able to accommodate men of Kalecki's individuality, notwithstanding certain celebrated exceptions. Moreover the intellectual climate of the early fifties was not conducive to dispassionate consideration of unorthodox ideas such as those espoused by Kalecki. Without going into the details of the matter, it must be noted that a situation was created in 1954 that led to Kalecki's resignation. Bitter as was the moment of his departure, he felt that it was a blessing in disguise to be relieved of the constraints on freedom of expression that any international civil servant must accept.

And yet these constraints had been readily accepted by him. In fact, although he was a man of exceptional originality and independence of mind, Kalecki had an austere concept of the discipline to be observed by an international civil servant in the discharge of his duty. As he saw it, the Secretariat could be expected to command the confidence of governments only if it abstained from judgments on their politics and policies. At the same time, reticence on political and policy matters should, Kalecki believed, be accompanied by complete objectivity and fearlessness in discussing the facts and the relationship of those facts to internationally agreed goals. Kalecki's scruples about not straying into the arena of political judgment will be illustrated subsequently in connexion with the Economic and Social Council's enquiry into the problem of inflation. Anyone familiar with Kalecki's strongly held views on political economy will readily appreciate how difficult it must have been for him at times to remain within the strict boundaries of objectivity that he had set for himself in writing about world economic trends.

The series of *World Economic Reports* to which he contributed from 1947 to 1954, as well as the more specialized studies of this period, are notable more for rigorous and detailed empirical economic analysis than for the broad sweep of policy conclusions reached. The facts are usually left to speak for themselves, and even the

* The views expressed in this lecture are those of the author and do not necessarily represent those of the United Nations Secretariat, of which he is a staff member. The author gratefully acknowledges valuable comments received from Stanislaw Braun, T. C. Chang, Eprime Eshag, Stein Rossen and Dudley Seers.

Note: For the sake of brevity, one section of this lecture which summarised Kalecki's report on Israel following his visit to that country in 1950 has been omitted. This fascinating report, which in many ways is characteristic of Kalecki's approach to development problems, has now been published in full in Michal Kalecki, *Essays on Developing Economies*, Essay No. 8, The Harvester Press Limited (1976). (*Ed.*)

manner of organising the material was, generally speaking, as neutral as possible. Thus, each *World Economic Report* had sections dealing successively with the United States, Western Europe, Japan, a group of Far Eastern countries, and a group of Latin American countries (the statistical requirements for adequate analysis were not yet available for African countries). For each of these countries and groups of countries there would be a schematic review of year-to-year changes in the gross national product and its major expenditure and sectoral components, followed by an analysis of accompanying shifts in employment and unemployment, and in prices and wages. Socialist countries and China were treated similarly, so far as possible, but here separate sections were devoted to analysis of the economic plans. Of considerable theoretical interest was the development of Keynesian[1] national income analysis of the market economy countries to a high stage of refinement—some of the features of that analysis will be discussed below.

Kalecki's reputation and professional brilliance made it possible for him to gather a remarkable group of collaborators around him. At one time or another these included Stanislaw Braun, T. C. Chang, Éprime Eshag, Sidney Glassman, Borje Kragh, S. Krestovsky, Samuel Lurié, Jacob Mosak, Surendra Patel, De la Peña, Lawrence Reed, Stein Rossen, Dudley Seers, Marjorie Tucker and S. Ting. In the course of the discussion that follows we shall be citing various passages in United Nations documents as illustrations of Kalecki's work in the UN. There is always a certain difficulty in making attributions of this kind where the work done is that of a team, and the document as a whole is published anonymously. Nevertheless, Kalecki's associates would readily agree that his was the guiding and controlling spirit not only as regards the theoretical framework of the work done but also in the practical analysis carried out. Unlike many theoretical economists of his generation, he was thoroughly familiar with the methods of statistics and econometrics, and he directed the analytical work on each and every country studied down to the last detail, and to an extent that was and is unusual for research directors. He also insisted on the greatest possible precision and conciseness of expression, and went over every single word of the text to that end.

All in all, the passages that have been selected for discussion below are typical of those on which Kalecki's influence was clearly preponderant, and we shall therefore attribute them simply to him. Kalecki himself would have been much more scrupulous, and would have insisted on giving more explicit recognition to his colleagues in each such case.

It has to be borne in mind that Kalecki's assignment in the UN was to direct the work of the 'Eonomic Stability Section': his primary concerns were therefore with current domestic economic problems resulting successively from the shortages of the immediate postwar period and the accompanying inflation, the recession of 1948/49, and the sequence of inflationary and deflationary events associated with hostilities in Korea. He and his team traced the domestic impact of these events throughout the world, in developed, underdeveloped and socialist countries alike,

[1] The term 'Keynesian' employed here reflects general usage, though as Mrs. Robinson and others have pointed out, Kalecki had a claim to priority in the discovery of the main principles of the 'Keynesian' system—a claim that he himself never pressed.

and those sections (usually Part I) of the six *World Economic Reports* from 1947 to 1952-53 which dealt with such matters were written by them.

Kalecki had little or no responsibility for the work on development or on international trade and payments,[2] so that Part II of the *World Economic Reports* was usually entrusted to other hands. Despite this, Kalecki did, as we shall see, contribute significantly to the identification and analysis of some of the basic issues of development and balance of payments problems.

Full Employment, Inflation and External Imbalances in Industrial Countries.

Kalecki's most important single preoccupation during his UN career was with problems of full employment and inflation. It is already difficult to recall the intellectual climate of that period—a period during which full employment was a main goal of the international community, and there was a tacit assumption that all other economic and social goals must be sought in a manner consistent with it. Several countries, including the United States, had written employment objectives into their domestic legislation.

In the immediate aftermath of the second world war, full employment in the industrial countries was assured by the pressure of pent-up demand and of reconstruction. It was clear, however, that these special supports to economic activity must come to an end sooner or later, and in March 1948 the Economic and Social Council requested the Secretary-General to obtain information from governments on their plans to maintain full employment and prevent a future economic decline, and to submit an analysis of that information.

Accordingly, Kalecki and his team prepared the first of a series of questionnaires to governments covering all aspects of the problem, and subsequently published analyses of the replies received. The questionnaires, the replies received from governments, and the analyses of the replies are a fascinating study in themselves—a means, in effect, of confronting governments with their responsibilities under the United Nations Charter, and under the resolutions on full employment that they had accepted. It is not possible to do justice to the material in the present context, but one of the issues raised is worth a passing reference. The questionnaire invited governments to indicate what measures they proposed to take in the event that an attempt to maintain full employment in the face of a decline in exports led to balance of payments difficulties.

The analysis of the questionnaire indicated that 'Almost all countries state that they would resort to import controls if faced with this contingency.'[3] Only the United States and Iran did not envisage a situation arising in which they might have to take measures to safeguard their balances of payments. And only Australia and Belgium referred specifically to the possibility of currency devaluation. The latter obviously reflects the unwillingness of most governments to mention devaluation as even a hypothetical possibility, but the readiness to contemplate

[2] An exception is the important analysis of 'Post-War Dollar Deficits in International Trade', which appeared as Chapter 9 of *World Economic Report 1949–50* and which was written by T. C. Chang under Kalecki's general supervision.

[3] [10].

tightening of import restrictions is certainly a far cry from the attitudes of the same governments today.

This question was the subject of a series of exchanges between R. F. Harrod and Kalecki in the Economic and Employment Commission's Sub-Commission on Employment and Economic Stability. Harrod was a member of the Sub-Commission[4] while Kalecki was its Secretary. In 1976 Harrod would chide the British Government for its refusal to make use of import restrictions in restoring full employment, but in 1949 he expressed disappointment at the readiness of Governments to resort to import restrictions for this purpose. Such an attitude, he felt, implied disregard of the ideas of international economic cooperation developed at Bretton Woods four years earlier. If necessary, international arrangements should be strengthened so that Governments would gain confidence in their effectiveness. For example, the resources of the International Monetary Fund should be increased and its tasks broadened through the addition of central banking functions. In reply, Kalecki pointed out that the reply of the IMF to the Secretary-General's questionnaire showed that that institution could not deal with a major downturn in business activity and that its capabilities were limited to the alleviation of minor recessions. Kalecki said that while Governments recognized that they should not export unemployment, and while import restrictions were not the first step they would take in stabilizing domestic employment, they had indicated that they would refuse to import unemployment and would, if necessary, introduce import restrictions to that end. The representative of the IMF, J. K. Horsefield, supported Kalecki's exposition of limitations on the IMF's capacity to deal with economic fluctuations. Ragnar Frisch added the comment that it was useless to rely on an armoury of weapons that could affect only the second decimal place of the problem.[5]

In August 1949, the Economic and Social Council invited the Secretary-General to appoint a group of experts to propose national and international measures required to achieve full employment.[6] The group met from October to December 1949, assisted by Kalecki and his staff. Although the group issued a unanimous report,[7] Kalecki was sceptical as to whether some of the proposals for international action were realistic—notably the proposal 'to stabilize international trade by maintaining external disbursements on current account in the face of internal fluctuations of effective demand'.[8] He was, however, in broad agreement with the analysis presented in the report, and with the domestic measures proposed.

It was on the basis of one of the group's recommendations, supported by Kalecki, that the Economic and Social Council called on each government to 'publish as soon and as precisely as is practicable the standard by which it defines the meaning of full employment as a continuing objective of policy, such standard

[4] Other members were L. Melville (Chairman), P. Chernyshev, R. Frisch, E. Goldenweiser and G. Leduc.

[5] Forty-fifth meeting of the Sub-Commission on Employment and Economic Stability of the Economic and Employment Commission. United Nations document E/CN.1/Sub.2/SR.45, pp. 10–15.

[6] Economic and Social Council resolution 221(IX)E, adopted on 11 August 1949.

[7] *National and International Measures for Full Employment*, UN Sales No.: 1949.II.A.3. The members of the group were John Maurice Clark, Nicholas Kaldor, Arthur Smithies, Pierre Uri, and E. Ronald Walker.

[8] *Ibid.*, paragraph 183.

being expressed, wherever possible, in terms either of employment percentages or of absolute numbers of unemployed or in ranges of such percentages or numbers; and thereafter publish such revised standards as may become necessary from time to time'.[9]

The adoption of this resolution marks the high water mark, internationally, of the full employment commitment. But its significance was short-lived and the resolution was not in fact generally implemented. Already in *Problems of Unemployment and Inflation 1950 and 1951* published in August 1951 Kalecki noted that 'only the United Kingdom reported that it had adopted a specific full employment standard within the meaning of the Economic and Social Council resolution'.[10] In another reply to the questionnaire, the United States reported that while the Government had not 'determined an employment standard as a definite and unalterable percentage of the labour force' it had by legislation adopted a procedure for announcing year-by-year employment goals which serve as a guide for economic policy. A number of other countries gave reasons for their inability to adopt a full employment standard, and one country, Canada, raised the objection that Article 55 of the Charter of the United Nations points to three goals, not one, namely 'higher standards of living, full employment, and conditions of economic and social progress and development'.[11]

The reluctance of governments to commit themselves to a full employment standard did not take Kalecki by surprise. As long ago as 1943, in his remarkable article on 'Political Aspects of Full Employment',[12] he had argued that while the economic measures required to achieve and maintain full employment were now well known, there would probably be strong opposition after the war to continuing full employment. Such opposition would reflect dislike of government intervention, especially in the form of public investment and subsidies to consumption, and dislike also of the social and political changes resulting from the *maintenance* of full employment. There would be a return to orthodox policies of cutting down budget deficits, leading to a slump in which government spending would again come into its own. The spontaneous trade cycle of the past would be replaced by what Kalecki called a 'political business cycle'.

One will not find the slightest hint of all this in any of Kalecki's written work on full employment at the United Nations. He was firmly determined to eschew political controversy, and saw himself and his team as technical experts on the analysis of economic trends and issues but not as participants in the debate about

[9] Economic and Social Council resolution 290(XI) adopted on 15 August 1950.

[10] The announcement of the standard was made in a Parliamentary statement on 22 March 1951, which indicated that 'It is the firm policy of His Majesty's Government to keep unemployment at the lowest level compatible with the avoidance of inflation'. The experience of previous years had indicated a level of about 2 per cent at the seasonal peak. However, the Government felt compelled to allow for the possibility that a decline in external demand for UK exports, or a shortage of imported raw materials, might make it impossible to maintain unemployment at such a low level. The Government therefore decided 'to express the full employment standard of the United Kingdom as a level of unemployment of 3 per cent at the seasonal peak'.

[11] [17].

[12] Published first in the Political Quarterly, 1943; reprinted in an abridged version in *Selected Essays on the Dynamics of the Capitalist Economy 1933–1970*, Cambridge University Press, 1971.

such issues. He recognized that the capacity of the Secretariat to influence governments on major questions of policy was quite limited.

He observed equally strict restraint in dealing with problems of inflation and deflation. He set out the dynamics of demand inflation in the remarkably concise introductory chapter of a study that, because it was written anonymously in association with others, is not very well known even to those familiar with his other works.[13] Yet it remains a model of rigorous exposition on the subject.

Kalecki was particularly concerned to distinguish between demand inflation and other types of inflation at a time when most governments and international agencies made no such distinction; they therefore regarded fiscal and monetary restraints as the principal weapons to be employed against inflation, regardless of whether or not there was an actual excess of effective demand. Although the distinction between excess effective demand and other sources of price increases is now commonplace, economists are not always as precise as they might be in diagnosing the origins of inflation or in drawing conclusions from that diagnosis as to the remedies to be applied. This is particularly noticeable in the emphasis often placed on budget deficits as a source of inflation, in abstraction from other features of the economy.

Kalecki invited particular attention to the contrast between those types of national expenditure that have, as a counterpart, currently produced supplies of goods for consumption, and those types that have no such counterpart. Since gross private income (after taxes but including depreciation) can be shown to be equal to the sum of personal consumption, gross private domestic investment, export surplus and budget deficit, it is evident that the demand for savings out of private income is equal to the last three items. These Kalecki refers to by the somewhat cumbersome expression 'net non-consumption payments' because they are payments not derived from the production of goods for personal consumption, and are net in the sense that government expenditures are net of government revenues.

The critical question in diagnosing demand inflation was to determine whether, with a given distribution of production and expenditure between consumption and non-consumption items, something had occurred tending to bring about a marked shift in these relationships. Thus an increase in the aggregate of non-consumption payments raises, and a decrease lowers, the pressure of demand upon supplies of consumption goods. At full employment, a reduction in the total of these payments will lead to a decline in output and incomes, while a rise pushes up prices and thus brings about a shift from wages to profits, thereby generating the required increase in gross private savings.

Demand inflation or deflation can also result from a shift in the proportion of private income tending to be consumed. During the early postwar period about which Kalecki was writing there was a large-scale pent-up consumer demand supported by accumulated liquid assets, so that the proportion of income tending to be consumed was abnormally high while requirements for savings were also high because of heavy investment in reconstruction.

Kalecki showed that inflationary pressure could also build up in response to a

[13] [14] pp. 5–14.

decline in the supply of consumer goods in circumstances in which requirements for savings were stable in relation to income. Such a decline in the supply of consumer goods might be the result of a crop failure, or a drop in productivity in consumer goods industries or a deterioration in terms of trade. Moreover even if the total supply of consumer goods were unchanged, a reduction in food supply could cause a rise in food prices and a fall in real wages.

Thus, whatever its origin, demand inflation tends to depress real wages. If workers respond by demanding higher money wages, an inflationary price spiral is initiated which can proceed indefinitely without recovery of average real wages. The process becomes intensified to the extent that price increases induce hoarding of commodities, thereby reducing supplies available for consumption. Hyper-inflation is a special case of a price spiral in the course of which confidence in money disappears: under these conditions no reduction in inflationary pressure is brought about by a shift from wages to profits because the additional profits are immediately spent on the hoarding of goods (or investment in inventories).

Kalecki was well aware that inflation in under-developed countries exhibits special characteristics, and we shall refer to these in a moment. First, however, we may take the discussion of inflation in industrial countries forward to 1952, when the Economic and Social Council asked the Secretary-General to 'prepare in the light of recent experience . . . a report on national and international measures designed to reconcile the attainment and maintenance of full employment with the avoidance of the harmful effects of inflation'.[14]

The episode was an interesting one, reflecting at once the rigorousness of Kalecki's thinking and his refusal to be drawn into what he considered to be political questions. In his report, Kalecki said that it was 'by no means easy to isolate in past experience the influence of the high level of employment from other factors'. In fact, rapid inflation had in the past been affected to a considerable extent by factors other than the maintenance of a high level of employment—for example by the short-run inelasticity in the supply of raw materials and foodstuffs during cyclical upturns, and after the outbreak of hostilities in Korea. Where inflation was accompanied by full utilization of resources—as during the war or early postwar years—the basic cause of inflation was the fact that a much higher proportion of the national product than normal was absorbed in purposes other than the production of consumer goods (or in 'net non-consumption payments', to use Kalecki's earlier terminology). In both types of situation cited, therefore, potent factors other than the high level of employment *per se* were involved. Consequently, Kalecki felt that analysis of past experience did not provide an adequate basis for discussion of the question that the Council had raised.

The report went on to say, however, that chronic inflation was nevertheless possible under full employment if wages rose faster than productivity. This could be due either to employers bidding for specific types of labour or because of the strengthened bargaining position of trade unions. If wages rose faster than productivity, labour costs would rise and these increases would be passed on by

[14] Economic and Social Council resolution 426B(XIV) adopted on 10 July 1952.

employers to the consumer in the form of higher prices. Thus real wages would not, generally speaking, rise faster than productivity, and the workers, disappointed in their expectations, might ask for new wage increases. The spiral would then continue, and might be aggravated by speculation in commodities.

Plainly, said Kalecki, unemployment could be kept sufficiently high to prevent such a situation from arising, but this would go counter to the obligations of governments under Articles 55 and 56 of the United Nations Charter. The prevention of a wage-price spiral without generating unemployment would therefore call for government intervention. It may be noted that Kalecki did not doubt that such intervention could be successful. He would certainly have disputed the proposition that there are circumstances in which maintaining a certain level of unemployment is the only way of preventing or halting a wage–price spiral.

Governments could choose between various types of measures. They could control wages—and this would probably necessitate price controls as well; alternatively, under 'highly specific conditions' governments might arrange for voluntary agreements for restraint to be concluded between workers and employers. A second alternative would be to allow wages to move freely but to control prices: this would squeeze profit margins and increase the pressure of demand, thereby making the controls more difficult to operate, and creating a need for additional taxation or reduced government expenditure.

The report concluded that 'The implications of either policy extend, it will be evident, into an area where political rather than economic judgment is involved. The institutional and administrative aspects of such policies vary greatly from country to country, being dependent on the character of trade unions and employers organizations, the ability and willingness of governments to administer price controls, the degree of dependence on foreign trade, etc.'[15]

Accordingly, Kalecki proposed that a study of the alternatives would best be entrusted to an expert group 'because in an experts' report divergent views on such a controversial subject could find expression.'[16] The Council decided not to appoint an expert group. Instead, governments submitted accounts of their experience of dealing with inflationary pressures associated with high levels of economic activity to the Secretary-General. An analytical summary of these accounts was then prepared by Kalecki as a basis for further discussion in the Council.

Kalecki's paper suggested that the statements received from governments had not in fact singled out full employment as an independent cause contributing to inflation. Most of the examples given related to cases of a general excess of demand, or of shortages arising in particular sectors, notably food.

Kalecki went on to analyse United Kingdom experience in detail. From 1946 to 1952, the United Kingdom had experienced both demand inflation and cost inflation. Kalecki noted that the major increases in labour costs had, with some

[15] [20] document E/2404, paragraph 13.
[16] *Ibid.*, paragraph 14.

lag, been correlated with upswings in import prices. He concluded this part of the analysis as follows:

> It may be noted that increases in labour costs may play either a passive or an active role in inflation. The fact that wage rates rise more quickly than productivity does not necessarily indicate that rising labour costs are an active independent source of inflation. The dynamic source of inflation rather may be excess demand or rising import costs. Accompanying increases in wage rates and per unit labour costs in such circumstances may be regarded more as an effect than as a cause of inflation. The pressure to raise wages here originates not in a favourable bargaining situation, but in the desire of wage earners to prevent a loss in real wages. The fact that real hourly earnings remained virtually unchanged in spite of improvements in productivity suggests that this was the case in the United Kingdom during the period 1946 to 1952 as a whole.[17]

In effect, Kalecki was saying that while he conceded the theoretical possibility that wage demands exceeding advances in productivity could result from the strengthening of workers' bargaining power at full employment, no evidence had been brought to his attention that this had happened in practice up to 1954. Where wages had increased faster than productivity, this had been caused by excess demand or by rising import costs, which had prompted workers to seek to protect themselves against a decline in their real wages. It is unlikely that Kalecki would have come to a different conclusion if he had been in a position to reconsider his analysis in the light of the experience of the next twenty years.

In *World Economic Report 1951–52*[18] Kalecki presented a study of the use of general fiscal and credit policy to deal with deficits in the balance of payments, using experience in Denmark and the Netherlands as a basis. The Danish Government had announced its intention

> to solve Denmark's future balance of payments problems by pursuing a monetary and fiscal policy which will reduce domestic demands both for investment and consumption, thereby releasing factors of production which may be diverted to production for export . . . a switch-over to export production is likely to involve transitional difficulties, and the level of unemployment is therefore expected to show a moderate increase in the coming period.[19]

The Netherlands Government was pursuing similar objectives, as indeed have many other governments since then, and up to the present time. The analysis is therefore of much more than historical interest.

Beginning late in 1950 or early in 1951, during the boom set in motion by the outbreak of hostilities in Korea, Denmark and the Netherlands sought to restrain private consumption by increases in both direct and indirect taxes, while private

[17] [21], paragraph 24.
[18] [5], pp. 37–43.
[19] Reply of Government of Denmark to United Nations questionnaire on full employment and related matters, covering the period 1950–51.

investment was discouraged by fiscal measures and by increased interest rates and credit restrictions.

In both countries the volume of imports declined about 12 per cent in 1951/52, or more than twice as much as the sum of real domestic expenditure and exports. This was due to a sharp drop in investment in inventories. However, the decline in domestic demand does not seem to have resulted in a diversion of resources to exports, largely because there was a simultaneous decline in import demand in other countries. Even in the Netherlands, where the volume of exports did increase, there was a decline in production in the export industries, which experienced significant unemployment and excess capacity. The report notes, however, that had demand for the exports of these countries continued to expand in 1951/52, 'there would have been a better chance that a substantial proportion of the resources freed by internal deflation might have contributed to swell the volume of exports'. On the other hand, reasons are given for doubting whether the deflationary policies had much effect on wage settlements.

The study concludes that it should not be inferred that restriction of internal demand is not important in dealing with balance of payments problems. The elimination of an external deficit tends to increase the pressure of demand, and if the economy is operating at full employment, an offsetting contraction in domestic demand is necessary to prevent inflation. But this does not mean that a cut in internal demand will always reduce the import surplus *pro tanto*, leaving the level of economic activity unaffected. Where exports are limited by foreign demand rather than by domestic supply, such a cut may merely lead to a slowing down of economic activity; and the balance of payments will improve mainly through the consequent decline in imports.

Inflation in Less Developed Countries

Writing in 1947, long before the monetarist–structuralist controversy in Latin America, Kalecki foresaw that,

> Any estimate of the course of events in India and Latin America in the near future must take into account the large-scale development schemes upon which these countries are likely to embark . . . If direct taxation is not increased, inflation will follow just as it did during the war. However, even if development expenditures are offset by direct taxation, the problem of inflation in food prices will not be solved, because taxation of higher incomes will hardly reduce the demand for food. In the long run, an increase in food production will doubtless constitute a very important part in the development programme of under-developed countries. This will require fundamental social and technical changes in the agricultural economies.[20]

Inflation was thus not incompatible with unemployment or underemployment, if there were bottlenecks in equipment or raw materials making it impossible to employ all the available labour. In such cases the expansion of supply needed to

[20] [12], pp. 5–6.

meet the pressure of demand could be realized only through an increase in imports.

Kalecki noted further that economic development reduces the relative, and often the absolute, size of the rural population by drawing off workers to the non-agricultural sectors. The remaining rural population was likely to increase its per capita food consumption so that unless there were a sufficient expansion of food output, the supply of food to non-agricultural workers would probably not increase as rapidly as their demand, based on rising incomes. If food imports were increased, this would accentuate pressures on the balance of payments, with inflationary consequences. Alternatively there would be a shortage of food with rising prices and a fall in real wages leading to an inflationary price–wage spiral.

Kalecki was not inclined to take inflation in underdeveloped countries lightly. Nowhere did he argue, for example, that inflation may be a necessary evil, a method of extracting forced saving. He emphasized, on the contrary, that persistent inflation provides incentives for the hoarding of commodities, flight of capital, currency speculation and distortion of the investment pattern. 'These primary effects of inflation', said Kalecki, 'may not only make inflation cumulative, but may also frustrate the very process of development by which inflation was originally caused.'[21]

In his analysis of government statements for the Economic and Social Council's discussion of inflation at its eighteenth session in 1954, Kalecki singled out the case of Chile as 'typifying in most respects the inflationary experience of countries engaged in accelerated economic development'.[22] While Chilean industrial production had expanded from 1940 to 1952 by about 60 per cent, recorded agricultural output had scarcely increased at all. This had led to severe inflationary pressures and a wage–price spiral, in the course of which real wages had generally risen very little: some advance in real wages in manufacturing, mining and commerce had been accompanied by little change in agriculture, construction and utilities, while real wages in public and domestic services had declined substantially.

Critical as Kalecki was of inflation, he was not disposed to accept orthodox prescriptions for dealing with it. As he saw it, the only way in which fiscal and monetary contraction could cope with inflation was by halting the development process that had generated inflation in the first place.

Kalecki considered that any development plan for a low-income country should be so constructed as to avoid inflationary increases in the prices of necessities and limit taxation on necessities and on the incomes of the poorest segments of the population. Avoiding inflation was not, in his view, a monetary matter. It depended on ensuring an appropriate structure of national expenditure. If such a structure were achieved, the monetary problems would take care of themselves. Non-inflationary development involved three basic requirements. *First*, the supply of food and other essentials must be expanded to the extent necessitated by the planned growth of income. *Secondly*, expenditure on non-essentials must be

[21] [20], Document E/2404, paragraph 19.
[22] [21], paragraph 27.

curbed to the extent required to release adequate savings for financing private and public investment. And *finally*, private investment must be held down sufficiently to make room for the financing of public investment. Once these conditions were satisfied, the required flow of resources from the private to the government sector would take place either through direct purchases of government securities or through the intermediation of the banking system, including the central bank.[23]

Socialist Countries

Kalecki's treatment of the socialist countries in United Nations documents calls for relatively little comment. During much of the time that he spent at the UN, the amount of data, both qualitative and quantitative, available from these countries was limited. As in the market economy countries, an account was given of general trends in the national produce in terms of its main expenditure and sectoral components. There was also discussion of the demand–supply position, and it was pointed out that where demand pressures built up, this was usually due to inadequacies in the supply of food. In this respect, experience in the Eastern European countries was strikingly similar to that in the less developed market economies. In *World Economic Report 1951–52*,[24] for example, it was pointed out that while industrial growth had been rapid in several Eastern European countries the expansion in agricultural production did not keep pace with large increases in non-agricultural employment. At the same time, the outflow of labour from agriculture to industry tended to increase the per capita food consumption of the remaining agricultural population; in other words, the shift in population from rural to urban areas was not accompanied by a commensurate shift in food supplies. In 1951–52, in such countries as Czechoslovakia, Hungary, Poland and Romania prices rose sharply on the free and black markets and to a lesser extent in government stores. As a result of these developments, a considerable redistribution of income between urban and rural populations took place.

Analyses of the development plans of the socialist countries were also presented in the *World Economic Report* from time to time. These were almost entirely factual in character. Kalecki was personally critical of the theory that maximum growth invariably requires the output of investment goods to increase faster than that of consumer goods, and there was no-one who would have sought to overrule him if he had seen fit to introduce a comment along these lines into the *World Economic Report*. But, rightly or wrongly, he was determined not to engage in this kind of controversy with any country, market economy or socialist. And it was not until he left the United Nations and returned to Poland that he published

[23] The above exposition is based on the paper entitled 'Financial Problems of the Third Plan: Some Observations', first published in *The Economic Weekly*, July 9, 1960 following a study undertaken in India at the request of Professor P. C. Mahalanobis from December 1959 to March 1960; this paper has now been reprinted in Michal Kalecki, *Essays on Developing Economies*, The Harvester Press (1976), Essay No. 9. The fundamental ideas contained in the paper had, however, been worked out much earlier, and had animated Kalecki's thinking about development problems while he was at the United Nations. See, for example, a summary of his lectures on 'The Problem of Financing Economic Development' given in Mexico City in 1953, published in the above-mentioned book, (Essay No. 5).

[24] [5], pp. 46–47.

his refutation of the theory on which virtually all the planning of socialist countries up to that time had been based.[25]

Likewise, in *World Economic Report 1952–53*,[26] attention was drawn to the difficulties that had arisen in the socialist countries as a result of imbalances between the growth of agriculture and industry, and within the industrial sector between the output of consumer and producer goods as well as between the growth of capacity in investment goods industries and the output and supply of fuel and raw materials. Kalecki's concern about structural imbalance, and the need to accelerate the growth of supplies of consumer goods, foreshadowed his main preoccupations after his subsequent return to Poland. Here again, he made no overt criticisms of the policies of the socialist countries in the *World Economic Report*. But once he was back in Poland, his pronouncements on the problems of balanced development became quite explicit. Particularly significant was his analysis of the Polish plan for 1966–70[27] in which he criticized several aspects of the policies reflected in the plan, and urged a reduction of 'productive investment' so as to make it possible to raise investment in housing and the rate of growth of consumption.

He was steadfast in insisting on the inclusion of material on China in the *World Economic Report*, despite strong internal and external pressures for omission on the grounds that the data were unreliable. He contended that he was not in a position to check the officially published data of any government, whether of China or of any other country, and that as an international official he must treat all governments alike.

An interesting point in the discussion of the first Chinese five-year plan (1953–57) in *World Economic Report 1952–53*[28] is the contrast drawn with the new plans for the Eastern European countries of that time. For the first time, the proportion of resources devoted to investment in the latter countries was to decline so as to permit the supply of consumer goods to be stepped up, whereas in China the output of producer goods industries and especially of the heavy industries, was to increase much more rapidly than output as a whole. The conclusion was drawn that 'the central purpose of this plan is to provide a foundation for future development of the economy by expansion of producer goods industries'.[29] Although the text does not say so in so many words, it is implicit in the account given that the concentration on heavy industry was considered reasonable in the Chinese context because of the primitive stage of industrial development thus far attained, and because there was still ample scope for the expansion of agriculture and light industry in the rural areas, making use of surplus rural labour.

Another point of interest in the same *World Economic Report* is to be found in the formula given for the relationship between increases in national product, net investment and increments in productive capacity.[30] Kalecki later informed his

[25] Ekonomista No. 5, 1956, Warsaw. Published in English in *Short Papers on Economic Growth*, Warsaw, 1962.

[26] [6].

[27] Zycie Gospodarcze, Warsaw, April 12, 1964.

[28] [6], pp. 52–53.

[29] *Ibid.*, p. 53.

[30] [6], p. 44.

former colleague Braun that this formula had constituted the first version of the equations later developed in his *Introduction to the Theory of Growth in a Socialist Economy.*[31]

Conclusion

The impression that restudying the various themes of the period has left with this observer is that for Kalecki the economic problems, whether of developed or of underdeveloped countries, and whether of market economy or of socialist economies, were much more readily solved than the political problems. If the commitment to full employment has weakened, and the degree of toleration of unemployment has increased, in the developed market economies, Kalecki would probably feel that this has little or nothing to do with problems of economic management, as some are inclined to think. It reflects rather a reordering of social priorities for reasons which have to be sought in political rather than economic analysis—a reordering, by the way, with which Kalecki would have had no sympathy. Similarly, the disappointed hopes of people in underdeveloped countries are due not so much to lack of resources, whether domestic or foreign, but rather to the absence in those countries of political forces capable of mobilizing those resources fully, particularly where this involves the need for social change and agrarian reform.

What Kalecki's ultimate diagnosis of the problems of socialist countries would have been it would be difficult to say; but here too he might well have concluded that the realization of the full potential of the people for economic progress and the solution of their economic problems depends largely on matching broad political and social evolution to the stage of development already attained.

Thus the most challenging problems brought to the fore by Kalecki's analysis of the world economy were precisely those which his self-denying ordinance had forbidden him to touch.

United Nations,
New York, N. Y.

REFERENCES

UNITED NATIONS PUBLICATIONS AND DOCUMENTS TO WHICH MICHAL KALECKI CONTRIBUTED

World Economic Reports

[1] *Economic Report: Salient Features of the World Economic Situation 1945–47*, pp. 24–28; UN Sales No. 1948. II. C. 1, January 1948.

[2] *World Economic Report 1948*, Part I Chapter 2; UN Sales No. 1949. II. C. 3.

[3] *World Economic Report 1949–50*, Part I; March 1951; UN Sales No. 1951. II. C. 1.

[31] Basil Blackwell, Oxford, 1969. The first Polish edition was published in Warsaw in 1963, and the second, from which the English version was translated, in 1968.

[4] *World Economic Report 1950–51*, Part I; April 1952; UN Sales No. 1952. II. C. 4.

[5] *World Economic Report 1951–52*, Part I; April 1953; UN Sales No. 1953. II. C. 2.

[6] *World Economic Report 1952–53*, Part I; April 1954; UN Sales No. 1954. II. C. 1.

Documents Prepared for the Sub-Commission on Employment and Economic Stability

[7] *Background Paper on National Measures concerning Full Employment*, UN document E/CN. 1/Sub. 2/2, November 1947.

[8] *Food Shortage and Economic Stability and Development*, UN document E/CN. 1/Sub. 2/5, November 1947.

[9] *The Structure of Full Employment*, UN document E/CN. 1/Sub. 2/10, March 1949.

[10] *The Problem of Balance of Payments Difficulties in the Maintenance of Full Employment*, UN document E/CN. 1/Sub. 2/11, April 1949.

[11] *Summary of Replies to Question 8 of the Questionnaire*, UN document E/CN. 1/Sub. 2/12, April 1949.

Other United Nations Documents

[12] *Survey of Current Inflationary and Deflationary Tendencies*, UN Sales No. 1947. II. 5, September 1947.

[13] *Postwar Shortages of Food and Coal*, UN Sales No. 1948. II. A. 3, July 1948.

[14] *Inflationary and Deflationary Tendencies 1946–48*, UN Sales No. 1949. II. A. 1, June 1949.

[15] *Maintenance of Full Employment*, UN Sales No. 1949. II. A. 2, July 1949.

[16] *Implementation of Full Employment Policies*, UN Sales No. 1950. II. A. 1, July 1950.

[17] *Problems of Unemployment and Inflation 1950 and 1951*, UN Sales No. 1951. II. A. 1, August 1951.

[18] *Governmental Policies Concerning Unemployment, Inflation and Balance of Payments 1951–52, Part A*, UN Sales No. 1952. II. A. 2, November 1952.

[19] *Analysis of replies of governments to the questionnaire on full employment, balance of payments and related policies, 1952–53*, UN document E/2445, June 1953.

[20] Report by the Secretary-General under Council resolution 426 (XIV) on *Measures designed to reconcile the attainment and maintenance of full employment with the avoidance of the harmful effects of inflation. Note by the Secretary-General*, UN document E/2404, April 1953. *Report by the Secretary-General*, UN document E/2449, June 1953.

[21] *Measures to prevent possible inflation at high levels of economic activity*, UN document E/2597, May 1954.

[22] *Summary Record of the Sub-Commission on Employment and Economic Stability of the Economic and Employment Commission, First to Fifty-second Meeting;* 19 November 1947 to 27 April 1949, UN documents E/CN. 1/Sub. 2/SR. 1 to 52.

[4]

KALECKI'S ECONOMICS OF SOCIALISM

By WLODZIMIERZ BRUS*

It seems appropriate to begin by justifying the subject: are there really reasons for dividing *theoretical* economics—so frequently presented as a general theory of efficient allocation of scarce resources—into economics of capitalism, economics of socialism and even economics of a mixed economy? Kalecki's answer to this question was unequivocal: 'the institutional framework of a social system is a basic element of its economic dynamics'—reads the opening sentence of one of his last papers presented in Cambridge in 1969 and published after his death [1]. Obviously this was not a matter of latter-day conversion: he always explicitly stated what kind of social system was taken as a framework and what changes in it were postulated in his analysis. Discussing the consequences of a fall in investment for employment and national income in a capitalist economy, which is crucial for understanding the truly substantive—as opposed to theological—significance of bringing social systems into economics, Kalecki says that in a socialist system 'full employment will be maintained through the reduction of prices in relation to costs', whereas 'in the capitalist system . . . the price-cost relationship . . . is maintained and profits fall by the same amount as investment plus capitalists' consumption through the reduction in output and employment. It is indeed paradoxical that, while the apologists of capitalism usually consider the "price mechanism" to be the great advantage of the capitalist system, price flexibility proves to be the characteristic feature of the socialist economy.' [2]

This may sound rather strange and calls for a brief elaboration. Assume a state of full employment and full capacity utilization in a capitalist economy. In diagram 1, a given level of profits (OA) on the vertical axis combined with a given share of profits in national income (P/Y) as determined by the price-cost relation, or price-wage relation if costs are reduced to wage-costs, corresponds to a given level of income (OC) on the horizontal axis. Profits equal investment (I) plus capitalist consumption (C_c); P/Y is represented by the slope of the straight line drawn from the origin O to B—the point of intersection of CD and AB drawn vertically and horizontally, respectively. By drawing a straight line at a 45° angle (OD) we can project national income also vertically (CD), and in this way derive the workers' consumption on the assumption that all wages are consumed; the latter is represented by BD i.e. CD minus CB.

What happens if for some reason there is a reduction in investment activity? Kalecki says, in line with the well-known argument, that this will lead to a fall in profits. Let the new level of profits be OA'; so far so good—this will happen in any economy, regardless of the social system. There is, however, a world of difference between different social systems as to the impact of a fall in profits. In a capitalist (laissez-faire) system the tendency will be to keep the share of profits at P/Y by

* The lecturer was until 1968 Professor of Economics in Warsaw University and is now University Lecturer in Modern Russian and East European Studies and Fellow of Wolfson College, Oxford.

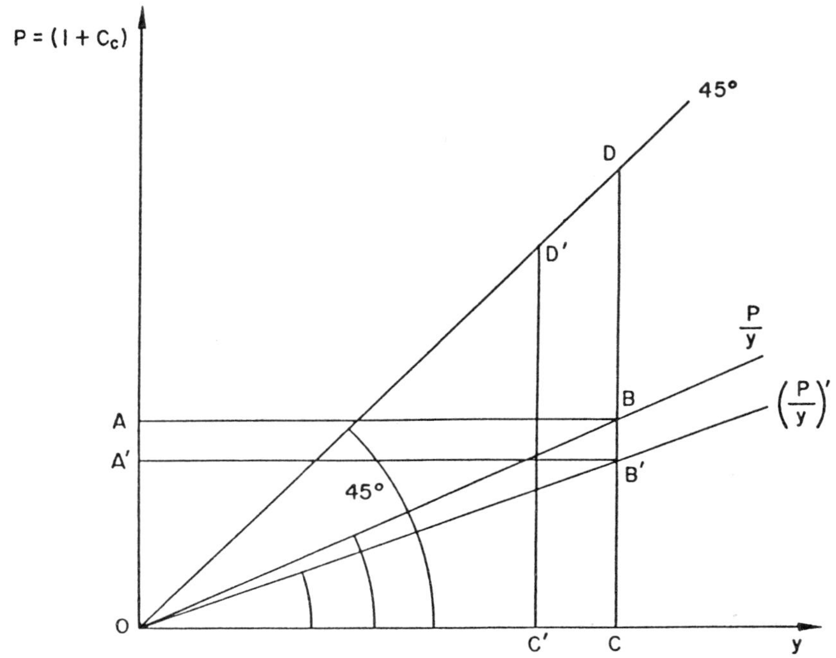

Diagram 1.

maintaining the existing price-cost or price-wage ratio. The effect would thus be to lower the level of national income to (OC′). In a socialist economy, on the other hand, there are no economic or political reasons for sticking to the old profit (or surplus) ratio; even the tyrants would not mind increasing the welfare of their subjects if the state lost nothing. Here the share of surplus could be reduced to (P/Y)′, in order to maintain the previous level of income (OC) with an increase in popular consumption from DB to DB′.

There are many simplifications in this example, but the essentials are correct: the two social systems differ in the way they react to a fall in the 'propensity to invest'. One reacts by adjusting output and employment to a given pattern of income distribution between wages and profits, and the other by adjusting income distribution to the capacity level of output and employment.

This in itself should not be taken as a conclusive proof of the superiority of socialism over capitalism; it might well happen in some cases that the full-capacity level of output under capitalism would be greater or of better quality or would match demand better than under socialism. But one thing should be clear: namely that socialism is economically capable of adjusting aggregate effective demand to productive capacities (in the framework of given organizational and other limitations). That is why one has to study a socialist economy as a *supply determined* economy, and this, as Kalecki always patiently explained, makes an enormous difference to the whole approach in economic theory and its application.

Full recognition of the role of the social system as a basic element of economic dynamics undoubtedly reflects, in a most general form, the Marxist foundations of Kalecki's economics. This is not a surprise to those who are familiar with his studies of capitalism, as other lectures in this series show. Let me only mention that among Kalecki's later publications one can find an attempt (maybe not entirely successful but very characteristic) to fit standard economic reasoning into a broad framework of the Marxist understanding of historical development [3]. One should in particular note his excellent essay on the importance of Marxian schemes of reproduction for modern economic analysis presented to the UNESCO symposium on the centenary of *Das Kapital* in 1967 [4].

While recognizing the enormous significance of the Marxist approach and of many Marxian tools of economic analysis, Kalecki never felt that he had to accept every component of Marxian economics or to retain those parts of it which have become obsolete in view of new experience and of the progress of economic theory. He felt, for example, a strong distaste for the Marxian theory of value, which he considered metaphysical and (if I am not mistaken) never wanted to discuss. Nor was he an institutional Marxist bound by 'authoritative' interpretations of the party leaders of the day, who were only concerned to find a quasi-theoretical justification for every twist in their policies, while at the same time refusing to submit socialism to Marxist dialectical scrutiny of contradictions. For Kalecki, socialism, however distinct from capitalism, was never a conflictless utopia.

Being aware of his rather special brand of Marxism, Kalecki came back to Poland in December 1954 with a firm intention to stay away from the economics of socialism which was still fettered by theological dogmas that we had only just started to discard. The situation changed with unexpected speed during the period preceding the Polish October 1956, and from spring 1956 onwards Kalecki became deeply involved both in most challenging theoretical debates on the economics of socialism and in tracing new policies and institutional reforms. Only then—but I must say to our credit, almost immediately—did we realize what a powerful intellectual asset we had acquired in this tiny man for the rising 'movement of socialist renewal', as the developments in Poland were called at that time.

Characteristically enough, Kalecki fought his battle against established dogmas on two fronts. The battle on the *first* front was against the so-called official 'law of faster development of department I', which produced producer goods, as an allegedly absolute condition for sustained growth. This dogma had just been re-established in the USSR after the fall of Malenkov in 1955. Kalecki chose this topic for his paper to the Second Congress of Polish economists in June 1956; the paper was called 'The dynamics of investment and of national income in a socialist economy' [5]. By using a simple growth-model, which was to be the starting point for his theory of growth under socialism, in combination with his own interpretation of Marxian reproduction-schemes, he showed how inadmissible the absolutist conclusions were. He demonstrated that, *first*, faster growth of the producer-goods sector must correspond to increasing the share of investment in national income. *Secondly*, under conditions of a constant incremental capital/output ratio, faster growth of the producer-good sector may be justified only when *acceleration* of growth (and not growth as such) is the strategy of the plan. *Thirdly*, it is necessary to assume a permanently increasing incremental capital/output ratio in order to maintain that a constant rate of growth requires an increasing share of investment and hence faster growth of producer-goods output. The introduction of foreign trade does not change anything if we are concerned with final disposable product. I shall always remember the strong impression Kalecki's paper made on the gathering, not because he endorsed or refuted a specific growth policy in absolute terms, but because he demanded that conclusions be derived from assumptions and interrelations clearly defined and without the vagueness which is a breeding ground for mystical beliefs planted behind a smoke-screen of pseudo-Marxism.

The battle on the *second* front was against some extreme reactions to the abominable experience of Stalinist central planning: disillusionment with a centralistic system made very popular the view that the solution lies in substituting a socialist market-mechanism for central planning. Kalecki was never attracted by theories which defended the economic rationality of socialism by trying to prove that full-fledged market operations can be introduced or imitated in it, or by those who claimed that the superiority of socialism over capitalism was to be sought in the fact that it was better equipped to create and safeguard the cherished textbook conditions of perfect competition and general equilibrium. For him the case for socialism rested, apart from distributional and other social considerations, upon central planning not as a device for perfect market-like allocation, but precisely because it enabled resource allocation to take place according to non-market, long-term macro-criteria, applied *ex ante* instead of *ex post*. As in many other situations, he had the courage to stand up not only against the establishment but also against the current of popular misconceptions.

This does not mean that Kalecki endorsed the centralistic model of central planning and opposed what became known as economic reforms. On the contrary, he devoted considerable time and effort to finding theoretical and practical solutions for: a reasonable devolution of economic decisions; curtailment of the number of obligatory plan-indicators and elimination of obviously harmful ones (like the discredited gross-output target); the introduction of economic incentives linked to profitability, and the active use of prices, credit policy and interest rates. He did not, in other words, oppose the idea of utilizing the market-mechanism, but considered it as a subordinate element in the running of the economy which should be planned centrally as far as the main lines of development were concerned. We worked very closely together in this field, particularly in the Economic Council (we were both vice-chairmen of this short-lived advisory body to the government) and in a small committee charged with the task of screening the individual statutes of the so-called 'experimental firms'.

One of the reasons why Kalecki adopted a constructive attitude towards economic reform was its interconnection with the establishment of workers' councils as one of the basic elements of the emerging (as it seemed at that time) system of operating the economy. He was very active in the preparation of the Workers' Council Act of 1956, and wanted to make it clear that a two-way interrelationship was at work. Without some decentralization, workers councils would not have any real scope for their activities. In an article published in December 1956 [6] he stressed that it was the 'extension of the rights of the enterprises which creates for the workers' councils the possibility of showing initiative in the organization of production'. On the other hand, the system of workers' councils combined with central planning seemed to him to provide the proper blend of factors indispensable for avoiding past degeneration in the economic mechanism and for creating the necessary conditions for the development of socialist democracy. As usual he warned against expecting too much too soon, but was deeply convinced of the validity of this path in the long run. When the movement in this direction was first arrested and later reversed, he felt deeply disappointed.

Notwithstanding all his interest and activity in running the economy, Kalecki's main preoccupation in socialist economics was in the field of long-term planning. As the scientific adviser to the chairman of the Planning Commission, head of the perspective-plan division of the Planning Commission, participant in the Comecon meetings etc., he was primarily involved in shaping the pattern of Polish long-run economic development. Some important publications emerged directly from this activity: 'The 1961–1975 Perspective Plan' (1958), 'Outline of a method of constructing a perspective plan' (1962), 'On the fundamental principles of long-term planning' (1963) and other papers [7]. All these papers are both a reflection of and a contribution to Kalecki's theoretical foundations of long-term planning, namely his theory of growth in a socialist economy. This obvious feedback between the practice of planning and the theory of growth constitutes one of the most characteristic features of his economics of socialism.

There is no need to describe in detail Kalecki's theory of growth under socialism. His *Introduction to the Theory of Growth in a Socialist Economy* has been published in English [8]. What is perhaps worth mentioning is his emphasis on the merely *introductory* nature of this work, which he believed needed further elaboration, and his deliberate effort to avoid over-sophisticated mathematical presentation. But the main points which I wish to make concern the question as to how his theory of growth fits into his overall approach to the economics of socialism.

The basic model of growth used by Kalecki as a starting point is very simple. The rate of growth of national income (r) is determined, on the one hand, by the rate of growth of productivity (α) and the rate of growth of employment (β). In approximate form $r=\alpha+\beta$. At the same time, r is determined by the share of investment in national income ($I/Y=i$) and the incremental capital/output ratio (m, or k, when not only investment in fixed capital but also in stocks are taken into consideration), and by two additional coefficients: a, which reflects the negative effect of scrapping of obsolete and worn out equipment and u, which stands for the improvement in utilization of existing productive capacities; both investment and national income are gross of depreciation. Thus we obtain the following formulae:

$$r=\alpha+\beta \quad (1)$$

$$r=\frac{1}{k}\cdot i-a+u \quad (2)$$

Formula (2) is presented on the simplifying assumption that no investment in stocks per unit-increment of output is needed, and thus $k=m$.

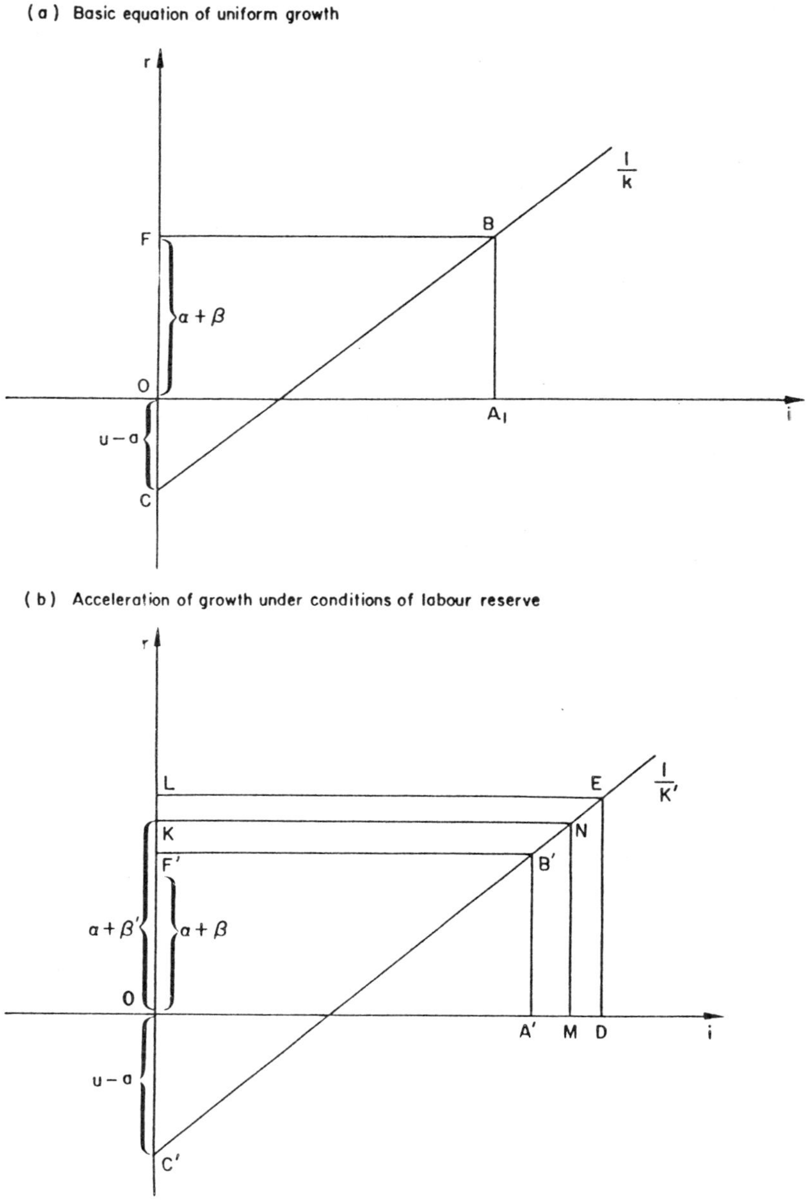
(a) Basic equation of uniform growth
r
F
B
1/k
α + β
O
A1
i
u − a
C
(b) Acceleration of growth under conditions of labour reserve
r
L
E
1/K′
K
N
F′
B′
α + β′
α + β
O
A′
M
D
i
u − a
C′

Diagram 2.

In graphical presentation (diagram 2a) i is measured on the horizontal axis, and 1/k is the slope of the line CB; C lying below the origin reflects the impact of $(u-a)$ on the assumption that $a>u$ (if $a=u$ point C coincides with 0). On the vertical axis we measure the rate of growth $r=\alpha+\beta$.

It is frequently pointed out that Kalecki's basic model of growth is similar to or even identical with the Harrod–Domar type of model. Formally speaking this may be true, but it is not very meaningful because such statements disregard the substantive interpretation and the analytical use made of the model. These are closely interrelated with the general approach to the economics of socialism discussed in the opening section. Kalecki himself, in 'Theories of growth in different social systems', already mentioned, maintains that Harrod–Domar types of model are inapplicable to capitalist economies because:

> problems of effective demand and utilization of resources are neglected. . . . They do apply to socialist economies where the problem of effective demand is really solved . . . The trouble, however, arises out of the fact that the models to which we refer do not concentrate frequently on essential problems rooted in the realities of socialist economies. [1]

He emphasizes two such problems: (1) the problem of *transition* from one growth-path to another, as opposed to the search for the so-called optimal, equilibrium growth-path of a uniformly expanding system; (2) the problem of long-run development *bottle-necks*. What he tried to do in writing on the theory of growth in socialism was mainly to tackle these two problems.

The first aspect of the problem of transition from one growth-path to another stems from the need to accelerate growth by using-up the accumulated labour reserve of the past. Practically all socialist countries had (and to some extent still have) such a reserve in an open or disguised form. Even in the simplest case, assuming a constant capital/output ratio, this involves several changes in the allocation of resources. First, the rate of growth of employment (β) is raised above the current rate of growth of the labour force in order to absorb the pool of unemployment. *Ceteris paribus*, this requires an increase in the share of investment in national income (i). From the point of view of the utilization of resources, the change should be as quick as possible, but this is not so simple because of its implications for current consumption apart from technical limitations in the structure of capacities. This is a political problem of trade-off between the present and the future, and it is here that Kalecki introduces for the first time his concept of the 'government decision curve', an ingenious explanatory device focusing on the inter-play between subjective (political priorities) and objective factors in the choice of long-term strategy. In any case, it is clear that the process of absorption of the labour reserve usually requires time, and time is also required for stepping down towards the normal rate of growth of employment. In the meantime, of course, conditions change and new 'equilibria' have to be sought.

The process discussed above is illustrated in diagram 2b. From the initial position as on diagram 2a (rate of growth $r=OF=OF'$, share of investment in national income $i=OA=OA'$) we move first to $i=OD$, corresponding to a rate of growth of employment higher than the current rate of growth of labour force. At a constant k (i.e. with the same slope of the straight line drawn from point C′) we arrive at a rate of growth of national income OL = DE. In other words, we move from point B′ to point E. Obviously this rate of growth of national income can be sustained only as long as the accumulated pool of unemployment is available. Afterwards the share of investment in national income has to be reduced to something like OM, which at the same k permits a rate of growth of national income of MN = OK.[1] In other words, we move from point E to point N along the line C′E. Of course, this presentation does not take into account all changes which would have taken place between the initial position and that corresponding to the normal rate of growth of employment.

Even more complex are the problems of transition from one growth-path to another when the change involves a change in the capital/output ratio or in the life-span of equipment. Kalecki devoted much attention to this problem, examining it very thoroughly with the help of his own version of a vintage-model.

There seem to be at least three main reasons for the special attention he devoted to this case of a change in the growth-rate. *First*, whereas acceleration of growth in the case of an economy with labour reserve can in itself not be questioned, and the problem of choice is actually reduced to the choice of speed, in other cases acceleration requires increasing labour productivity at the cost of a higher capital-output ratio or of 'rejuvenation' of equipment. Here there is a more fundamental decision to make: whether or not to raise the rate of growth.

Secondly, the element of relativity is stronger also because, in the case of acceleration with the same incremental capital/output ratio, the gains in the long-run are rather certain, and what may make one cautious is the scale of the short-run sacrifices. By contrast, in his vintage model, long-run gains will materialize only when certain rigorously defined conditions are met. People brought up on all kinds of 'golden rule' considerations may not fully appreciate the significance of this point, but under the circumstances existing in Eastern Europe this opened a new dimension in thinking about long-term planning-variants. I have mentioned the 'golden-rule', but I hope that this will not lead to any misunderstanding. Kalecki did not concentrate his attention on finding a 'golden rule' solution, which for him could, under some assumptions regarding the type of technical progress, only indicate the upper limit of efficient variants. He says, 'the key problem in the choice of capital intensity is the standard of living *in the course* of recasting'[2] (i.e. gradually changing the capital equipment from lower to higher level of capital intensity). The careful reader of the appropriate chapters of *Introduction to the Theory of Growth in a Socialist Economy* will also notice that in this case the rate of growth (and all its corresponding parameters) does not switch from one level to another at some turning points only, but it changes virtually all the time during the transition period. This explains, among other things, why Kalecki contrasted his approach with that of conventional growth theory, maintaining in his essay on

[1] It is assumed that the rate of increase in employment will be higher now than it was prior to the acceleration of the rate of growth to OL i.e. $\beta' > \beta$.

[2] See [8] in *Selected Essays* etc., *op. cit.*, p. 69.

'Theories of Growth in Different Social Systems' that 'most of the stuff on long-run economic growth is written in terms of "comparative statics".'

The *third* reason for Kalecki's concentration on the 'recasting' and/or 'rejuvenation' problem was its close links with the question of the choice of techniques and the criteria for project selection in a socialist economy. It is in this connection that he examines critically the argument presented by Maurice Dobb and Amartya Sen in favour of raising, under certain assumptions, the capital/output ratio even in the case of an unlimited supply of labour. Kalecki argues that when the impact of technical progress during the transition period is taken into account, the Dobb-Sen solution cannot be of any major practical significance, but acknowledges their contribution to widening the scope of theoretical discussion of the subject. Consistently he advocates the view that the 'marginal recoupment period'—a macroeconomic accounting parameter for project selection—should be determined in such a way as to achieve minimum investment compatible with an equilibrium in the balance of supply and demand for labour and in the balance of payments, if an open economy is considered [9].

So much—or rather so little—for the primary importance of the transition problems in socialist growth-theory. As far as the second specific problem is concerned—that of the long-run development bottlenecks—its significance in a supply-determined, expanding economy is clear:

> When national income grows at a high rate the expansion of certain industries lags behind that of demand for their products because of certain organization or technological factors, for instance shortage of an appropriately trained personnel or difficulties in adaptation of technical improvements (the latter is especially the case in agriculture). The resulting gaps have then to be made good by foreign trade and to maintain the balance of the latter either some exports have to be increased or some imports replaced by home production. These operations will be usually accompanied by higher outlays of capital and labour and in this way affect profoundly the problems of economic growth. [1]

Consistently, he incorporated the impact of bottlenecks into the mainstream of theoretical analysis, modifying his model appropriately at every stage.

For Kalecki careful consideration of bottlenecks was a condition of realistic planning, which should prevent breakdowns (particularly harmful to the standard of living) and secure a higher long-term growth than by using the 'Charge of the Light-Brigade' methods of planning. His orthodox critics, however, accused him of defeatist attitudes; albeit no one thought it trendy in the late 1950's to invoke literally Stalin's slogan that 'there are no such fortresses which cannot be taken by the Bolsheviks', but the actual meaning was identical. The assault was successful in the sense that Kalecki's perspective plan for 1961–75 was abandoned; much less successful were the practical consequences for the national economy, but this is a different story, which we cannot pursue here.

The subject of this lecture was so vast that I did not dare stop to quote some of Kalecki's favourite anecdotes. This is the more regrettable as Kalecki rarely emerged from a serious economic session without a witty epigram, of which he was no less proud than of a good piece of economics. Yet in spite of this self-imposed discipline, I have been unable to refer to any of Kalecki's numerous empirical studies of social and economic phenomena, e.g. brief but outstanding summaries of research on changes in income distribution and on economic crimes. As for Kalecki's theoretical work, I have only presented his approach to theoretical questions rather than the content of his theories.

It would be wrong to create an impression that Kalecki's approach was entirely flawless. He may, for example, be criticized on the following points: he always assumes a given structure of consumption in his growth models, and his only attempt to formulate the criteria of choice in this respect could hardly be regarded as satisfactory [10]; the relation between the production-curve, widely used by him,[3] and a conventional neo-classical isoquant remains unclear; the treatment of technical progress as an entirely exogenous variable leaves out some important economic interrelations and social feedbacks. However, in general, I regard Kalecki's approach as a most fruitful one, focusing our attention on issues of primary relevance to the economics of socialism.

This focus on relevant issues explains, at least in part, why Kalecki so often found himself in the centre of political controversies, despite the fact that he was never a member of a political party and always tried to stay away from direct involvement in politics. In 1964 he was violently attacked from the highest quarters for proposing some modifications in a five-year plan which, implemented without change, finally sparked-off the workers' revolt in December 1970. In 1968, in the wake of Czechoslovak Spring and the Polish March-events, the blow was directed against Kalecki's theories and his school of economics. All sorts of motivations, sometimes very base, were behind this assault, although it would be wrong not to see a kind of logic, or instinctive reflex in it. From the point of view of a totalitarian system and its vested interests, this man was dangerous, and his whole approach was politically loaded. His emphasis on relativism, on conflicts, on constraints, and on choice were anathema to irrational fetishism, arbitrariness and monocentric insistence on a uniquely legitimate no-alternative-path. This reaction has to be acknowledged as a peculiar but valid tribute to the power of Michal Kalecki's economics of socialism and, despite everything, seen in historical perspective, as a source of optimism.

Wolfson College,
Oxford.

REFERENCES

[1] 'Theories of Growth in Different Social Systems', *Scientia*, Vol. CV, May–June 1970.

[2] 'Determination of National Income and Consumption', in: *Selected Essays on the Dynamics of Capitalist Economy 1933–1970*, Cambridge 1971, p. 97.

[3] 'Econometric Model and Historical Materialism', in: *On Political Economy and Econometrics. Essays in Honour of Oskar Lange*, Warsaw 1964.

[3] See [8], Appendix.

[4] 'The Marxian Equations of Reproduction and Modern Economics', *Social Science Information* 7(6), Paris 1968.

[5] 'The Dynamics of Investment and of National Income in a Socialist Economy' (in Polish), *Ekonomista* No. 5, 1956.

[6] 'Workers Councils and Central Planning' (in Polish), *Nowe Drogi* No. 12, 1956.

[7] 'An Outline of a Method of Constructing a Perspective Plan', in: *Essays on Planning and Economic Development.* Research Papers of the Center of Research on Underdeveloped Countries, Vol. I, Warsaw 1963.

[8] *Introduction to the Theory of Growth in a Socialist Economy*, Oxford 1969, and in: *Selected Essays on the Economic Growth of the Socialist and Mixed Economy*, Cambridge 1972.

[9] 'Investment Planning and Project Selection', in: *Selected Essays on the Economic Growth of the Socialist and Mixed Economy, op. cit.*, part II.

[10] 'On Optimum Structure of Consumption' (in Polish), *Gospodarka Planowa*, No. 7, 1963.

[5]

MICHAL KALECKI*

By EDWARD LIPIŃSKI

1.

Oskar Lange wrote somewhere that progress in science is not achieved by wholesale rejection of old theories and their replacement by new ones, but rather by painstaking enhancement and improvement of what is already available. This rule certainly held for Ludwik Krzywicki. Michal Kalecki, on the other hand, was if anything the exception that proves it. He treated old theories as highly suspect and it was not by studying them that he began his career as a theorist; instead he directed his efforts towards the observation of economic life itself. True, before he wrote his first theoretical study, he had read one or two economic works: Tugan-Baranovsky's well-known history of crises and Hobson's and Lenin's studies of monopoly capitalism. But it may be that they too were of greater interest to him for their empirical than their theoretical content. For it was facts, not arid theories, that absorbed Kalecki first and foremost. He sought knowledge of the tree of life via statistics. His classic work on market theory was preceded by a detailed, painstaking and extraordinarily labour-consuming inquiry into the world and the Polish economy and economic policies. At the time when he turned to economic theory, Kalecki already had behind him the experience of several years' work in the Business Cycle and Prices Research Institute, a body undertaking systematic statistical enquiries, and an apprenticeship as an economic journalist. Back in 1927, he started writing for *Przegląd gospodarczy* (Economic Review), and later for *Polska gospodarcza* (Economic Poland). Most of his contributions were analyses of particular commodity markets (fifty survey articles being devoted to non-ferrous metals alone). But as well as giving a photographic impression of the market in question, he always tried to detect monopolistic tendencies and linkages and the international contradictions they were breeding. At the Institute, Kalecki collaborated with Ludwik Landau on two pioneering studies of national income in Poland. In addition he wrote essays on investment trends and indices, the formation of trusts in Polish industry, consumption indices etc. His monthly analyses of the economic situation published in the Institute's *Bulletin* were always masterly.

Kalecki was to continue this statistical work during his period abroad, first, during the war, at the Oxford Institute of Statistics, then after the war in the ILO office in Montreal, and later, in the economic department of the UN secretariat, where he prepared reports on the world economy. Nor did he abandon this field of research after his return to Poland in 1955, as may be illustrated, for example, by the series of studies of contemporary capitalism of which he was the moving spirit.

* This article was first published in *Polish Perspectives*, No. 9, September 1971. We are grateful to the author for his permission to reproduce it here.

Another way in which Kalecki got to know the inner workings of economic behaviour and policy was through his stints of service as adviser to governments and planning commissions. It was not his custom to give advice that was not based on his own research. His brief and succinct reports were invariably preceded by personal investigations of the problems involved.

Thanks to all this, Kalecki knew exactly what economics was about and was able to speedily extract the most important elements from a complex set of phenomena. This profound insight played an important part in the formation of his theories. For the great strength of Kalecki as an abstract thinker was his close knowledge of life. Some people familiar only with his basic works look upon him as a great master of deductive reasoning, a logician of a mathematical cast of mind (to say nothing of those who regard him as a formalist without any real contacts with life). Anyone who worked with him or has read him more attentively, however, is bound to see that he possessed an almost ideal blend of inductive and deductive powers. Even in his most general mathematical formulas, one could feel the presence of real life.

I recall the impression Kalecki's theoretical capacities made on me the first time I had the chance of seeing them in action after his return to Poland. It was in June 1956, under the dome of the Planning Commission building, during the memorable economists' congress that took place there. All the speeches were about reviving the Polish economy and urged a creative, as opposed to dogmatic, approach to Marxism. The contradictions of socialist economy, socialist relations of production, bourgeois economy and Marxist economy, degeneration, apologetics —there was no shortage of forceful language, Kalecki did not take any part in the general debate. Somewhat aloof, he delivered a sober, businesslike report on growth and investment. He did not invoke Marx, but he did use his methods. Though he made no mention of social relations, the latter were implicit in his observations about the contradiction between consumption and accumulation, etc. For me, his paper was a classic example of Marxist analysis of economic phenomena (as I wrote at the time).

Kalecki always made use of mathematics in economic argument. Thanks to his technical education, he found this easy. In the last fifteen years of his life Kalecki's independent efforts coincided with a veritable mathematical invasion in economics. This invasion has brought with it certain gains, but even greater losses. I have contended as best I can with the havoc it has wrought, the empty formalism, the pseudo-mathematical flight from reality. But it never occurred to me to attack Kalecki; for he never made excessive use of mathematics in his work. Kalecki was an ally; being an excellent mathematician, he was much better than I at exposing formalism. He struck terror into the hearts of the pseudo-mathematical pseudo-economists. Like any other strong personality, Kalecki had his epigones, no doubt, as well as followers and disciples. But can he be held responsible for them? No one ever flayed epigonism more mercilessly than Karl Marx. But even in his case, it was to no avail. The ranks of Marxists epigones swearing by their supposed master are innumerably vast. Michal Kalecki made use of Marx's work, but took good care not to place himself among the Marxist epigones.

2.

Two Polish thinkers have made seminal contributions to modern economic theory (on a par with Florian Znaniecki and Bronisław Malinowski in sociology and ethnography respectively). This was the first time that Polish achievements had succeeded in spanning the linguistic gap (even Copernicus' economic discovery has remained to this day associated with the name of Sir Thomas Gresham). It gives me a feeling of pride to recall that Kalecki's theory of the trade cycle emerged before my very eyes, if not actually under my observation. This may be a good occasion to acknowledge frankly that I did not fully understand Kalecki's discovery until Keynes' similar theory had made the basis for effective stimulation of market forces. However it did not take me long to recognize Kalecki as an independent theorist with a formidable gift of deduction, who deserved to be supported. But, outside a small group of friends who were similarly associated with the extreme left (Ludwik Landau, Antoni Pański, and later, Marek Breit, and among the non-socialists, Jan Wiśniewski; all were killed during the war), Kalecki was not understood. From the vantage-point of the present day, I shall attempt to explain why this was so.

One of the sources has been pointed to by Joan Robinson. The ideas of the new economics, as she reminds us, are essentially simple and accessible. The main obstacle to their acceptance was that created by the old ideas that had been so deeply rooted in neo-classical education. It was difficult to penetrate through the 'thick fog of orthodoxy'. The same thing could be observed in economists' circles here. Perhaps we could even illustrate it by reference to two of Kalecki's close friends. Ludwik Landau was an excellent statistician, who, though he had never shown any inclination towards the study of contemporary economic theory, understood the Kalecki theory of the trade cycle immediately. And indeed, in the review of Kalecki's *Próba teorii koniunktury* (An Essay in Trade Cycle Theory) which he published in the journal *Ekonomista*, Landau gave special emphasis to the broader implications which that slender volume had for the general theory of capitalism. In the case of Breit, by contrast, the process of conversion to Kalecki's style of reasoning lasted for some years. Breit was manifestly impeded by his own neo-classical and Wicksellian erudition (for all that Wicksell anticipated Keynes in more than one point). It is not surprising in view of this, that the older generation of economists fought its way through the fog of orthodoxy with even greater difficulty. Curiously enough, the dogmatism that was characteristic of Marxist economic theory at this time created a similar fog of orthodoxy and similar difficulties, even though the new theory represented a return to Marx at many points.

But there were other impediments as well. Economists engaged in practical work as economic advisers ran into special difficulties of their own when confronted with the new theory that stemmed directly from the character of the views that Kalecki and the Keynesians presented. What did the new theory say? Perhaps we could try to convey something of it by introducing a few of Kalecki's paradoxes, which, though they cannot be regarded as adding up to a good summary of the new theory, nonetheless capture its spirit splendidly.

1. It is often said: why should we build new factories when the old ones are still not fully exploited?[1] Kalecki replied to this by saying that in order to employ existing capacity, it is necessary that it be expanded. Let us suppose, said Kalecki, that—as is frequently the case in the United States—two towns are connected by two railway lines, both of them little used. What should be done? A third railway line should be built, for then the first two can be put to use carrying men and materials needed for building the third. And what when that third line is completed? Then one should build a fourth. And then a fifth. Kalecki warned his readers that the example was paradoxical in the sense that some other investment near the two railways would obviously be better. Nonetheless, he emphasized, this example 'reflects the laws of overall capitalist development splendidly'. (*Polska gospodarcza*, 1933, No. 37).

2. Investments have a stimulating effect on the economy only during the period while they are being carried out. The 'productive' character of investments, on the other hand, tends to check, and finally to reverse the original upswing. Kalecki saw it as being one of the most noteworthy paradoxes of capitalism that the increase of productive capacity, and hence of the community's wealth bears within it the seeds of crisis (*Polska gospodarcza*, 1935, No. 42).

3. 'Increased consumption by capitalists means an increase in their profits, which clashes with the widespread belief that the more one consumes, the less one saves.' (*Próba teorii koniunktury*, Warszawa 133, pp. 21–22).

4. The question is often raised where the money for increased investments comes from, if the consumption of capitalists is not curtailed, so that purchasing power is made available for purposes of investment. It may sound paradoxical, but such investments 'finance themselves'. (*Place nominalne i realne*—Nominal and Real Wages, Warszawa, 1939).

Since the days of the Utopian socialists and Karl Marx, this was the first such formidable dose of paradoxes that had been aimed at the head of capitalist economy. It was necessary first to become used to them before they could be incorporated into economic policy. Early socialist thinkers had familiarized us with the idea that an increase in wealth can go in hand with an increase in poverty, that a superfluity of labour can be accompanied by a superfluity of capital, and so on. A lot more water had to flow under the bridges before the socialist themselves grasped the idea that poverty could be countered within the framework of capitalism, and that the relief of poverty might become one of the objectives of economic policy.

The reason why it was particularly difficult for economists working as advisers to accept the new theory was that they were bound to develop a predilection for considering economic magnitudes in the terms in which they actually encountered them. Funds had to be sought for financing investments. Expenditure on investment and the freezing of resources during the period of construction were naturally looked upon as a necessary evil on the road to gaining an increased flow of goods and services at a later date. Particularly if 'sound finances' were taken as a principle. The economist with broader social horizons does not want to hear

[1] Points 1–4 are taken virtually word for word from Kalecki himself.

of this capitalist logic. Even when he does not actually condemn maximizing of profits as the aim of individual behaviour, he himself always wants to be useful to the whole of society, to his state or his people, and not just to the capitalists. The crazy world of capitalism he accepts like a spell of bad weather during which something useful might yet be done for the community as a whole. At first, however, it seemed that the new theory demanded brutal cynicism on the part of the economic adviser. Here was someone seriously advocating the construction of pyramids, or worse still, the burying of bottles filled with bank-notes, simply in order to be able to dig them up again later.

Obviosuly 'contestation' would have been another and more logical answer; and Kalecki's paradoxes might have been an excellent argument for contemporary militants. But instead the new theory gave them vertigo. I still remember one case in point. Kalecki had just published an article about the consequences of lowering wages during a depression in what must have been one of the first issues of *Przegląd socjalistyczny* (Socialist Review). This provoked an attack in the columns of *Wiedza dla wszystkich* (Knowledge for Everyman), accusing Kalecki of appealing to the bourgeoisie's reason and trying to convince them that they were behaving foolishly since a reduction of wages would not be of any benefit to them. This was seen as being 'harmful opportunism' masking a bourgeois content. Thus even in the 'contestation' of those days the idea could not sink in that the capitalist world had gone so crazy that the bourgeoisie were acting against their own interests.

I have used the expression 'new theory' to refer both to Kalecki's ideas and Keynes' *General Theory*, even though the first of them was a socialist, and the second a bourgeois reformist. The new theory arose in two quite different social environments independently. Some were to regard this as one further proof of the soundness of the theory, just as Krzywicki had seen the fact that both socialists and conservatives began to use historical materialism as one of the most cogent arguments in favour of the doctrine. Others, however, to this day regard the coincidence as justifying the assignment of Kalecki and Keynes to the same camp.

While on the subject, let me recall to mind another incident testifying eloquently to the confusion that was reigning in the minds of Polish economists in the thirties. When the *General Theory* appeared in 1936, the journal *Ekonomista* devoted two separate articles to it. From London, Kalecki despatched a proclamation to the effect that this was 'a turning point in the history of economics'. Władysław Zawadzki, on the other hand, reassured himself and his readers by saying that Keynes had already changed his views at least twice, and that one could therefore be quite confident that the *General Theory* did not represent his final word either.

3.

To read Kalecki's writings is an aesthetic pleasure, not so much because of any elaborate choice of words, but rather because of the striking concentration of content. Even when not making use of models and equations, Kalecki always wrote in the language of mathematics. Nor did his early career in journalism corrupt him in this respect, even though for some time pay-by-the-line was his only source of livelihood. Evidently *Przegląd gospodarczy* and *Polska gospodarcza* paid for net and not gross product. Or perhaps Kalecki himself had already committed himself at that stage to Mark Twain's recipe for writing: if you want to write well, say what you have to say, and then cross out the unnecessary words as though you had to send the rest by telegraph from America to Australia. It should be added, incidentally, that Kalecki also spoke with a remarkable laconic precision, which his listeners invariably found captivating. Many people can recall his embarrassment on the famous occasion when he was invited to give a course of 15 one-hour lectures at Cambridge: 'But I'd have to prepare for it for years,' he said. For Kalecki would only expound conclusions which he had arrived at himself. If he referred to the works of other people, it was only in order to rebut them, or more rarely, to indicate that they had a similar opinion to his own.

4.

Kalecki was a man of quite exceptional intellectual independence. I used to even suspect that his early experiences as a theoretician developed in him the habit of regularly exercising his independence. In the thirties, he belonged to a very small group of economists who had pitted themselves against a number of prejudices that were deeply rooted in the minds even of the most highly trained economists. He could scarcely have failed to notice later, however, that the whole Keynesian revolution achieved little more than narrowing the wall of myths enclosing man's thinking about economics; that even the most heavily attacked fallacies lived on, if at a greater distance from the main thoroughfare of economic thought. And thus there was developed in Kalecki a distinctive distrust for all views that were not exposed to the most comprehensive criticism. This is the way I would be inclined to explain his permanently polemical approach to everything, including even his own earlier statements. This seems to explain, for example, the remark made to me by a foreigner after a conversation with Kalecki: 'What a strange fellow! The minute you start agreeing with him, he stops agreeing!' A conversation with Kalecki really was an effort; it was dialectics as Zeno would have understood it. Kalecki's distrust of myths, especially elegant, theoretical myths, was far stronger than his tolerance. One felt his attitude towards views differing from his own was one of at best forbearance.

5.

From the early thirties on, Kalecki was identified with the socialist movement, with its intellectual rather than its working-class wing. *Przegląd socjalistyczny*, to which Kalecki contributed articles on economic and political themes, was a somewhat exclusive journal. These articles were critical essays on the political and economic irrationality of capitalism. And it is here that Kalecki's socialist motivation should be sought. His critical, rationalist and sceptical mind was markedly prone to pessimism, and decidedly impatient of utopian dreaming. He was for socialism because he felt it might be a better system. And that it might be made even better. He did not expect that system to fulfil any ideals, but merely to bring some improvement. As with economic matters, so too with social ones, he did not pursue absolute solutions. Eschatology was alien to him. Both in relation to economic and social problems, he felt great distaste for slogans which could not be backed up by available resources. He fought against 'heroic' planning to the best of his ability, and several times, both in Poland and abroad, was able to feel a certain wry satisfaction from the subsequent course of events. In planning matters generally, he usually came down on the side of caution. In practice, it happened again and again that optimism had to be replaced by a pessimism which far outstripped Kalecki's original reserve on the issue. At first, Kalecki was inclined to draw more satisfaction than anything else from these episodes. He still felt convinced that 'humanity' learns by its mistakes.

Practical observation of economic life led to Kalecki's forming a remarkable allergy. He didn't like good harvests, for example; because they produce planner's euphoria, and if this happens to come at a time when long-term decisions are being taken, the results are disastrous.

In the last fifteen years of his life, Kalecki wrote extensively about socialist economy. His work on growth theory is probably the best thing of its kind available in socialist literature; his *Zarys teorii wzrostu gospodarki socjalistycznej* (Introduction to the Theory of Growth in a Socialist Economy), which has been translated into a number of foreign languages, may well become as much of a classic as the earlier *Teoria dynamiki gospodarczej* (Theory of Economic Dynamics). In addition, he published a number of articles devoted to, among other things, the functioning of socialist economies. It is doubtful whether one could extract any 'Kalecki system' from these writings. But their general tendency is well known. In the fiery debates of the post-October period (1956–57), his contributions were consistently aimed against the propensity, wide-spread at the time, to overestimate the possibilities of sweeping systemic change. In his view, the system of economic management, as it had existed up till then, was in large measure the product of economic tensions caused by faulty planning allocations. While defending central planning against the attacks of the extreme decentralizers, he took a very active part, at the same time, in the work of the Economic Council and the Planning Commission on producing a new model for the economy which would be a departure from the old system of bureaucratic centralism. He was very eager to ensure that the conditions of decentralization and automatization should not be dictated by lower-rank managers, and that decentralization should mean an increase in self-management for the workers' collective as well. For this reason, among others, he felt that workers' councils should be installed as high as the level of the group of enterprises. Perhaps he saw the conflict between workers' councils and central planning more clearly than any of us. This is what he wrote about the synthesis model of workers' councils combined with central planning which was foreshadowed at the time:

'We ought not to delude ourselves that a system of this kind is free of contradictions and will be easy to run. On the one hand there will be the danger that the workers' councils will be weakened and the whole system of management bureaucratized. On the other, it could happen that the workers' councils will exert such pressure that it will become necessary to slow up the tempo of development, or to make maintenance of the growth rate dependent on aid from abroad, or again that there will be a period of chaos, after which things will be tidied up with the aid of a return to the system of bureaucratic centralism.' (*Nowe Drogi*, 1956, No. 11/12).

Kalecki was keenly interested in the problem of the proper deployment of the different units of the central planning authorities. Particularly important, in his view, was the question of the proper organization of the more important investment decisions, of ensuring that planning should be a matter of choice between genuine alternatives. To eliminate the element of fiction from this area, Kalecki regarded it as essential that one or more autonomous centres be set up, staffed by experts completely independent of the industrial and administrative hierarchy. This advice was not taken, though it would seem to have been the most important conclusion that his years of experience as an economic adviser had led him to.

Kalecki was not only a theoretician. He was a natural expert adviser. He spoke about hope and disillusionments he had in that connection on the occasion of his jubilee. One of the few dreams he ever permitted himself was for a socialist *Il Principe Nuovo*, who would be prepared to listen carefully to the advice of his counsellors, and to value their independence of mind and devotion to society above devotion to his own person.

Kalecki looked for such a prince from Havana to Delhi.

6.

In itself, death need not be tragically sad—if the life in question has been a successful and fruitful one. If there has been fulfilment. If one's life-work has already assumed definite and lasting contours, death can be accepted as something natural, a kind of reuniting with nature. This is what all the sages teach us. But death becomes inexpressibly sad, when one can see no obvious continuation of that life-work, when death becomes a caesura, and not just the end to a particular life.

Half a century ago I was convinced that Poland was the most impoverished country in Europe as far as economic theory was concerned: 'The development of economic theory in Poland,' I wrote, 'leaves an infinitely large amount to be desired. Practical and political concerns dominate research, and most of what is published is either descriptive or popular; attempts at independent theoretical enquiry are a rarity. . . A special theory has even emerged in this country which sees this predominance of practical concerns as being symptomatic of the Polish mind in general.' (*Przedświt*, 1920, No. 3). These were bitter words, but words written with hope, for I regarded Polish political economy as an unworked, but fertile field. The fact that it had not been ploughed I regarded as being largely due to Poland's long years of subjugation.

Then came the 'fertile' years of hope. In the thirties, new ideas and tendencies began to make their appearance, simultaneously with or even preceding developments in the homeland of classical political economy and Scandinavia. Suddenly there was a whole group of young and talented economists and statisticians, the most gifted among whom soon began to be important names in the international literature.

War thinned their ranks; and soon after came the years of mythology. Polish economic thinking would have to be sought out in the distant past.

But in fact that whole period was relatively short. And then, in the mid-fifties, Polish economics suddenly exploded onto the scene, vibrant with new ideas and conceptions. Michal Kalecki returned to his homeland. Oskar Lange descended to this earth. Schools were created. Warsaw began to be known as the 'socialist Cambridge'. People came to Warsaw from all over the world to study economic theory and planning, and in some cases, to breathe the Warsaw air with its heavy charge of intellectual tension. Our voice counted for something at international conferences. It was a brief interlude. But long enough to produce theoretical works of lasting value. We felt proud; and linked the outburst of creative effort with the conditions provided by the new social system.

Michal Kalecki has left us. Oskar Lange before him. But there is no need for Polish theoretical economics to become a provincial Cinderella again. Social conditions obviously play an important role in the development of economics as a discipline. The state of economic science does not therefore depend only on the members of the academic world; but they are certainly largely responsible. Our tradition is the richer for the contributions of Michal Kalecki and Oskar Lange. If their work is continued, we will be able to cry: *Non omnis moriar!*

[6]

KALECKI'S POLITICAL ECONOMY: A COMPARISON WITH KEYNES*

By ÉPRIME ESHAG

Kalecki's view as to what the proper function of economic theory should be was rather similar to that of Keynes. In a sense they were both 'political economists' interested in analysing and providing solutions to concrete economic problems. For them economic theory had to be directly concerned with the analysis of real economic phenomena whether small or large and whether of past, present or future occurence. According to this approach, the significance of a theory is to be judged not by the complexity of the mathematical techniques embodied in it, but solely by reference to the practical importance of the economic problems it sought to solve and the adequacy of the solutions provided. For this reason, despite their large store of mathematical and statistical knowledge, neither Kalecki nor Keynes indulged himself in building abstract economic models based on unrealistic assumptions which could not be factually illustrated and verified.[1] They were both what David Worswick calls in his lecture 'serious' economists.

Although the models of the determination of employment and income in capitalist economies constructed by Kalecki and Keynes were similar in all important respects, there were some differences in the presentation and explanation of their models which Joan Robinson has discussed in her lecture. But the more significant differences between Kalecki and Keynes are to be sought in the practical political messages contained in their writings rather than in their theoretical models. This can be explained largely by differences in their social and intellectual backgrounds. Kalecki came from a Jewish family in Lodz, Poland, and when his father (a local mill-owner) lost his business, Kalecki was forced to abandon his engineering studies and seek employment for his livelihood; he was largely self-taught in Economics. He had witnessed and experienced material deprivation, had read some Marxist literature, noted by Lipiński, and fully appreciated the Marxist contribution to economic and social analysis. Kalecki was in fact an outstanding example of a scientific socialist dedicated to improving the lot of the mass of the people. Keynes on the other hand was born into a well-to-do and established upper middle class academic family. He went to Eton and King's College, Cambridge, and enjoyed all the amenities of the British upper class academic circles. He never seriously studied Marxist literature, but this did not generally prevent him from dismissing Marxist writings on economic and political problems as low grade intellectual exercises. He was politically an enlightened liberal intellectual interested in preserving all the essential elements of the free enterprise economies.[2]

* I am grateful to the Editors and to Stanislaw Braun, W. Brus and David Worswick for their valuable comments.

[1] In this, Keynes was strongly influenced by Marshall's attitude on the proper role of mathematics in economics. See *Memorials of Alfred Marshall*, Ed. A. C. Pigou, pp. 12, 24–26 and 312–14.

[2] For a more detailed description of differences in social and intellectual backgrounds of Kalecki and Keynes, see George R. Feiwel, *The Intellectual Capital of Michal Kalecki*, University of Tennessee Press (1975), Chapter II.

These differences in Kalecki's and Keynes's social and intellectual backgrounds go some way in explaining important differences in the political tone and content of their writings summarized below under three broad headings.

1. *The purpose and scope of government intervention.* Although both writers had demonstrated that market forces could not ensure full utilization of productive resources, and therefore advocated state action, their motives for doing so differed significantly and so did the type of intervention they envisaged. Keynes's primary purpose in advocating interference with the free operation of market forces was to prevent the needless waste caused by unemployment and to save the free enterprise system. Without government action there was the danger of periodic depressions and mass unemployment which threatened the existence of an individualistic system. He would confine state intervention to such measures as would ensure full employment and would leave the allocation of resources and the distribution of income to market forces. He says: 'It is in determining the volume, not the direction, of actual employment that the existing system has broken down';[3] and concludes his case for state intervention by adding:

> Whilst, therefore, the enlargement of the functions of government, involved in the task of adjusting to one another the propensity to consume and the inducement to invest, would seem to a nineteenth-century publicist or to a contemporary American financier to be a terrific encroachment on individualism, I defend it, on the contrary, both as the only practicable means of avoiding the destruction of existing economic forms in their entirety and as the condition of the successful functioning of individual initiative.[4]

Unlike Keynes, Kalecki had no particular interest in preserving the free enterprise system and his advocacy of state intervention was motivated by a socialistic desire to improve the economic conditions of the broad masses of the population. For him, market forces failed to ensure not only full utilization but also a rational allocation of resources from the point of view of the welfare of the community as a whole. He would therefore extend the scope of state intervention to a regulation of the pattern of investment and to redistribution of income without being unduly concerned about consequential changes in the character of the free enterprise system entailed by such a policy. It was not enough to maintain full employment by raising government expenditure which he (like Keynes) saw would help to assure some stability to modern capitalism. It was equally important to consider the impact of such expenditure on the economic welfare of the community. In his address to the Reunion of Latin American Schools of Economics in 1965 he summarized his long-held position thus:

> Let us now consider the direction of government expenditure undertaken in order to maintain full employment. From the point of view of creating demand this does not matter as said above; the most rational course, however,

[3] J. M. Keynes, *The General Theory of Employment, Interest and Money*, p. 379.
[4] *Ibid.*, p. 380.
For Keynes's earlier pronouncements on this subject, see Eprime Eshag, *From Marshall to Keynes*, Blackwell (1963) pp. 90–91.

and this would occur under a socialist system, would be to spend on investment and thus to accelerate the development of the economy; or to contribute through government expenditure (or reduction of taxation) to the increase in consumption of the broad masses of the population. However, under capitalism, this does not necessarily happen.[5]

2. *Distribution of Income.* As Joan Robinson points out, Keynes showed little interest in the classical question of the distribution of income between the different classes of the community. Following the tradition of the classical economists, he strongly disapproved of the income accruing to the rentier class, but he considered 'the rentier phase of capitalism as a transitional phase which will disappear when it has done its work'.[6] As a progressive liberal he held that 'there is social and psychological justification for significant inequalities of incomes and wealth, but not for such large disparities as exist today'.[7] He was by and large satisfied with the system of distribution of income in a free enterprise economy and not particularly interested in closely examining its rationality and morality.

On the other hand, for Kalecki, the subject of the distribution of income was a crucial one and he devoted considerable attention to it. But although in a broad sense a Marxist, he made no use of the classical labour theory of value and of Marx's concept of exploitation based on it. Instead, he used his own macro-model to demonstrate that under a free enterprise system workers' income and consumption are determined for them by capitalists, whereas capitalists determine their own income by *their own* investment and consumption decisions. As a socialist, Kalecki could find no moral ground for justifying this system of income distribution.

3. *Relative importance of ideas and vested interests.* The third and probably the most important single difference between Kalecki and Keynes concerned the relative weight attached by them to institutional and political factors as compared with pure knowledge, or ideas, in determining economic policy and developments. Despite his solid pragmatism and intellectual brilliance, Keynes, as a western liberal intellectual, tended to exaggerate the importance of the role played by the progress of economic ideas in shaping economic policy. He says:

> The ideas of economists and political philosophers, both when they are right and when they are wrong, are more powerful than is commonly understood. Indeed the world is ruled by little else. Practical men, who believe themselves to be quite exempt from any intellectual influences, are usually the slaves of some defunct economist. Madmen in authority, who hear voices in the air, are distilling their frenzy from some academic scribbler of a few years back. I am sure that the power of vested interests is vastly exaggerated compared with the gradual encroachment of ideas.[8]

Kalecki, on the other hand, recognized the limitations of ideas in influencing economic policy and the course of events. Perhaps the most important single lesson he had learned from studying Marxist literature and from his own experience

[5] Michal Kalecki, *Essays on Developing Economies*, The Harvester Press, (1976) p. 22.
[6] J. M. Keynes, *op. cit.*, p. 376.
[7] J. M. Keynes, *op. cit.*, p. 374.
[8] Keynes, *op. cit.*, p. 383.

concerned the close organic interrelation that existed in every society between the structure of the economy, political institutions and what may be called the 'prevailing wisdom'—the ideas (whether expressly professed or implicitly accepted) which underlie economic policy and are propagated in the community. For him, the influence of economic ideas in shaping policy was severely constrained by the prevailing social and political institutions, which included the media of information and learned journals. He says:

> The assumption that a Government will maintain full employment in a capitalist economy if it only knows how to do it is fallacious.[9]

Kalecki's approach gave him a deep insight into the complex process of policy formulation and a clear vision of the future. It enabled him, as noted above, to foresee as early as 1943, the difficulties of maintaining full employment in 'capitalist democracies' in peacetime conditions because of the opposition of vested interests; this prophecy has been amply verified by the economic developments in the industrial countries of the west during the last decade.

Keynes who believed that 'the power of vested interests is vastly exaggerated' could not foresee these developments. For the same reason, he would probably have been somewhat surprised at certain important developments in economic ideas and policies in recent years—some forty years after the publication of the *General Theory*. One need mention only two such developments: *first*, the wide popularity gained by the neomonetarist school among some academic circles and almost all policy makers of the West with its heavy emphasis on the control of the supply of money as a means of curing *all* price inflations and regulating the volume of aggregate demand and production in the short run; *secondly*, the re-emergence of the orthodox doctrine of 'sound finance' which in addition to demanding a strict control of the money supply, also views with disfavour any growth in budget deficits without much regard to the prevailing level of unemployment. It is interesting to note that the policy of reducing the budget deficit, which nowadays forms a major plank of both the Conservative and Labour governments in the United Kingdom, has in recent years enjoyed the blessing even of some Keynesian economists in Cambridge, England. But none of these developments came, or would have come, as a surprise to Kalecki, who had foreseen as early as 1943 that the political forces ranged against the maintenance of full employment 'would probably find more than one economist to declare that the situation' of full employment 'was manifestly unsound'.[10]

Kalecki as a Man

Enough has been said about Kalecki's intellectual power, his creative genius and his contribution to economics. Something should now be said about his character as a man, since this had a direct bearing on his work and career. But first a few words about his personality in general. In his looks and voice, Kalecki bore a striking resemblance to Bertrand Russell: both were of rather small stature,

[9] *Selected Essays on the Dynamics of the Capitalist Economy*, Cambridge University Press (1971) p. 138.

[10] Michal Kalecki, *Selected Essays*, *op. cit.*, p. 144.

with large heads and prominent noses, and both spoke in a loud voice, Kalecki's being at least one decibel louder, but not as high-pitched as that of Russell. Kalecki was rather shy in appearance, and like most other great people had little time for small talk. This was best exemplified in the way he answered his telephone in the United Nations which usually took the form of a loud and clear challenge, 'Yes?' His loud voice, combined with his impatience with small talk, at times put off newcomers who took him for a somewhat odd and aloof person. But those who knew him better never failed to enjoy his warm company, his engaging conversation and his sense of humour. He was in addition a generous, loyal and kind-hearted person and was genuinely appreciative of the smallest gesture of friendship to himself or his wife. Kalecki was a born democrat and treated all those with whom he had any dealings, irrespective of their rank, with equal consideration.

What had a more direct bearing on Kalecki's work, however, was his character. He was a proud and dignified man of exceptional integrity and courage. Perhaps the most important occasion on which he was called upon to demonstrate these qualities was during his service with the United Nations Secretariat (1946–54). In his work at the United Nations, Kalecki was reputed for his objectivity and impartiality in the analysis of world economic developments and in all other work assigned to him. In this, Kalecki was of course adhering to the solemn oath, which he, in common with all other United Nations employees, had to take, swearing to work exclusively in the interest of the Organisation and to refrain from taking instructions from outside bodies and governments. What is not generally known, but perhaps needs to be related here, is the difficulties encountered by Kalecki in maintaining this independent course of action which finally led to his resignation.

The last years of Kalecki's service with the United Nations coincided with the worst phase of the cold war which culminated in the political witch-hunts of Senators McCarren and McCarthy in the United States. It would be difficult for those who did not actually work in the United Nations Headquarters in New York to imagine the atmosphere of terror that hung over the Secretariat in those years. Anyone daring to criticize, or even failing to co-operate with, McCarthyism, left himself open to the serious accusation of being a communist or a fellow traveller. A number of Kalecki's colleagues were dismissed by the Secretary General (Trygve Lie) for undeniably political reasons.[11] Many others were successfully terrorized into active co-operation with McCarthyism or into abject silence. The independence of the Secretariat, enshrined in the United Nations Charter, was eroded to a point where Trygve Lie permitted the FBI agents to enter the diplomatically immune United Nations Headquarters to interrogate not only United States citizens, but also many Latin American members of the Secretariat. There is ample evidence to suggest that most members of the other nationalities were also under close surveillance both at the Headquarters and outside.

Throughout this period Kalecki was under strong pressure to abandon his independent stand, by altering the contents, tone and presentation of Part I of the *World Economic Reports*. But Kalecki stubbornly refused to budge. His duties as

[11] Some of those who were dismissed appealed to the Administrative Tribunal of the United Nations against the Secretary General and were awarded compensation for wrongful dismissal.

an international civil servant, as he rightly saw them, were to give a broad picture of economic developments in the world by publishing and analysing all data received from official government sources; he was going to do no more and no less than this. It was because of this uncompromising attitude, that eventually his superiors decided to push him out of the United Nations, or at least to 'clip his wings' as was openly declared by some of them.

There was some improvement in the morale of the United Nations staff when Dag Hammarskjold succeeded Trygve Lie in 1953; among other things, the FBI activities in the Secretariat were manifestly curtailed. But even Hammarskjold was not prepared to go far enough to safeguard Kalecki's position. The opportunity for pushing Kalecki out of the United Nations finally came when a scheme for the reorganization of the Secretariat was introduced under which a number of senior Director posts were created. Because of his seniority and his exemplary services to the Secretariat, Kalecki would in the normal course of events, have been entitled to promotion to one of these senior posts from his rank of Assistant Director. But instead, under the reorganization plan Kalecki's post, which carried the responsibility of producing Part I of the *World Economic Report*, was eliminated and he was asked to perform the lower grade functions of a Chief of Section. It was said that the *World Economic Reports* were in the future to be written by outside experts and Kalecki and his staff were to have the simple duty of collecting and presenting the data to these experts.

Kalecki was thus presented with the option of being humiliated into accepting a sinecure with a lower status or resigning. He decided to resign and to return to Poland against the advice of some of his close friends who feared for his material well being in a Stalinist Poland where he was considered by the authorities to be a 'bourgeois Keynesian economist'. This was the measure of Kalecki's integrity, pride and courage. It need hardly be added that, once Kalecki was safely out of the way, the *World Economic Reports* continued to be written as before by the United Nations staff; not a single issue was written by the outside experts.

After his resignation, Kalecki was urged by some of his friends to stay out of controversial issues on his return to Poland, advice which he seemed to have heeded during the old oppressive régime. With the change in the Polish political climate that took place in the course of 1956, however, Kalecki was given the opportunity of participating in the debate on the problems of the Polish economy. As explained in Brus's lecture, he utilized this opportunity to the full and became the undisputed intellectual spokesman of the critics of the orthodox dogmatism and of bureaucratic centralism. Once Kalecki had thrown himself body and soul into this struggle, he was not prepared to withdraw from it because of the swing of the political pendulum towards the establishment of a new centralized bureaucracy. He continued to advocate his theories of growth and planning despite the apparent hostility of the authorities. Kalecki was prepared to suffer political ostracism and violent criticism rather than compromise with the authorities by endorsing their policies. At the same time, he continued to oppose those Eastern European economists like Oto S̄ik who advocated the replacement of central planning by some form of market mechanism.

The attacks on Kalecki, as Brus has related in his lecture, became progressively more violent during and after the Czechoslovakia crisis in 1968 and finally ended in the liquidation of his famous School by making most of its senior members redundant and forcing some of them out of the country. Kalecki was by that time suffering from ill health and his sole response to all these attacks was to opt for an early retirement as a gesture of protest, although he continued with his research and published a number of papers after his retirement. It was no more to the credit of the Polish authorities to drive Kalecki into retirement than it had been to the credit of the United Nations Secretariat authorities to drive him into resignation in 1954.

In 1969, the year before his death, Kalecki spent one term as Visiting Fellow in Cambridge, England, where he was treated with the greatest consideration and honour by the members of the Faculty of Economics; his wife Ada was with him. I visited them for a week-end just before they returned to Poland, and had the opportunity of talking to him about his recent experiences in Poland. He was somewhat depressed and withdrawn, partly no doubt because of the poor state of his health and partly because of the disappointments he had suffered as economic adviser to the Polish Government. He talked at length about his recent work in Poland; he was sad and disappointed, but rather philosophical and in no way bitter. This was not surprising, because Kalecki had for many years stressed the relative insignificance of knowledge and reason, as compared with the vested interests of the socio-political institutions, in shaping the course of economic policy. He could see that this important proposition was equally true of the Polish communist régime in the 1960's. Soon afterwards he returned to Poland, and died in April 1970.

No account of Kalecki's life and work, no matter how abridged, can be complete without a mention of the important part played in his life and work by Ada, his wife, who survives him. They were a devoted couple, and Ada, apart from taking meticulous care of Kalecki's health, was able to give him considerable practical help by editing his work and providing him with translations. But it was the moral support that Kalecki received from his wife that had a significant bearing on his decisions concerning his career and his work. Throughout Kalecki's life, but more particularly in crisis periods, he received constant encouragement from his closest companion to follow the dictates of his conscience, and for this, Kalecki's pupils and admirers owe a big debt to Ada Kalecki.

Wadham College
and
Institute of Economics and Statistics,
Oxford.

[7]

KALECKI'S REVIEW OF KEYNES' *GENERAL THEORY**

FERDINANDO TARGETTI and BOGULSLAWA KINDA-HASS

Bocconi University and Trento University, Gdansk University

I. Introduction

At the beginning of 1933 Kalecki published in Polish a small book on business cycles. In October of the same year he discussed his model of the business cycle at the International Econometric Society at Leyden in the Netherlands. Because of the interest created by his paper he was awarded a one year grant by the Rockefeller foundation to continue his research in the West. He chose to go to Scandinavia, where he arrived in 1936, intending to develop his 1932 ideas and write a book on the theory of production and business cycles. He chose Scandinavia not only because his English at that time was not good, but also and more importantly, because of the work being developed there on the theory of crises and cycles. In Sweden, following Wicksell's tradition, Myrdal had been working for some years on the problem of the process from an *ex ante* disequilibrium to an *ex post* equilibrium and by 1933 he had already published a book on this subject. Lindal, Ohlin and Lundberg were also working on similar lines. Lundberg, for example, finished his Ph.D. on the analysis of processes of disequilibria in 1937. Another important element in Kalecki's interest in Scandinavia was Frisch in Norway. Frisch and Kalecki had already met in Leyden in 1933. Together with Aftalion, Frisch had an important influence on Kalecki's early work. Frisch, however, had applied his model only to shipbuilding cycles while Kalecki's model was related to the whole economy.

Sweden may have been important for Kalecki; he does not, however, seem to have had an appreciable effect on Swedish economists. According to Lundberg in his Mattioli Lectures, Milan, May 1981, Kalecki kept himself apart partly due to his character, but also because he was "angry with the bourgeois attitude of the economists in Sweden". Lundberg added: "I regret this because I see the greatness of Kalecki's contribution *ex post* but not *ex ante*".

Soon after arriving in Scandinavia Kalecki received a copy of Keynes' *General Theory* which had been sent to him by Jòzef Zagòrski from London as soon as it was published. Having read the book he was shocked to find that Keynes had written the book he had wanted to write ("for three days I felt ill" he told G.L.S. Shackle [46, p. 127]) and so it happened that he never wrote his "General Theory". However, he wrote

* While we assume the entire responsibility for the translation and the propositions reported in this article, we should like to thank Jorge Fodor for his criticism, suggestions and aid in writing this paper. The article has been written jointly by both authors. However Boguslawa Kinda-Hass is principally responsible for the translation of Kalecki's review and the introduction (sections I and II), Ferdinando Targetti for the comments (section III).

a review of the book in the year of its publication in the Polish journal *Ekonomista*. This review has never been fully translated into English — there is a partial translation in Feiwel [4, pp. 62-66]. The aim of this brief introduction is to present it to English speaking readers. Together with J.R. Hicks in the *Economic Journal*, Abba Lerner in the *International Labour Review* and W.B. Reddaway in the *Economic Record*, Kalecki was one of the few to review the *General Theory* as early as 1936. In Poland as elsewhere Keynes's work was received with mistrust; for instance, the Walrasian mathematical economist Wladyslaw Zawadzki thought that it was not necessary to undertake the task to understand the *General Theory* because Keynes was known to change his opinion regularly [39, p. 502]. Kalecki by contrast understood perfectly the importance, the message and the new method of the book.

In the next section, we present the first English translation of the whole of Kalecki's review article of the *General Theory*. In the final section, we add some explanatory notes on bibliography and some comments on Kalecki's own approach and its relationship to Keynes.

II. SOME REMARKS ON KEYNES' THEORY[1] *by M. Kalecki*

1.

Mr. Keynes' book *The General Theory of Employment, Interest and Money* is, without any doubt, a turning point in the history of economics. It can be roughly divided into two fundamental parts:

1) the determination of short period equilibrium with a given production apparatus, once the level of investment (per unit of time) is given;
2) the determination of the volume of investment.

It seems that the first problem has been solved in Keynes' theory very satisfactorily, even if some reticences and inexactitudes of exposition could give rise to some doubts. In this article I present my own interpretation of this part of Keynes's theory, arriving at his basic conclusions, following a slightly different route.

The matter is quite different as far as the second fundamental problem is concerned, namely, the analysis of the factors determining the level of investment. It is not only the exposition, but the construction itself, that reveals serious deficiencies, so that the problem remains, as we shall see, at least partly unsolved.

Before dealing with the key questions one should say a few words about the basic concepts and hypotheses of Keynes's theory. Furthermore, some supplementary hypotheses should be added to ease the task of presenting his theory.

The notion of a "given production apparatus", which we have previously used, gives rise to some doubts, which should be cleared up. It has often been argued that we

[1]English translation of [13]. Reprinted in [39, pp. 265-274]. In section II the footnotes designated by an arabic numeral are footnotes of the translator, those designated by roman numerals are the footnotes of M. Kalecki.

cannot assume a certain state of the production apparatus in the considered period of time, because — if we do not deal with a case of a stationary state — the investment itself changes the magnitude and the structure of this production apparatus. The answer to this objection is simple. The analysis should concern a period short enough for the change of production apparatus to be small enough to allow us to ignore its influence on output, income and so on. These magnitudes are actually measured in the unit of time and hence they do not depend on the length of the period of time which we take as given, while the growth of the production apparatus is, *ceteris paribus*, proportional to this length.

Next we have to take into account that Keynes considers all the time a closed system thus omitting the influence of foreign trade. We furthermore presume that workers do not save (nor do they live "beyond their means"). The saving of workers surely does not play any important role in economic processes, whereas if we take this saving into account, it will obscure some typical characteristics of the functioning of the capitalist economy in general, and above all it makes Keynes's theory less clear.

Keynes uses as *numéraire* the so-called wage unit, that is, the payment per one man-hour, and he assumes for the sake of simplicity that the payments for various kinds of work remain in a constant relation to one another. Thus if the wage unit is, let us say 50 gr[2], and the price of a kilogramme of one commodity is 2 zl, it means that the price of this commodity is 4 wage units. This way of accounting for the value of commodities has a deeper significance, because Keynes, in a subsequent part of his theory, shows that a movement of wages induces a proportional movement of prices. Therefore, by expressing everything in wage units, Keynes eliminates one of the most important factors in the general movement of prices. We shall return to this matter later. For the time being the reader can consider the wage unit as constant, that is to say, that nominal wages do not vary. Not until later shall we consider the effect of a change in the wage unit.

A fundamental aspect of Keynes' theory is the hypothesis of the existence of a reserve of unemployed workers, which is in strict relation to the previous considerations. If the fall in nominal wages due to unemployment leads to an equi-proportional fall in prices, there is no tendency to absorb unemployment. However, for the time being, as we have just pointed out, we assume nominal wages to be constant, "until further notice"; therefore we can assume the existence of a reserve army of unemployed workers without any further consideration.

2.

Let us take the production apparatus as given. The level of production with this apparatus depends on the amount of employment and on the allocation of the labour force in the particular sectors of this appartus. In every firm the level of production is determined by the intersection of the curve of marginal prime costs[3] and the curve of marginal revenue (in the case of a free competitive market the curve of marginal

[2]The Polish money unit is zloty (zl). The hundredth part of the zlotty is the grosz (gr).
[3]In Polish and English in the text.

UWE, BRISTOL LIBRARY SERVICES

revenue will be a horizontal line with its abscissa equal to the price; here we will deal with a more general case, which includes also imperfect competition).

We show the intersection point between the marginal revenue curve and the marginal cost curve as follows. From both prices and costs we deduct raw material costs and the part of the apparatus which is used up in production[i]; in this way, we get the curves of marginal value added[ii,4] and of labour costs. It can now be said that the production of the firm is determined by the intersection of the marginal value added curve and the curve of marginal labour cost. Both value added and labour cost are expressed in wage units.

Let us now define the short-term equilibrium as the state in which the curves of marginal value added and of marginal labour cost do not shift. Given the production apparatus the position of the marginal cost curve is settled. Therefore given the production apparatus, the short-term equilibrium is reached through the shifting of the marginal value added curves and equilibrium is reached when these curves do not tend to move any further.

FIGURE 1

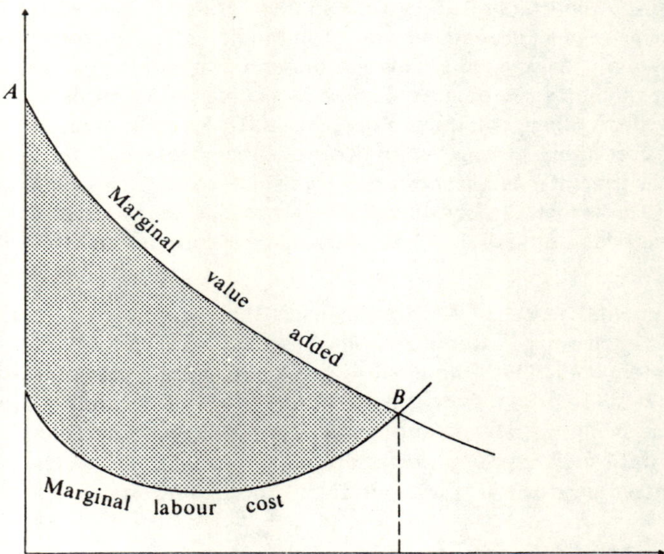

In Figure 1, the area *OABC* will be equal, as one can easily see, to the total value added (in wage units) obtained by the firm producing *OC*. The shaded area is the income of the capitalists (entrepreneurs and rentiers) of this firm, whereas the non-

[i]But not the obsolescence which is independent of use.

[ii]It is not the term used by Keynes.

[4]In Polish and English in the text.

shaded area is the income of the workers. Therefore the sum of the areas *OABC* of all the firms of the economic system we have considered gives us the national income, expressed in wage units; while the sum of all shaded areas is the global income of the capitalists, and the sum of the unshaded areas is the global income of the workers. At the same time social income is equal to the value of consumption plus investment; and, because we have assumed that the workers do not save, the sum of all non-shaded areas coincides with the value of workers' consumption, while the sum of the shaded areas coincides with the value of capitalists' consumption and investment.[iii]

We are already able to show the crucial role of the expenditure of capitalists on consumption and investment in the determination of the short-term equilibrium. In this equilibrium the curve of marginal value added remains, *ex definitione*, in a certain given position. As we have just shown, the sum of shaded areas amounts to capitalist expenditures for consumption and investment while the non-shaded areas are equal to the expenditure on consumption by workers. A spontaneous change in worker expenditure cannot happen because (as we have assumed) they spend exactly as much as they have earned. But when capitalists are considered, a spontaneous change in expenditure is highly probable either by means of spending reserves or by contracting new debts. Let us suppose that they raise their expenditure by a certain amount in a unit of time. Then the marginal value added curves will shift up to the point where the sum of the shaded areas matches the higher value of capitalist expenditure for consumption and investment. And since the sum of the shaded areas is at the same time the total income of capitalists, their higher expenditure "will force" a higher income of the same amount for them.

Naturally, in the new short-period equilibrium, the employment and income of workers, and therefore the value of their consumption (measured in wage units), are higher than before. It follows that the demand for every kind of goods, both for investment as well as for consumption by capitalists and workers, has grown; therefore the shift of the curves of marginal value added has had to take place in all branches of industry.

Therefore we see that the sum of capitalist expenditure determines the position of the value added curves in such a way that the sum of the shaded areas, that is, of capitalist income, is equal to their expenditure. Thus the level of expenditure (expressed in wage units) is the crucial factor in determining the short-term equilibrium.

3.

We have shown earlier that capitalist expenditure "forces" an income equal to the amount of this expenditure. Because this expenditure is formed by consumption and investment, and income is formed by consumption and savings, we can say also that

[iii]The income of capitalists and investment are both gross. Therefore in order to calculate both the income of capitalists and net investment, one must deduct that part of amortization which does not depend on the utilization of the productive equipment, but depends on "physical" and "moral" aging (*i.e.*, as a result of technical progress).

investment "forces" savings whose value is equal to the same value of this investment. It is clear that, generally, the capitalists who invest are not the same ones who save. The investment of the former creates equal savings of the latter.

Now let us assume that the capitalists have a given saving habit; this means that to each level of capitalists' global income, expressed in wage units, will correspond a precisely determined distribution of this income between consumption and savings. As a result of the above, each level of global savings corresponds also to a determined level of capitalist consumption. And furthermore it is easy to provide that the global value of investment, expressed in wage units, determines the total amount of capitalist expenditure. In fact the level of investment, I, "forces" an equal level of savings and, if capitalist consumption is, let us say, smaller than the level C corresponding to savings I, the capitalists will consume more; in this way they "push" their income up to the level $C+I$, at which the proportion between their consumption C and their savings, I, will correspond to their saving habit.

4.

Now we see that investment I, expressed in wage units, determines "grosso modo"[5] the short-term equilibrium once the production apparatus is given. In fact, given their saving habits, investment, strictly speaking, determines the capitalists' consumption, C. We have therefore the sum of capitalists' expenditures $C+I$ and its distribution between consumption and investment. To determine the short-term equilibrium in all its details we should also know the structure of investment (and not only its total value) and the "tastes" of capitalists and workers. If we take the "tastes" as given, the only element not yet determined by the short-term equilibrium, corresponding to a given amount of investment expenditure I (expressed in wage units) in the unit of time, will be the distribution of these expenditures among the various kinds of investment. However it seems to us that the change in the structure of investment expenditure will be of a relative minor importance in relation to the global employment and social income Y, expressed in wage units. That is to say, we do not make a serious mistake in writing:

$$Y=f(I),$$

where f is a growing function and its shape is determined by the dimension and the structure of the production apparatus, by the capitalist saving habit and by the "tastes" of capitalists and workers. The derivative of this function:

$$dY/dI=f'(I),$$

is the so-called Keynesian multiplier[6]. If investment changes from the given level I to $I+\triangle I$, where $\triangle I$ is a small increase, income will change to the level $Y+\triangle If'(I)$.

[5]In Italian in the text.
[6]In Polish and in English in the text.

5.

Now let us see what Keynes's theory as expounded above (even if in a slightly different way from the original) offers. First of all, we can see that investment is the factor which decides the short-term equilibrium, and hence, at a certain moment, the size of employment and of social income. In fact their amount will decide the amount of the labour force which will be absorbed by the existing production apparatus[iv]. So we must look for the answer to the question why we have high or low levels of employment and of production in the analysis of factors governing the amount of investment. The second part of Keynes's theory which we will discuss later, is devoted to this analysis.

For the time being we must stress that, following the previous reasoning, saving does not determine investment but, on the contrary, it is precisely investment which creates savings. The equilibrium between demand for "capital" and supply of "capital" always exists, whatever the rate of interest, because investment always "forces" savings of the same amount[v]. Hence the rate of interest cannot be determined by the demand for and the supply of "capital". Its level, according to Keynes's theory, must therefore be determined by other factors, namely the supply of and demand for means of payment. If, for instance, a given amount of money is in circulation and social income grows, the demand for the means of payment will increase and the rate of interest will rise as much as it is necessary to bring about the use of the same quantity of money despite the higher level of activity. This is a very general sketch of Keynes's theory of the rate of interest, which we do not want to deal with in detail here.

Before dealing with the analysis of factors determining the size of investment, the problem of nominal wages still remains to be considered. We will do this also in a very general way. Hitherto we have assumed that the wage unit is a constant magnitude. What changes will the short-term equilibrium depicted above undergo if, for instance, this unit decreases because of a fall in the nominal wage? If we assume that the value of investment, expressed in wage units, does not change, it is obvious that nothing will change also in the short-term equilibrium as a whole, which, as we have previously shown, is completely determined by investment. Employment and production will remain unchanged; prices only, if expressed in money terms, will be reduced proportionally to the wage unit.

But is it really likely that investment, expressed in wage units, will not change if nominal wages, for instance, decrease? Keynes argues that this is what actually happens, but his arguments on this point are not sufficiently convincing. The most important counter-argument that can be put forward here is that a decrease in wages raises profitability and that may induce a rise in the amount of investment. Keynes, however, as we shall see later on, does not take sufficient account of the influence of *current* profitability on investment, and therefore he does not analyse this problem at

[iv]The proposition that investment decides the global dimension of the production has been proved by myself in a similar way to Keynes' in [7, pp. 20-21].

[v]An analogous idea about the demand for and supply of capital has been given by myself in [7, pp. 22 and 23].

all, which is here, beyond any doubt the most crucial one. But, despite these deficiencies in his arguments, Keynes's statement, that the nominal wage magnitude does not influence, at least directly, the determination of short-period equilibrium, seems correct. In order to show the likelihood of this it is enough to assume that the entrepreneurs do not infer *immediately* the consequences from an increase in profitability due to a decrease in wages in their investment activity. For if they do not raise investment immediately, short-period equilibrium remains unchanged in the meantime, and prices will drop in the same proportion as wages. Therefore the improvement in profitability which reach will turn out to be illusory and the basis for the growth of investment vanishes. If after the wage reduction entrepreneurs do not increase immediately the amount of investment, they will not increase it later either. In this way the movement of nominal wages cannot be a factor having any influence on the short-period equilibrium.[vi].

6.

The fundamental concept of the Keynesian theory of investment is the marginal efficiency of a given object of investment. Keynes defines it as that discount rate of the future expected gross income (the difference between proceeds and expenditures) of this object over its "life" which makes the present value of those expected receipts equal to its actual market price. If for instance, we buy machinery worth 1.000 zloty and we forecast that it will be used for 5 years and during these years it will probably produce for us an income of 300 zl, 320 zl, 350 zl, 350 zl, and 300 zl, its marginal efficiency will be the discount rate, by means of which one gets 1.000 zl as the actual value of the income of these 5 years. Naturally the bigger the expected income and the lower the price of investment goods the higher will be this marginal efficiency of investment, which subsequently we will call expected profitability. The size of investment then is determined in Keynes's analysis by the equalization of the expected profitability and the rate of interest. If the expected profitability is at a certain moment of time greater than the rate of interest, investment is attractive and its level will rise. But owing to the greater demand for investment goods their prices will rise and hence expected profitability will fall. Investment finally reaches the level at which prices of investment goods equalize the expected profitability and the rate of interest.

This simple concept has two serious deficiencies. First, it does not say anything about the sphere of investment *decisions* of the entrepreneur, who makes his calculations in "disequilibrium" on the basis of *existing* market prices of investment goods. It shows only that if the expected profitability, calculated on the basis of this price level, is not equal to the rate of interest, a change in the level of investment will occur. This will transform the existing situation into one in which expected profitability *is equal to* the rate of interest. Using the terminology of Swedish economists, one can say that Keynes's theory determines only the *ex post* level of investment, but that it does not say anything about *ex ante* investment.

[vi] I have also shown the independence of production from the movement of nominal wages in [7, pp. 45-47].

But this is not the end. In the subsequent analysis new difficulties emerge. Let us suppose that in the original situation the expected profitability was higher than the rate of interest and that investment increases. This provokes such a rise in the prices of investment goods, that the expected profitability, calculated on the basis of these new prices and of the expected incomes in the *initial situation*, is equal to the rate of interest. Now we must take into account the fact that the growth of investment does not provoke only an increase in the prices of investment goods, but that, according to the first part of Keynes's theory which we have explained above, it also stimulates a general recovery, provoking a rise of prices and production in all sectors. However, because, as Keynes holds in another part of his book, "the elements of the present situation have a striking influence on the formation of long-term expectation"[7], the expectations will become more optimistic and a difference between the marginal efficiency of investment and the rate of interest will arise again. "Equilibrium" then is not reached and the growth of investment will still persist (we are dealing here, as easily can be seen, with a cumulative Wicksellian process).

Therefore we see that the Keynesian concept, which tells us only how high investment should be in order that a certain "disequilibrium" may become "equilibrium", meets a serious difficulty along this way also. In fact the growth of investment does not result at all in a process leading the system toward the "equilibrium".

Therefore it is difficult to consider Keynes' solution of the investment problem to be satisfactory. The reason for this failure lies in an approach which is basically static to a matter which is by its nature dynamic. Keynes takes as given the state of the expectations of returns and from this he deduces a certain determined level of investment, overlooking the effects that investment will have in turn on expectations. It is here that one can see a sketch of the road one must follow in order to build a realistic theory of investment. Its starting point should be the solution of the problem of investment decisions, of *ex ante* investment. Let us suppose there to be at a given moment of time a certain state of expectations as to future incomes, a given price level of investment goods and finally a given rate of interest. How great then will be the investment that entrepreneurs intend to undertake in a unit of time? Let us suppose that this problem has been solved (despite the fact that it seems impossible to us to do this without introducing some special hypothesis about the psychology of the entrepreneurs or even, an hypothesis about money market imperfections). A further development of the theory of investment could be as follows. The decisions concerning investment, corresponding to the initial state, will not generally be equal to the actual level of investment. Therefore in the next period the size of investment will generally be different and the short-period equilibrium will change together with it. Therefore we should now deal with a state of expectations that in general will be different from that of the initial period, different prices of investment goods and a different rate of interest. From these a new level of investment decisions will result and so on.

[7]Translation from Kalecki. We have not been able to find the precise quotation in the *General Theory*. Though several times a similar point is made, see, *e.g.* [40, p. 51].

The detailed analysis of this dynamic process goes beyond the scope of this article; one must accept that the first part of Keynes' theory still keeps its validity. The level of investment in the dynamic process sketched here is subject to continuous change, but at every level of investment, employment and production will be determined on the basis of the first part of Keynes's theory. Keynes did not explain precisely what causes changes in investment, but, on the other hand, he has fully examined the close link between these changes and global employment, production and income movements.

III. Bibliographical Note and a Comment

1. *Bibliographical Note*

The largest work on Kalecki's thought, life and scientific production is Feiwel's *The Intellectual Capital of M. Kaleki* [4]. He does give a complete bibliography, but does not specify when a certain article or a book reproduces a part already published elsewhere.

During the 1930s Kalecki published frequently in English essays which contained parts of older works (translated often from Polish) and the English speaking reader who wants to have a chronological understanding of his intellectual development can be easily confused. It is for such a reader that this bibliographical note is intended.

In January 1933 Kalecki published in Poland his first essay on business cycles.[8] From that date to the appearance of the *General Theory* a few more articles[9] followed which together form a complete theory of short-period equilibrium of a capitalist open and mixed economy. In two subsequent periods Kalecki revisited his theory: in the periods 1937/39[10] and in the periods 1941/54[11]. The final publication of his work in

[8]The book [7] is divided into three parts: the framework of the theory, the mathematical analysis, the consequences on money markets, prices and wages. A synthesis of this paper, translated in German, was discussed in Leyden. The English version is the article [12], which is a synthesis of the first part of the Polish book [7], and presents a development of the mathematical analysis of the second part. In the French version [9] Kalecki left aside the mathematical aspects of the problem and instead enlarged the monetary aspects. A great deal of the first part of [7] and the parts on monetary markets which were extracted from [9] were reprinted in Polish in1962 [33] and in English for the first time in 1966 [34] chap. 1, and subsequently in 1971 [38] chap. 1.

[9]Kalecki's theory of foreign demand was originally published in Polish [8] and subsequently translated into English as "On Foreign Trade and 'Domestic Exports'", which was published in [34] as chap. 3 and then in [38] as chap. 2. In 1935 Kalecki published in Polish two articles [10] [11] which were in effect a popular version of his theory of effective demand. The English translation of these articles, "The Mechanism of Business Upswing" and "The Business Upswing and the Balance of Payments" were published in [34] as chapters 3 and 4 and subsequently in [38] as chap. 3. Finally Kalecki's theory of the effects of tax variation on income and employment is stated in [15] and reprinted in [38] as chap. 4.

[10]In 1939 Kalecki published a book [19] which consists of six essays: "Distribution of the National Income" (reprinted from [17]); "Investment and Income"; "Money and Real Wages" (the argument was further developed in a Polish booklet published in the same year [20]; and subsequently translated in English in 1966 [34] as chapters 5 and 6); "The Principle of Increasing Risk" (reprinted from [16]); "The Long term Rate of Interest"; "A Theory of Business Cycle" (reprinted from [14]) which is a new formulation of his 1933 theory of the business cycle [7].

[11]In this period Kalecki published two books. The first, published in 1943 [25], is a reprint of papers published in the previous five years: part I, entitled "Prices, Interest and Profits" is a reprint with some alterations of three articles [21], [22], [23]; part II, entitled "Business Cycle and the Trend" is reprinted from [14]. In the 1954 book [30], part I, II, IV, V, entitled "Degree of Monopoly and Distribution of Income", "Determination of Profits and National Income", "Determination of Investment", "The Business Cycle" are new developments of old subjects; part III, "The Rate of Interest", was previously published in [25], part VI "Long Run Economic Development" is a new subject.

1971 is a collection of papers from the three stages 1933, 1939, 1954 to which he added some more recent papers about long-term problems[12]. In the above mentioned works, together with a few other works on the war economy[13], on full employment[14] and on hyperinflation[15] we have Kalecki's theory of capitalism[16].

We do not wish here to perform either the difficult tasks of comparing Keynes with Kalecki in general or their formal models and their vision of capitalism[17]. We only wish to make some remarks on the differences between the two authors, using mainly Kalecki's review of the *General Theory*, and his theory of short-period equilibrium which he developed in his first two stages (1933 and 1939), that is, before and after the appearance of the *General Theory*. First, we briefly summarize Kalecki's theory of the determination of income. We then compare his theory with Keynes's theory on some issues.

2. *Kalecki's theory*

(i) *The determination of profit*: In the 1933 Polish booklet [7], given a classical saving function (*i.e.* wage-earners consume all their income), the autonomous expenditure of capitalists (consumption and accumulation) divided by the propensity to save out of profit by capitalists determines the level of profits[18]. Allowing for the effect of their different consumption functions, this result is akin to the Keynesian multiplier. Investment and consumption decisions of capitalists determine profits and not the other way round. If the propensity to consume out of profits is stable, what determines investment decisions is what rules the roost!

(ii) *Investment decisions*: In the 1933 booklet [7] investment decisions, given stationary expectations, are, on one hand, directly correlated with the actual level of profit, and, on the other hand, indirectly correlated with the actual stock of capital goods[19]. The actual level of profit is determined by present accumulation which in turn is influenced by the investment decisions taken in the past by capitalists.

[12]In Kalecki's last book [38] parts I and II, as we have seen, are reprints of parts of his previous three books [34], [19], [30]; part III, which is devoted to long-terms problems, consists of three essays: "Political Aspects of Full Employment" (reprinted fro [24]); "The Problem of Effective Demand with Tugan-Baranowski and Rosa Luxembourg" (originally published in Polish [35]); "Class Struggle and the Distribution of National Income" (reprinted from [37]); "Trend and the Business Cycle" (reprinted from [36]) which is a reformulation of his ideas discussed in part VI of [30] and in [32].

[13]The book [29] is a collection of papers published from 1940 to 1944 in the *Oxford Bulletin of the Institute of Statistics*.

[14]The most important articles are [18], [27], [28].

[15]See especially [31].

[16]It is known that Kalecki's theoretical contribution goes beyond that, as he has contributed to the theory of socialist economies, of developing countries economics and also to mathematical theory. The whole of Kalecki's collected writings are in the process of being published in Poland. Up to now two books have been published. This translation of Kalecki's review of *The General Theory* is based on the version in the first volume [39].

[17]For the largest work on this subject see [4] part I, chapters 1 and 2. For the deepest see Joan Robinson, especially [45].

[18]In this 1954 book [30, part II] the level of profit at a certain date is entirely and solely determined by past decisions to invest.

[19]In his 1954 book [30, part IV] the investment function is dependent on the level and the rate of change of economic activity.

(iii) *The rate of interest and the financing of investment*: Kalecki deals in his 1933 booklet with the problem of financing investment. He holds that investment is financed through a 'credit inflation'[20]. This has similarities to Kaldor's thesis that the supply of money is determined by the demand for money. Consequently Kalecki drops the rate of interest from the determinants of investment decisions because its fluctuation is in tune with, but at a lower level than, the rate of profit. Only an exogenously tight monetary policy will adversely affect investment decisions. In the 1939 book he makes a distinction between the short-term and the long-term rate of interest[21]. The former is affected by monetary policies but its change has virtually no effects on investment. Conversely, changes in the long-term rate of interest have effects on investment, but, because he considers that this rate of interest is highly stable, its influence on investment decisions is negligible. The rate of interest is not an endogenous limit to investment expansions. This occurs in the 1933 booklet [33] through the depressing effect which the stock of capital accumulation has on investment decisions. In the 1939 book [19] it happens through the principle of 'increasing risk': when the higher is the level of investment and the more illiquid the borrower investor becomes there are negative consequences for new investment decisions.

(iv) *The business cycle*: The theory of the business cycle is directly deducible from the determinants of investment. In the 1933 booklet [7] the upswing is due to a reflationary cumulative effect: accumulation (investment *ex post*), influences positively the level of profit, which in turn has a positive influence on investment decisions (investment *ex ante*). The downswing is due to the fact that the deflationary effect of accumulation prevails over this reflationary effect. Investment (*ex post*) increases capacity utilization which depresses investment decisions (investment *ex ante*). In the 1939 book [19] the deflationary task is undertaken by the principle of increasing risk[22].

(v) *Degree of monopoly, distribution and level of income.* Kalecki followed in 1933 and 1939 two different ways to determine the level of income and employment. In 1933 [7] Kalecki argued that the rate of profit is identical to the share of profit multiplied by the output/capital ratio (the degree of productive capacity). Over the course of the cycle all three change in the same direction. At every point of the cycle investment and the stock of capital are known. Given the relation between the investment and the profit level the rate of profit is also known. Hence by the first identity one obtains the degree of utilization of productive capacity and then the level of national income. In 1939 [19] the way he follows is to determine, by means of the degree of monopoly, the distribution of income and then its level. Following Lerner he defines the degree of

[20]In his 1954 book he further develops the subject in the chapter, "The finance of investment" [19, p. 107].
[21]In his 1939 book the same argument is put forward in part III.
[22]In his 1954 book [30] the cycle depends on a new version of the investment function (footnote 20 here); the principle of increasing risk has a new formulation in chap. 8 "Entrepreneurial Capital and Investment". Kalecki investigates in this book the characteristics of ceilings and troughs of cycles and the structure of their fluctuations.

monopoly as the difference between the price level and the marginal cost divided by the price level. In aggregate the average degree of monopoly is given by the relative share of gross capitalist income and salaries in aggregate turnover (which is the sum of national income and the value of raw materials). (This proposition holds insofar as the economy, as normally happens in a capitalist economy, runs below full capacity and then the marginal cost curve is reverse L-shaped[23]). The sum of gross capitalist income and salaries equals the national income less the wage bill. By simple algebra he obtains an inverse relation between the share of wages in national income and the degree of monopoly and the ratio of the materials bill to the wage bill [24, p. 51]. In the business cycle the share of wages is approximately constant because in the upswing the degree of monopoly *cet. par.* falls while the price of raw materials increases and *vice versa* during the downswing.

Now we can summarize the causal structure of Kalecki's determination of short-term equilibrium. Given the propensity to consume, capitalist investment determines the profit level; given stationary expectations and a passive monetary authority, the profit level in its turn has a positive effect on the decisions to invest. This process is endogenously cyclical because of the depressing effect of increasing productive capacity or increasing risk. Given the degree of monopoly, which is exogenous in the short run, he obtains the share of wages and the distribution of income. Once the level and the share of profits are known the levels of income and employment are determined.

(vi) *Real wages, money wages and income.* In 1933 Kalecki held that, in a closed system, the cyclical fluctuations of the share of profit were independent of the struggle for wages. In 1935 Kaleki criticized the orthodox theory according to which a reduction of wages is recommended as a way to overcome the depressions [10, paragraph 1]. He developed the point in 1939, [19] and [34] in the chapters on "Money and Real Wages". If free competition prevails and the marginal cost curve is upward sloping the only consequence of a fall in wages will be a proportional fall in prices, without any effect on capitalist expenditure. As a result the real wage rate and employment will be constant. Furthermore a fall in prices makes it difficult for firms to service their debts and as a consequence may lead to an increase in the long-term rate of interest which has negative effects on investment[24]. If imperfect competition or cartels are prevailing the result of a wage fall is even worse. When the marginal cost curve is flat (below full employment) a fall in money wages is accompanied, as a result of price rigidity, by an increase in the degree of monopoly and a consequent reduction in real wages. The wage good industry reduces its output and employment, while employment in the industries producing investment goods and capitalist consumer

[23]In his 1954 book [30, part I] Kalecki developed this theory: he distinguished between prices determined by costs and prices determined by demand. Moreover, he analyzed the structural causes of change in the degree of monopoly and hence in the share of wages.

[24]Five years later Kalecki returned to this argument. See [26].

goods remains unchanged. As a consequence the real income of capitalists does not rise, but real income of the workers falls[25].

3. *Comparison between Keynes and Kalecki*

The first problem we wish to discuss, raised by Kalecki's review of the *General Theory* is the micro foundations of macro equiibria. In chapter III of the *General Theory* the theory of effective demand is a Keynesian version of the Marshallian theory of the competitive firm. It has been shown [2] and [42] that in the Keynesian model it is possible to aggregate expected demand and supply functions of single firms as well as to reach an equilibrium below full employment that is determined by the equalization of aggregate supply, aggregate expected demand and aggregate expenditure only under the assumptions that firms produce a single good and all firms have the same price expectations.

Kalecki in his review of the *General Theory* also deals with a micro foundation of macro equilibrium by means of a upward sloping curve of marginal cost of labour for the firm. However, his attempt to deal with a more general case which includes also imperfect competition is an important advance, but raises some problems. At the micro level the equilibrium is given by equality between marginal revenue and marginal cost. Once the costs of raw material inputs are subtracted the equilibrium gives also the distribution of value added between profit and wages. However, a serious problem of aggregation arises. If, from an equilibrium point, the capitalists' autonomous expenditure grows, the marginal value added curves of firms shift north-east and output and income will grow and a new distribution at the level of firms will take place. At the macro level there must be both equality between autonomous capital expenditures and total profits as well as between these profits and the sum of all profits of all firms; but there is no guarantee that the equilibria at the micro and macro levels will be compatible[26].

Kalecki in all his subsequent works (see v above) solves the problem of aggregation by assuming at the micro level constant returns to scale (because of imperfect competition) and a constant degree of monopoly (in the short run). But, unless we are dealing with stationary equilibria, it is difficult to think of a constant degree of monopoly as production grows. However, these assumptions are not less strong than the ones mentioned above which are necessary to solve the problem of aggregation in the Keynesian model.

[25]Kalecki returned to the argument at the end of his life. He criticized in [37] the orthodox theory according to which when wages are raised, profits fall *pro-tanto*. If perfect competition and increasing marginal cost prevail a rise in wage rates must cause a proportional rise in prices without having effect on level of output. Consequently output and distribution remain unaffected. If imperfect competition prevails, the firms form their prices by marking up their direct costs. If wage bargainings occur at an industrial level a rise in wage rates will lead either to a price inflation in the industry or to a change in mark-up. That is to say that only under imperfect competition can a rise in wages lead to a redistribution of income. However, from this follows, contrary to the precepts of neo-classical economics, an increase in employment.

[26]A similar argument is put forward by A. Chilosi [3].

A second matter of comparison concerns investment. Kalecki in his review was the first[27] to point out Keynes' confusion in chapter XI of the *General Theory*, between *ex ante* and *ex post* investment and the erroneous (given the premises) method by which investment reaches the equilibrium point. Keynes's argument is that as investment rises the marginal efficiency of capital falls because the price of capital goods increases and this process leads investment to the equilibrium point at which the marginal efficiency of capital is equal to the rate of interest. Kalecki not only rejects the necessary hypothesis of increasing marginal cost curves of capital goods industries but his critique goes deeper, holding that the rise in prices is an effect of a realized investment (investment *ex post*), whereas the marginal efficiency of capital is a determinant of the decision to invest (investment *ex ante*). Moreover, if Kalecki's theory that investment determines profits is tantamount to Keynes's theory that investment determines savings, and if for both theories stationary expectations prevail and if the marginal efficiency of capital is a rate of discount of expected profits, then realized investment increases and does not depress the marginal efficiency of capital (see ii above). The process is cumulative: the growth of investment is not a process leading the system to an equilibrium point. The conclusion is then either the equilibrium is a very short one and the investment must be taken as exogenous or, if the theory commits itself to offer an investment function, it must take into account that investment increases the productive capacity and the matter becomes dynamic 'for its own nature', as in Kalecki's theory of the cycle (see iv above).

A final problem with which we wish to deal, concerns two relations; between investment and the rate of interest, on one hand, and between wages and level of activity on the other. In Keynes's theory, stated in terms of equilibrium, the macroeconomic equilibrium is reached at the point at which a decreasing marginal efficiency of capital equalizes the rate of interest and in which today's rate of interest is determined by the expectations of tomorrow's (long-term) rate of interest. This fact and the lack in the *General Theory* of a theory of distribution of income has led many economists to reformulate Keynes's theory in neoclassical terms[28]. The rate of interest of IS/LM equilibrium in fact turns out to be the marginal productivity of capital[29], if rigidities from the labour market and from the money market are excluded[30]. A further argument supporting this thesis could be found in the relation, put forward by Keynes himself, between the wage rate and the level of activity. Keynes by relying on a Marshallian production function with decreasing productivity of labour (despite the existence of unemployment) is forced to say that a higher level of employment must be associated with lower real wages. But, if equilibrium is a state in which every economic agent is not willing to change his position and if in a state of involuntary unemployment workers are willing to work for the current wage, then a true full equilibrium of underemployment cannot exist[31]. To this proposition Keynes can only

[27]Subsequently, among others see [44] and [1].
[28]The first and most famous is Hicks [6].
[29]This has been clearly shown by Garegnani [5].
[30]These two elements characterize Keynes' "particular case" for neoclassical economists, see [41].
[31]A proposition held by D. Patinkin since 1948, see [43].

object that the process to a full equilibrium at lower real wages must be undertaken through a process of inflation due to a change in aggregate expenditure, whereas it cannot be undertaken *via* a wage prices reduction. But if the theory is formulated in terms of equilibrium instead of processes the "true" equilibrium of full employment will be reached also by means of a wage-price reduction and the Pigou effect will win the game.

Kalecki, instead, has been quite clear throughout his work (and in his reveiw to the *General Theory*) to argue for a pure monetary determination of the rate of interest and in maintaining that the link between the rate of interest and investment is weak, (see iii above). Furthermore, he did not rely upon a neoclassical production function and, as a consequence, his cumulative process could lead to a situation in which higher real wages are combined with higher level of activity and higher employment, (see vi above) and note 25. And this makes Keynes's message itself even stronger.

First version received September 1981
Final version accepted May 1982
(Editors)

References

1. A. Asimakopulos, "The Determination of Investment in Keynes' Model", *Canadian Journal of Economics*, vol. 4, 1971.
2. C. Casarosa, "Un contributo all'analisi dei fondamenti microeconomici della teoria keynesiana della domanda effettiva", *Rivista di Politica Economica*, November, 1978.
3. A. Chilosi, Introduction of *Kalecki* (Edited by A. Chilo si), (Bologna: Il Mulino, 1979).
4. G.R. Feiwel, *The Intellectual Capital of M. Kalecki* (Knoxville: The University of Tennesse Press, 1975).
5. P. Garegnani, *Valore e Domanda Effettiva* (Torina: Einaudi, 1979).
6. J.R. Hicks, "Mr Keynes and the Classics: a Suggested Interpretation", *Econometrica*, vol. 4, 1937.
7. M. Kalecki, *Proba teorii knoiunktury* (An essay on the theory of business cycle) (Warsaw, Instytut Badania Koniunktur Gospodarcych i Cen, 1939).
8. M. Kalecki, "O handlu zagranicznym i 'eksporcie wewnetrznym'" ("On foreign trade and 'domestic exports'"), *Ekonomista*, n. 3, 1933.
9. M. Kalecki, "Essay d-une théorie du mouvement cycliques des affaires", *Revue d'Economie Politique*, n. 2, 1935.
10. M. Kalecki "Istota poprawy koniunkturalnej" (The mechanism of business upswing), *Polska Gospodarcza*, n. 43, 1935.
11. M. Kalecki, "Koniunktura a bilans platniczy" (The business upswing and the balance of payments), *Polska Gospodarcza*, n. 45, 1935.
12. M. Kalecki, "A Macrodynamic Theory of Business Cycles", *Econometrica*, vol. 3, 1935.
13. M. Kalecki, "Pare uwag o teorii Keynesa" (Some remarks on Keynes' theory), *Ekonomista*, n. 3, 1936.
14. M. Kalecki, "A Theory of Business Cycle", *Review of Economic Studies*, vol. 54, 1937.
15. M. Kalecki, "A Theory of Commodity, Income and Capital Taxation", *Economic Journal*, vol. 47, 1937.
16. M. Kalecki, "The Principle of Increasing Risk", *Economica*, vol. 4, 1937.
17. M. Kalecki, "The Determinants of Distribution of the National Income", *Econometrica*, vol. 6, 1938.
18. M. Kalecki, "The Lesson of the Blum Experiment", *Economic Journal*, vol. 48, 1938.
19. M. Kalecki, *Essays in the Theory of Economic Fluctuations* (London: Allen & Unwin, 1939).
20. M. Kalecki, *Place nominalne i realne* (Money and real wages) (Warsaw: IGS, 1939).
21. M. Kalecki, "The Short Term Rate of Interest and the Velocity of Cash Circulation", *Review of Economics and Statistics*, vol. 23, 1941.

22. M. Kalecki, "The Theory of Long Run Distribution of the Production of Industry", *Oxford Economic Papers*, June 1941.
23. M. Kalecki "A Theory of Profits", *Economic Journal*, vol. 52, 1942.
24. M. Kalecki, "Political Aspects of Full Employment", *Political Quarterly*, vol. 4, 1943.
25. M. Kalecki, *Studies in Economic Dynamics* (London: Allen & Unwin, 1943).
26. M. Kalecki, "Prof. Pigou on 'The Classical Stationary State'. A Comment", *Economic Journal*, vol. 54, 1944.
27. M. Kalecki, "Three Ways to Full Employment" in *Economics of Full Employment* (Oxford: Basil Blackwell, 1944).
28. M. Kalecki, "Full Employment by Stimulating Private Investment?", *Oxford Economic Papers*, March, 1945.
29. M. Kalecki, *Studies in War Economics* (Oxford: Basil Blackwell, 1947).
30. M. Kalecki, *Theory of Economic Dynamics: An Essay on Cyclical and Long Run Changes in Capitalist Economy* (London: Allen & Unwin, 1954).
31. M. Kalecki, "A Model of Hyperinflation", *Manchester School of Economics and Social Studies*, vol. 72, 1962.
32. M. Kalecki, "Observations on the Theory of Growth", *Economic Journal*, vol. 72, 1962.
33. M. Kalecki, *Prace z teorii koniunktury 1933-1939* (Studies in the theory of business cycles 1933-1939) (Warsaw: PWN, 1962).
34. M. Kalecki, *Studies in the Theory of Business Cycles 1933-1939*, with introduction by Joan Robinson (Oxford: Basil Blackwell, 1966).
35. M. Kalecki, "Zagadnienie realizacji u Tugana Baranowskiego i Rozy Luksemburg" (The question of Realization in Tugan-Baranowski and Rosa Luxemburg) in *Woko teorii ekonomicznych "Kapitalu"*, (About Economic Theories of *Capital*) (Warsaw: PWN, 1967) and in *Ekonomista* n. 2, 1967.
36. M. Kalecki, "Trend and Business Cycles Reconsidered", *Economic Journal*, vol. 78, 1968.
37. M. Kalecki, "Class Struggle and the Distribution of National Income", *Kyklos*, vol. 24, 1971.
38. M. Kalecki, *Selected Essays on the Dynamics of the Capitalist Economy 1953-1970* (Cambridge: Cambridge University Press, 1971).
39. M. Kalecki, *Kapitalizm, koniunktura i zatrudnienie*, (Capitalism business cycles and employment) (Warsaw: PWN, 1979).
40. M. Keynes, *The General Theory of Employment, Interest and Money* (London: Macmillan, 1936).
41. F. Modigliani, "Liquidity Preference and the Theory of Interest and Money", *Econometrica*, vol. 12, 1944.
42. S. Parrinello, "The price level implicit in Keynes' effective demand", *Journal of Post Keynesian Economics*, vol. 3, 1980.
43. D. Patinkin, "Price Flexibility and Full Employment" *American Economic Review*, vol. 38, 1948.
44. J. Robinson, "Kalecki and Keynes" in *Collected Papers*, vol. III (Oxford: Basil Blackwell, 1965).
45. J. Robinson, "Michael Kalecki", on the Economics of Capitalism", *Oxford Bulletin of Economics and Statistics*, February, 1977.
46. G.L.S. Shackle, *The Years of High Theory* (Cambridge: Cambridge University Press, 1967).

[8]

PETER J. REYNOLDS

Kalecki's degree of monopoly

Over the past few years there has been a revival of interest in the work of Michal Kalecki.[1] Indeed, economists of the post-Keynesian tradition frequently credit Kalecki with providing much of the foundation of the new paradigm in economics.[2] Yet, one aspect of his work remains something of an anomoly. The "Degree of Monopoly" theory of distribution, while central to Kalecki's own ideas, has often been ignored or misrepresented by subsequent writers.[3] Consequently, Kalecki's theory of profits is often taken

The author is Senior Lecturer in Economics, North Staffordshire Polytechnic. Much of this paper derives from work on his Ph.D. thesis (Sheffield University, 1979). He is grateful to Professor J. L. Ford for continued help and guidance. Nick Adnett, John Bridge, John Burbidge, and Sidney Weintraub all provided useful comments on an earlier draft of this paper. All, of course, are absolved from any errors that remain.

[1] See, for example, the Michal Kalecki Memorial Issue of *Oxford Bulletin of Economics and Statistics*, 1977, *39*(1); Asimakopulos (1975); Weintraub (1979).

[2] See especially Eichner and Kregel (1975).

[3] Of particular note is Kaldor's (1955-56) important paper in which he states

> In the later revisions of his theory Kalecki . . . was content with a purely tautological approach. . . . Unless the "degree of monopoly" can be defined in terms of market relationships of some kind . . . and an attempt is made to demonstrate how these market relationships determine the relation between prices and costs, the theory does not provide a hypothesis which could be affirmed or refuted. (pp. 92-93)

To the extent that subsequent post-Keynesian literature has focused on steady-state analysis, whereby the distribution of income is seen to depend on the (exogenously determined) ratio of investment to output and the differing savings propensities of "capitalists" and "workers" (following Kaldor, 1955-6; Robinson, 1956; and Pasinetti, 1962), the role of the degree of monopoly in affecting the pricing decision—which is a short-run decision—is necessarily forced into the background. This was recognized by Joan Robinson (1960), who appears to be much more sympathetic toward Kalecki's analysis than does Kaldor.

as his theory of distribution, leaving no role for the degree of monopoly.

Kalecki's theory of prices and distribution

In the introduction to *Selected Essays on the Dynamics of the Capitalist Economy* (1971), Kalecki states that throughout the formation of his ideas on economics, his views on distribution have remained unchanged. Unfortunately, in the different published versions of his work there are some subtle differences in the way in which the analysis is presented which appear to have contributed substantially to some of the misinterpretations. In the *Theory of Economic Dynamics* (1954), Kalecki set out for the first time a meaningful, internally consistent theory to explain how firms set prices and consequently how *manual* labor's share of the output in the manufacturing sector is determined. This analysis was subsequently included in the important collection *Selected Essays.*

The core of the analysis is as follows: Firms set a markup on unit prime costs which represent manual workers' wages and material costs and are assumed to be constant over the relevant range of output. The markup subsequently represents payments for overheads and profits. Consequently, for a given ratio of raw material to wage costs, the lower the markup, the lower profits' share, and the higher manual labor's share. The crucial point is in the way in which markups are determined. Short-run profit maximization is not assumed.[4] Instead firms will add a markup, the extent of which is influenced by the institutional nature of the environment in which the firm operates. These institutional factors are clearly spelled out by Kalecki:

> First and foremost the process of concentration in industry. . . .
>
> The second major influence is the development of sales promotion through advertising, selling agents, etc. (1954, p. 17; 1971, pp. 49-50)

Kalecki also suggests that the level of overheads and the power of trade unions must be considered.

If changes in overheads are immediately reflected in markups, then it is meaningless to suggest that prices are determined by

[4] In Kalecki's analysis, long-run profit maximization is not assumed either, though it can be argued that the behavior outlined is consistent with long-run maximization of profits.

a markup on prime costs. However, careful reading indicates that this is not Kalecki's intention. Rather, in times of depression—when overheads are relatively high—the institutional nature of the industry may be such that firms enter into tacit agreements to protect profits by raising prices relative to prime-costs. Whether this occurs will depend entirely on institutional aspects of the specific industry.

Powerful trade unions affect markups in that high ratios of profits to wages may strengthen their bargaining position, enabling them to obtain higher wage rises and consequently deterring firms from entering these wage rises in higher markups for fear of their competitive position being eroded. Although in his early work Kalecki did not explain precisely how such trade union influence may manifest itself, in his later work he made it clear that "this power manifests itself in the scale of wage rises demanded and achieved" (1971, p. 162).

Hence it is the institutional environment in which the firm operates that determines the degree of markup that the firm adds to prime-costs. Such institutional/environmental factors are treated as exogenous to the firm, and thus exogenous to the theory of prices and distribution. Unfortunately, full appreciation of this point is not helped by Kalecki persistently referring to these institutional/environmental factors as "the degree of monopoly." Kalecki uses the term "degree of monopoly" to refer to the sum total of these influences. Thus, a high degree of monopoly means that firms are in a position to add high markups; a low degree of monopoly means that the institutional/environmental pressures on them are such as to keep markups constrained to low levels.

Any theory which explains how a markup is added to prime costs, independently of the output decision, is consistent with a Kaleckian theory of distribution. Kalecki presented two main pricing models. "Costs and Price," originally published in *Studies in Economic Dynamics* (1943), was subsequently included by Kalecki in his 1954 and 1971 volumes, immediately preceding his chapter on distribution. The pricing hypothesis is as follows:

> the firm takes into consideration its average prime-costs and the price of other firms producing similar products. (1971, p. 44)

This is represented by the equation:

(1) $$p = mu + n\bar{p},$$

where u = unit prime costs, p = price, and $\bar{p}$ is a weighted average of prices of other firms producing similar products (in the "industry"), using output as weights. "The coefficients m and n characterising the price fixing policy of the firm reflect what may be called the degree of monopoly of the firm's position" (1954, p. 13; 1971, p. 45). This is to be interpreted as meaning that such institutional factors as concentration, tacit agreements, advertising, or weakness of unions can cause m and/or n to increase.

Provided that all firms in the industry are in equilibrium as regards their price fixing, that is to say that they have taken account of all institutional pressures on them, then the ratio of average price ($\bar{p}$) to average unit prime custs ($\bar{u}$) for the industry as a whole will be equal to $\bar{m}/1 - \bar{n}$, where $\bar{m}$ and $\bar{n}$ are the weighted averages of the individual firm's pricing parameters using prime costs and output, respectively, as weights.

The theory of the distribution of the product of an individual industry, and then (by aggregation) of the manufacturing sector, can be developed from the above pricing theory, using Kalecki's analysis, as follows:

W = aggregate wages;
k = ratio of prices to prime costs ($k = \bar{p}/\bar{u}$);
$j = M/W$;
F = overheads;
M = aggregate cost of materials;
ω = relative share of wages in value added;
V = value added = $F + \pi + W$;
π = profits.

Manipulation of the above definitions yields an identity for ω:

Prime costs consist of $W + M$;

$$\therefore \text{aggregate proceeds} \equiv k(W + M);$$

$$\therefore F + \pi \equiv k(W + M) - (W + M);$$

$$\therefore \omega \equiv \frac{W}{V} \equiv \frac{W}{W + (k - 1)(W + M)};$$

$$\therefore \omega \equiv \frac{1}{1 + (k - 1)(1 + j)}.$$

It is worth stressing that (2) is an identity. However, since k is determined by exogenous and environmental factors—which Kalecki referred to as the "degree of monopoly"—it is indeed meaningful to say that the degree of monopoly determines the distribution of income.

Unfortunately, appreciation of the behavioral content of the analysis is often obscured by reference to an early version of the degree of monopoly theory which appeared in *Econometrica* (1938, reprinted in *Essays in the Theory of Economic Fluctuations*, 1939, reissued in 1972). This early version of the degree of monopoly theory differs from the later presentation in that the concept of Lerner's measure of the degree of monopoly, defined as

$$(3) \qquad \mu = \frac{p - m}{p} \qquad \text{(where } m = \text{marginal cost)},$$

is introduced and, following Lerner (1934), is related to the elasticity of demand. This introduces an inconsistency into the analysis and consequently leaves it open to more than one interpretation. The problem arises because implicit in the Lerner measure is the assumption of short-run profit maximization which is inconsistent with the behavioral hypothesis contained in Kalecki's theory of costs and prices (1943 and 1954) set out above.[5]

Kalecki's empirical analysis

Kalecki illustrates his degree of monopoly theory (1954, pp. 30-41; 1971, pp. 65-77) with reference to the behavior of manual labor's share of the proceeds of manufacturing industry in the United States over 1879-1937 (using seven observations) and 1928-37 (using five observations), of National Income in the U.K. in the periods 1881-1924 and 1938-39, and of gross income of the private

[5] A second, slightly different, version of Kalecki's pricing equation, which is also consistent with his theory of distribution, appeared in "Class Struggle and Distribution of National Income," also published in the 1971 volume. Of course, there are plenty of alternative pricing hypotheses. Eichner (1973, 1975), Wood (1975), Harcourt and Kenyon (1977), Shapiro (1981), and Ong (1981) have all set out models in which the need to obtain funds for the financing of investment enters the pricing equation. Although these models could be combined with Kalecki's distribution identity to provide a modified Kaleckian theory of distribution, they suffer from the weakness—identified by Weintraub (1981)—of relying on an untapped potential of unexploited monopoly power. There is a further problem when we attempt to integrate the distribution theory into a more complete Keynes/Kalecki framework whereby the level of income/profit is determined by *past* investment decisions.

sector in the United States for the period 1929-37.

However, in no way does his analysis represent a testing of his theory. When dealing with census data for U.S. manufacturing he *defines* k as the ratio of proceeds to prime costs and obtains series for k' and j' adjusted to reflect changes in industrial composition. He then derives a series for ω' by using the distribution identity, (2), and compares his series ω' with a series of ω. Kalecki then *explains* changes in ω as occurring as the combined result of changes in j and k and industrial composition. This approach is summed up in the following section in which he interprets the long-run statistics for the U.S. economy. (Exactly the same approach was taken when dealing with the manufacturing sector for the depression years.)

> It appears that ω, the actual relative share of wages, in the value added, suffered a considerable though not quite continuous fall over the period considered. This fall resulted mainly from the increase in the "adjusted" ratio of proceeds to prime costs, k' which in our interpretation reflects a rise in the degree of monopoly. The "adjusted" ratio of the materials bill to the wages bill, j', tended to fall rather than to rise and thus in general its change mitigated the decline in ω. (1954, p. 32; 1971, p. 67)

Similarly, when interpreting data on U.K. National Income, he simply suggests how the observed movements could be consistent with his theory.

As has already been established, the variables j, k, and ω are linked by an identity. It is therefore an inescapable fact that the time series will be related in the way that Kalecki showed. Examination of the time series is interesting in highlighting the extent to which changes in income distribution were due to changes in the ratio of raw materials to wage costs, to changes in the ratio of aggregate proceeds to prime costs, or—for U.S. data only—changes in industrial composition. However, they do not provide us with a test of the crucial hypothesis that it is changes in the degree of monopoly—interpreted as environmental/institutional factors—that were responsible for the changes in the ratio of aggregate proceeds to aggregate prime costs. To verify this hypothesis, we would need to specify, and identify precisely, the relationship postulated and to obtain the appropriate time series for the degree of monopoly factors. Kalecki completed neither of these tasks and hence has not provided empirical verification of his theory. In fact, using his analysis merely to rationalize observed movements in the time series has been partly responsible for the criticism that his analysis is tautological.

Nonetheless, Kalecki's failure to provide rigorous econometric support does not invalidate his degree of monopoly theory. It simply remains for someone to provide the necessary econometric support.

The Riach-Asimakopulos interpretation: the short run and the long run

In Kalecki's analysis prices are set (in the short run) in accordance with the degree of monopoly in the particular industry in which the firm operates. As unit prime costs are assumed constant, the ratio of price to unit prime cost is thereby determined by the degree of monopoly. However, Riach (1971) and Askimakopulos (1975) put a different interpretation on the "degree of monopoly," which they still consider to be "Kaleckian."

Riach's analysis departs from Kalecki's when Riach attempts to move into the long run. However, in Kalecki's view "The long-run trend is but a slowly changing component of a chain of short-period situations" (1971, p. 165). The important point (I think) Kalecki was making is that the distribution of income is determined by the relation

$$\omega = \frac{1}{1 + (k - 1)(j + 1)},$$

where k is determined by the environmental/institutional factors which comprised his "degree of monopoly."

In any short period, there will be a given value of j and a given value of k, determined by the degree of monopoly for that period. For any industry, if we choose the period short enough, k will be constant over the period. If we choose a longer period, k will be a weighted average of the shorter periods' ks. The distribution of the income stream generated in any period will depend on what k happened to be—on average—for that period. As k, for any short period, is determined by the interim degree of monopoly, then it clearly follows that over any longer period, the distribution of income depends on the extent of the degree of monopoly over that longer succession of shorter periods.

Riach adopts a different approach. He argues that "difficulty arises when we move into the long-run where the capital stock is variable" (p. 53). He subsequently argues that in the long run it is not a firm's ratio of profits to sales that would be protected, but rather that

> we would expect long-run planning and profit objectives to run in terms of profit on invested capital rather than in terms of Kalecki's ratio of profit to sales proceeds. In which case it would be a high rate of return on capital which would attract entry, but be retainable in firms snug behind entry barriers. (p. 53)

Asimakopulos makes a similar point:

> It is emphasised that what a higher degree of monopoly makes possible, and protects, is the higher profitability of firms in the industry. This is not, in general, as Kalecki's use of the term implies, the same as the ratio of price to prime-costs. (p. 315)

Thus, following Riach and Asimakopulos, in the long run, in the absence of entry barriers we would expect capital mobility to equalize the rate of return on capital; but where entry barriers exist, we would expect the protection of high profit rates. After considering some of the empirical evidence (Bain, 1956; Mann, 1966) Riach argues:

> But to the extent that monopoly power is exercised we would logically expect that in the long run this would be directed towards obtaining a higher rate of return on capital rather than a high ratio of profits to sales proceeds, and, . . . we are on strong grounds for preferring this rather than the share of profits in sales proceeds as the corporate profit goal, and thus the "beneficiary" of protected entry. (p. 54)

Although Riach recognizes that Kalecki does not assume maximization of $(p - u)/p$; it is important to stress that the ratio of profits to sales proceeds does not enter into Kalecki's analysis as a corporate objective in any sense. It is merely the outcome of the influence of the exogenous environmental/institutional "degree of monopoly" factors on the pricing decisions of the firm, which are short-run decisions.[6] Firms will not aim to increase p/u beyond

[6] An examination of the implications of maximizing $(p - u)/p$ serves to highlight the absurdity of considering the ratio as an objective in any sense. With constant marginal costs and a downward-sloping demand curve, $(p - u)/p$ can always be increased by reducing sales and hence raising p. The ratio would then be maximized at an infinitesimally small level of output!

that level that is prudent, given the environmental/institutional factors of industrial concentration, advertising, union influence, and possibly entry barriers that exist in their industry. That is, they set prices above unit prime costs in accordance with the degree of monopoly factors. Output then depends on demand, and the level of profit is determined accordingly. The rate of profit on capital then depends on the capital-output ratio, which will be dependent on investment decisions taken in the past.

In the short run, prices are fixed according to the appropriate "degree of monopoly" factors, which may include entry barriers —though this later influence was not considered by Kalecki. We may add the assumption that in the long run, capital will move between industries so as to seek the highest return, in which case the "entry barrier" components of the degree of monopoly factors may protect industry profit rates.

The crucial point is that it is the relationship between prices and unit prime costs—particularly wage costs—that determines how "value added" is divided up between manual workers and others. This is determined as the outcome of the price-fixing process based on short-run considerations. This year's short-run considerations determine the distribution this year, next year's next year, etc.

So, what differs in the long run? If we take the long-run maximization of the profit-capital ratio to be the criterion for allocating capital funds between different industries, then we may incorporate this into the Kalecki pricing and distribution model. For example, if there are two firms in different industries each making the same rate of profit, (π), on sales (Y), but with firm (A) having a lower profit-capital ratio than firm (B), then capital—in the long run—will move into industry (B). This may simply be an expansion of production in response to high levels of demand causing high rates of capital utilization and hence high profit rates. Alternatively, it may represent an attempt to displace labor, causing the capital-output ratio in industry (B) to rise. The adoption of more capital intensive techniques will mean less labor input, thereby causing prime costs to be reduced. New prices will then be determined in accordance with the price-fixing equation. As m and n are fixed parameters, price will change to the extent that capitalization has affected unit prime costs, and the ratio of price to unit prime-costs will be equal once again to $m/1 - n$. Thus, the share of profits in value-added for that industry remains unchanged, except for any substitution of capital altering the ratio of wage costs to material costs, j. However, if more capital is being used per unit of output, π/K will fall. Long-run mobility of capital between industries may lead toward the equalization of the rate of return on capital for different industries, but the share of profits may still differ between industries according to differing degrees of monopoly.

A critical assumption in obtaining these results is that m and n are independent of the capital-output ratio of the industry. It is recognized that although a high rate of profit on capital may attract more capital from existing firms, especially large corporations with diversified interests in a number of industries, if entry barriers are low, it may also attract new firms. An increase in the number of firms may then reduce concentration and induce lower markups, thereby affecting distribution.

It follows that there is possibly a long-run reason for a high correlation between entry barriers and profit rates. The degree will depend on the extent to which existing versus new firms capitalize on the higher profit rates by increasing investment in those industries. This could affect industrial concentration which would affect markups and distribution. In a situation of long-run equilibrium, with capital mobility one could expect differences in profit rates to be eliminated, but markups on sales could vary due to dissimilar market structures and union influences.

For any industry, entry barriers may affect the long-run rate of return on capital, but the degree of monopoly sets the markup and calls the distribution tune.

REFERENCES

Asimakopulos, A. "A Kaleckian Theory of Income Distribution." *Canadian Journal of Economics*, August 1975.

_________. "Themes in a Post Keynesian Theory of Income Distribution." *Journal of Post Keynesian Economics*. Winter, 1980-81, *3*(2).

Bain, J. *Barriers to New Competition*. Cambridge, Mass.: Harvard University Press, 1956.

Cowling, K. *Oligopoly and the Distribution of Income*. University of Warwick Research Paper No. 69, June 1975.

Eichner, A. S. "A Theory of the Determination of the Mark-up Under Oligopoly," *Economic Journal*. December 1973, *83*.

_________. *The Megacorp and Oligopoly: Microfoundations of Macro Dynamics*. Cambridge: Cambridge University Press, 1976.

Harcourt, G. C., and Kenyon, P. "Pricing and the Investment Decision." *Kyklos*, 1976, *29*.

Holtermann, S. E. "Market Structure and Economic Performance in U.K. Manufacturing Industry." *Journal of Industrial Economics*. December 1973, *22*.

Kalecki, M. "The Determinants of Distribution of National Income." *Econometrica*, April 1938, *6*(2).

_________. *Essays in the Theory of Economic Fluctuations*. 1939. Reissued: New York: Russell and Russell, 1972.

_________. *Studies in Economic Dynamics*. Aberdeen: University Press, 1943.

_________. *Theory of Economic Dynamics*. 1st ed. 1954; Revised 2nd ed., London: Unwin University Books, 1965.

_________. *Selected Essays on the Dynamics of the Capitalist Economy*. Cambridge: Cambridge University Press, 1971.

_________. "Class Struggle and Distribution of National Income." *Kyklos*, 1971 (reprinted in *Selected Essays*).

Khalilzadeh-Shirazi, Javad. "Market Structure and Price-Cost Margins in United Kingdom Manufacturing Industries." *Review of Economics and Statistics*, February 1974.

Lerner, A. P. "The Concept of Monopoly and the Measurement of Monopoly Power." *Review of Economic Studies*, 1934.

Mann, H. M. "Seller Concentration, Barriers to Entry, and Rates of Return in Thirty Industries 1950-1960." *Review of Economics and Statistics*, 1966, *48*.

Ong, N. P. "Target Pricing, Competition and Growth." *Journal of Post Keynesian Economics*, Fall 1981, *4*(1).

Pasinetti, L. L. "Rate of Profit and Income Distribution in Relation to the Rate of Economic Growth." *Review of Economic Studies*, October 1962, *29*(4).

Riach, P. "Kalecki's 'Degree of Monopoly' Reconsidered." *Australian Economic Papers*, 1971, *10*.

Robinson, J. *The Accumulation of Capital*. London: Macmillan, 1956.

_________. "The Theory of Distribution." In *Collected Economic Papers*. Vol. 2. Oxford: Basil Blackwell, 1960.

Shapiro, N. "Pricing and the Growth of Firms." *Journal of Post Keynesian Economics*, Fall 1981, *4*(1).

Weintraub, S. "Generalizing Kalecki and Simplifying Macroeconomics." *Journal of Post Keynesian Economics*, Spring 1979, *2*(3).

_________. "An Eclectic Theory of Income Shares." *Journal of Post Keynesian Economics*, Fall 1981, *4*(1).

Williamson, O. E. *The Economics of Discretionary Behaviour: Managerial Objectives in a Theory of the Firm*. Chicago: Markham Publishing Co., 1964.

Wood, A. *A Theory of Profits*. Cambridge: Cambridge University Press, 1975.

[9]

CLAUDIO SARDONI

Some ties of Kalecki to the 1926 "Sraffian Manifesto"

Sraffa's famous article, "The Laws of Returns under Competitive Conditions" (1926), which has been called the "Sraffian Manifesto" by Shackle (1967, p. 12), was intended to provide a critique of the neoclassical theory of value.[1] Sraffa rejected the traditional hypothesis of perfect competition as unrealistic and dealt with the problem of price determination within a more realistic framework characterized by conditions of "imperfect competition."[2]

Sraffa's analysis, though mainly concerned with the theory of value, had relevant implications for macro-theory. In particular, Sraffa pointed out some fundamental factors which limit the long period growth of firms. Because of this, his analysis has pregnant insights into the macro-problems of investment and effective demand. I shall argue that Kalecki's investment theory was significantly influenced by Sraffa's work.

Demand limiting expansion

Sraffa pointed out that, in those industries characterized by a large number of independent, relatively small firms, each individual firm

The author is a researcher at the University of Rome. He wishes to thank K. Bharadwaj, G. Harcourt, and the late S. Weintraub for their constructive and helpful comments on an earlier version of this paper. Errors that may remain are of his own commission.

[1]Cf., e.g., Bharadwaj, 1976, pp. 38-67.

[2]On Sraffa's influence upon the theory of imperfect competition, cf. Shackle, 1967, chap. 3-6, and Dobb, 1973, pp. 203-204.

faces a downward sloping demand curve. It is this that represents the major obstacle to firms' expansion in the long period, even though they work under conditions of individual *diminishing* costs. In other words, demand blocks firms' growth.

> The chief obstacle against which they have to contend when they want gradually to increase their production does not lie in the cost of production—which, indeed, generally favours them in that direction—but in the difficulty of selling the larger quantity of goods without reducing the price, or without having to face increased marketing expenses. This . . . is only an aspect of the usual descending demand curve, with the difference that instead of concerning the whole of a commodity, whatever its origin, it relates only to the goods produced by a particular firm. . . . This method of regarding the matter appears the most natural and that which adheres to reality of things. (Sraffa, 1926, p. 543)

In the long period the existence of obstacles to increasing production blocks, of course, the growth of firms' size and, hence, the firms' investment. Within Sraffa's realistic market framework, *demand poses the major determinant of investment.*

A diminishing returns aspect

Market conditions affect firms' investment decisions also in another way. Sraffa suggested that the more than proportional increase in the expenditure which a firm has to incur to acquire additional means of production might be another important obstacle to impede investment. He observed, however, that such an increase in the firm's expenditure is only an effect of the existing market conditions. Sraffa's analysis deals with the demand for factors in general, but he paid particular attention to financial markets.

> . . . the limited credit of many firms, which does not permit any one of them to obtain more than a limited amount of capital at the current rate of interest, is often a direct consequence of its being known that a given firm is unable to increase its sales outside its own particular market without incurring heavy marketing expenses. (1926, p. 550)

If the firm was known to be able to expand its market share without a relevant increase in its marketing expenses, it "could encounter no obstacle in a free capital market" (1926, p. 550).

Sraffa also noted that capital markets were not "free," so that a firm would meet barriers even though it had no problems in expanding its market share. A firm, producing at falling costs, without encountering selling difficulties, is expected to earn abnormal profits. In this situation,

> . . . if a banker, or the owner of land on which a firm proposes to extend its own plant, or any other supplier of the firm's means of production, stands in a privileged position in respect to it, he can certainly exact from it a price higher than the current price for his supplies, but this possibility is still a direct consequence of the fact that such a firm, being in its turn in a privileged position in regard to its particular market, also sells its products at prices above costs. (1926, p. 550)

Capital markets, in other words, are also imperfect, so that firms privileged from the demand point of view meet some walls to their expansion and investment because of increasing cost in obtaining funds, deterring their investment.

Manifestly, it is "imperfect competition" which, in Sraffa's analytical framework, limits the firms' expansion and investment. In "free" fully competitive markets there would be no impediment to investment by firms. At the macro-level, this would imply that firms, as a whole, tend to invest at the highest possible rate, with the productive capacity of the capital good sectors being the only constraint to the process at any given time. Inevitably, the economy would achieve full employment.[3] But this can be barred under "imperfect competition."

Sraffa and Kalecki

The macro-theory in Sraffa's analysis appears to be quite lucid even if Sraffa did not underscore his observations. As Maurice Dobb commented, few economists assessed Sraffa's macro-implications. In Dobb's opinion, Kalecki was one of the few exceptions for he developed a theory of income distribution based upon the "degree of monopoly"[4] which clearly allowed for non-competitive markets.

But it seems to me that Sraffa's work exerted a wider influence on Kalecki. Beyond the idea of imperfect competition to explain production in the short period, Kalecki entered into an analysis of the limits to firms' growth and a theory of investment where demand and market imperfections resemble Sraffa's analysis.

Kalecki, in "Money and Real Wages" (1966), extended Sraffa's

[3]This also applies if unit costs are constant. For more details cf. Sardoni, 1983.

[4]Cf. Dobb, 1973, pp. 203-204, and 214-215.

neoclassical cost critique to the short period analysis.[5] There was the problem of the firms' behavior—in the short period—under the realistic assumption of constant marginal costs. Within this framework, it is possible to determine production levels below full utilization of the firms' productive capacity only if it is also imposed that individual firms face falling demand curves. Kalecki held that this was the case in many industries which operate under conditions of "imperfect competition." Here Kalecki explicitly referred to Sraffa's article.[6]

Kalecki also exposed the problem of firms' expansion and investment in a way analogous to Sraffa's approach. In the *Theory of Economic Dynamics* (1968), Kalecki, like Sraffa, rejected the idea that increasing costs are the main obstacle to firms' growth. He accepted the idea that it is market demand which limits the firms' size, although he stressed that this factor alone cannot explain the existence of multi-sized firms within the same industry.

> Two factors are usually mentioned as limiting the size of a firm: (1) diseconomies of a large scale; and (2) limitations of market, the expansion of which would require unprofitable price reductions or increase in selling costs. The first of these factors seems to be rather unrealistic. . . . The limitation of the size of the firm by the market for its products is real enough but it leaves unexplained the existence of large and small firms in the same industry. (Kalecki, 1968, p. 91)

Sraffa was preoccupied with the problem of the firms' expansion within industries to which the definition of perfect competition seems to apply because of the existence of numerous small, independent firms. Therefore, Sraffa did not have to cope with Kalecki's second problem involving a perspective on the limits in all sorts of industry. Kalecki also had to explain why in some industries firms of different sizes prevailed.

The factor invoked by Kalecki to rationalize the phenomenon, however, appropinquates Sraffa's observations on capital markets. Kalecki remarked:

> There is, however, another factor which is of decisive importance in limiting the size of a firm: the amount of the entrepreneurial capital, i.e., the amount of capital owned by the firm. The access of a firm to the capital market . . . is determined to a large extent by the amount of its entrepreneurial capital. . . . The variety in the size of enterprises in the same

[5] "Money and Real Wages" was first published in Polish in 1939.

[6] Cf. Kalecki, 1966, pp. 51-52, and p. 52n.

> industry at a given time can be easily explained in terms of differences in entrepreneurial capital. (1968, pp. 91-92)

Entrepreneurial capital limits the firms' expansion because it fixes the firm's borrowing capacity and, secondly, firms may not use their full borrowing potential because of the "increasing risk" of investment with respect to the size of their entrepreneurial capital. The higher the investment/entrepreneurial capital ratio, the graver the risk of expansion. Thus growth turns on the limited access of firms to the capital market.

> The limitation of the size of the firm by the availability of entrepreneurial capital goes to the very heart of the capitalist system. Many economists assume, at least in their abstract theories, a state of business democracy where anybody endowed with entrepreneurial ability can obtain capital for starting a business venture. This picture of the activities of the pure entrepreneur is to put it mildly, unrealistic. The most important prerequisite for becoming an entrepreneur is the ownership of capital. (1968, pp. 94-95)

Kalecki's "business democracy" clearly intends perfect competition in the capital markets, with each firm having free access to capital. The reality is that firms find high hurdles to their expansion because they are not able to obtain the desired capital. The similarity between Kalecki's and Sraffa's reasoning is apparent: all firms are effectively limited by the "imperfections" in the capital market, that is, the acts of capital suppliers to ration financial capital and enhance its cost.

In the industries isolated by Sraffa, firms were small and very similar to one another so that, as a consequence, their own entrepreneurial capitals were comparable in size, and no individual firm could grow at a far faster pace than the others. In Kalecki's framework, firms' entrepreneurial capital can vary so that ultimate size could differ.

Combining Sraffa's and Kalecki's assessments, we may properly conclude that, under "imperfect competition," demand stands as the major obstacle to investment and growth of every firm. Some firms, however, may not find themselves vulnerable to stiffer selling resistance, and only financial "imperfections" block the firms' expansion. A (minor) way out could be open to those firms loaded with internal funds. They can hasten their growth rate, so that we observe, in some industries, firms of different size.

The unemployment aspect

If the firms' investment is limited by demand and "imperfections" in the capital market, this implies that there is no reason why the economy as a whole should experience the exact level of aggregate investment with which full employment is contingent. Thus the unemployment mess turns out to depend on the micro-foundations of demand and financial markets. In fact, Kalecki developed a theory of this nature.[7]

For Kalecki investment decisions depend on *current* profits, the rate of *change* of profits, the speed of adaptation of productive capacity, and other long-run factors (e.g., technical progress). The variables reflect the influence upon investment which is exerted by the available entrepreneurial capital and by market demands. There exists no inherent reason why the actual amount of investment should necessarily suffice to the amount of investment required for full employment.

In his own method, Kalecki thus achieved results which largely coincide with those obtained by Keynes in the *General Theory*. The level of effective demand may drive the economy to a state involving idle labor and idle capital.

However, the important difference between the two K's, Keynes and Kalecki, is that the former based his analysis upon a theory of investment which devolves from the concept of the marginal efficiency of capital that still includes some marginalist origins, including its micro-foundations.[8] Kalecki's theory emanates on different grounds, namely, on his and Sraffa's *critique* of the marginalist micro-foundations.

Some assessments

Keynes's theory of investment is subject to several relevant criticisms, mainly because it is inconsistent with a satisfactory explanation of underemployment equilibria. It was Kalecki who, in 1936, actually criticized Keynes's theory of investment in a very incisive way.[9] Keynes, like Kalecki, well knew Sraffa's work on imperfect competition, and his neoclassical critique. Yet Keynes bypassed Sraffa's contribution in order to develop his own theory of investment. His analysis would rest on much more solid foundations by invoking the more realistic market conditions.

Why did Keynes shut out the implications of Sraffa's work? One

[7]On Kalecki's theory of investment, cf. Kalecki, 1968, pp. 96-108, and Asimakopulos, 1977.

[8]It was Keynes himself who recognized the similarities between his concept of the marginal efficiency of capital and Marshall's "marginal net efficiency of a factor of production." Cf. Keynes, 1936, p. 139.

[9]Cf. Kalecki, 1982, and Asimakopulos, 1971.

possible answer is that Keynes was not completely successful in his "struggle" to escape the old ideas "which ramify, for those brought up as most of us have been, into every corner of our minds." He, too, was not able to eject some aspects of the traditional theory, despite the fundamental insights into market capitalism.

Sraffa and Kalecki were much less attached to neoclassical economics, and their theories were a critical response to the prevailing doctrines. Both derived their work from the classical and Marxian traditions, and they were able to provide a vision of capitalist economies without any recourse to the neoclassical thought.

In his neoclassical critique, Sraffa provided significant judgements to provide a comprehension of how actual capitalist economies work; in particular, he saw factors that limit the firms' investment and growth. His analysis is undoubtedly relevant for macrotheory and makes it clear that demand and capital market constraints are quite capable of impeding the full employment objective.

Kalecki's work was influenced by Sraffa; his theory of investment and analysis of underemployment equilibria embody most of Sraffa's concepts. For Kalecki, too, demand and imperfect capital markets constitute the major obstacles to investment and growth by firms.

Sraffa and Kalecki can provide very helpful analytical tools for polishing Keynes's theory of effective demand and unemployment. They allow us to insert the fundamental results achieved by Keynes into a more general and rigorous framework which is in some radical contrast to the neoclassical relics that still pervade orthodox thought.

REFERENCES

Asimakopulos, A. "The Determination of Investment in Keynes' Model." In *Canadian Journal of Economics*, August 1971.

__________. "Profits and Investment: A Kaleckian Approach." In *The Microeconomic Foundations of Macroeconomics*. Ed. by G. C. Harcourt. Macmillan, 1977.

Bharadwaj, K. *Classical Political Economy and Rise to Dominance of Supply and Demand Theories*. New Delhi, 1976.

Dobb, M. *Theories of Value and Distribution since Adam Smith*. Cambridge University Press, 1973.

Kalecki, M. *Studies on the Theory of Business Cycles*. Oxford, 1966.

__________. *Theory of Economic Dynamics*. New York, 1968.

__________. "Some Remarks on Keynes' Theory." In *Australian Economic Papers*. December 1982. [English translation of M. Kalecki. "Pare uwag o teorii Keynesa." *Ekonomista*, 1936, (3).]

Keynes, J. M. *The General Theory of Employment, Interest and Money*. Macmillan, 1936.

Sardoni, C. "Marx and Keynes on Say's Law." Rome, unpublished manuscript, 1983.

Shackle, G. L. S. *The Years of High Theory*. Cambridge University Press, 1967.

Sraffa, P. "The Laws of Returns under Competitive Conditions." *Economic Journal*, December 1926.

[10]

Galbraith symposium

Galbraith, Sraffa, Kalecki and supra-surplus capitalism

E. RAY CANTERBERY

Introduction

An interesting and forceful connection suggests itself between the economics of John Kenneth Galbraith and the economics of Piero Sraffa. In turn, there is a connection with Galbraith's work and that of Michal Kalecki, the Polish economist whose view of production conforms with Sraffa's subsistence model. These connections occur with respect to Galbraithian notions of producer sovereignty and power.

Sraffa, in his most celebrated work, nullifies demand theory and leaves open the theory of personal income distribution. In Sraffa's view, the orthodoxy's opposition of cost and demand is an untenable hybrid of objective and subjective elements. Given the notion of consumer sovereignty, the subjective elements of marginalism overwhelm the objective production elements. Galbraith, introducing something more akin to producer sovereignty, fills the demand vacuum left by Sraffa. In this way, Galbraith is the source of demand theory that derives from the extension of the objective forces of production institutions. Sraffa moves from the classical subsistence economy to a production surplus economy; Galbraith moves on to the affluent society, a *supra*-surplus economy.

Kalecki's simplification of the income distribution, dividing income only between workers and capitalists, compels us to go beyond

The author is Professor of Economics at Florida State University. He thanks Susan Williams for her superb (even dedicated) editing advice and Paul Davidson, the scissor wizard, for suggestions that shortened the article even while improving it. Paul has added new meaning to the "cutting edge" of Post Keynesianism. Both are exonerated for anything that might have gone wrong.

Kaleckian subsistence into the more complex distribution of supra-surplus capitalism, where we must recognize the role of power in economic relations—a role epitomized by Kalecki's (and Weintraub's) price mark-up. As it turns out, Kalecki's "degree of monopoly" dovetails with Galbraithian "power." The configuration of a potential paradigm is drawn with some further intimations of the most realistic theoretical constructs of demand and income distribution.

The necessary economy: from Sraffa to Kalecki

Sraffa's neo-Ricardian view of production and value

Sraffa's invocation of David Ricardo is an abstraction of the system of production only and of the way that the real value of goods is decided. After introducing a classical subsistence model in Chapter 1, Sraffa (1960) moves on to a production surplus economy, one that produces commodities in excess of labor's physiological necessities plus actual depreciation of all the means of production. In Sraffa's model of the surplus economy, basic commodities or goods that appear as inputs *and* outputs are necessities only in a technological sense.

Demand, although (abstractly) affecting the level of production, plays no role in deciding prices. Prices are production prices or physical costs, not market prices. A move in the wage (and profit) rate, one of which is given, leaves the ratio of net output or economic surplus to means of production unaltered because productivity is determined solely by the technical conditions of production rather than from the distribution of product or income between wages or profits.

In the surplus economy *non*-basic commodities or goods and services entering only into final demand include both consumer necessities *and* luxuries. Only in Sraffa's subsistence model are basic commodities necessities in consumption as well as in production. In his surplus economy, Sraffa makes no attempt to separate the allocation of the extra-subsistence wage between necessary and "luxury" consumer goods. Moreover, Sraffa's treatment of labor as neither a basic nor a nonbasic service in the surplus economy raises additional serious questions about the nature of demand. Nonetheless, his notion of a standard commodity group comprised of those basic commodities that enter into production in the same proportion that they exit production drives a wedge in the neoclassical system sufficiently wide to allow room for a new theory of demand *and* of income distribution.

What then are the central propositions from Sraffa of interest to Post

Keynesians? In an industry in which equal amounts of, say, labor are always combined with a unit of capital, the marginal product of capital evaporates. Profits can no longer be said to be a return on capital. (In an interindustry model the value of heterogeneous capital cannot be determined anyway.) Moreover, this neo-Ricardian theory tells us that relative production price movements are driven by changes in the income distribution and technology rather than by demand movements. Finally, the income distribution can be altered without changes in the economic surplus relative to the available means of production. There is little room for the usual supply-and-demand considerations so central to neoclassical price theory, because the wages-to-profits relation becomes a social-political question to be answered elsewhere (possibly by Galbraithian power).

Kaleckian income distribution within Sraffa's subsistence model

In Kalecki the national *income* is divided between profits received by capitalists and wages received by workers. The national product is divided among the investment *and* consumption spending of the capitalists and the consumption expenditures of the workers (Kalecki, 1971). If we simplify by saying that *all profits* are diligently plowed back into the business to purchase new investment goods, *saving*, as well as investment, is equal to profits. The capitalist is the lone saver in this simple economy.

A Kaleckian view of production can be made to conform with Sraffa's subsistence model, if we divide Sraffa's output sector into two distinct industries, one producing necessary consumption goods, the other producing necessary investment goods. Although Sraffa does not prefer his model of physiological subsistence, in it nonetheless the amount of business investment in capital goods and the prevailing production technology would decide the level of employment as well as the division of labor between the production of consumption necessities and production necessities (investment goods). This technology and the prevailing level of production capacity (of the vintage technology) also decide the total amount of each class of good produced.

The introduction of subsistence wages into Sraffa's subsistence model transforms it into a Kaleckian world of income distribution. Subsistence wages decide the quantity of consumer necessities manufactured. Since investment goods are combined with labor at a given technology, the demand for consumer necessities and investment goods determines the employment level. The distribution of income between workers and capitalists (between wages and profits) becomes the mirror image of the distribution of national output between consumer necessities and investment goods. We next want to consider what happens to Kalecki's theory when Sraffa's production system produces surpluses and (with a demand theory addendum) the "working class" receives a larger share of the national income than required for subsistence. When wages (perhaps bolstered by interest and rents) become substantially greater than those required for subsistence, the surplus economy is on the way to becoming Galbraith's affluent society.

Beyond Kaleckian subsistence

Ironically, then, a critical insight into the advanced economy lies hidden in the model so quickly dismissed by Sraffa, his subsistence model in which both necessary consumption and necessary capital goods coexist. Such a model reveals that labor is best treated as a basic "commodity" or, better, basic service, because labor is still necessary to produce subsistence commodities.[1] Labor is an input *and* an output in the (at least) self-reproducing economy. Nevertheless, in the long run, just as the standard commodity must change with new technology, the quantity of consumer "necessities" must change as what is necessary is redefined.

Whether necessities are a constant or a variable market basket of goods and services, their quantities and market prices will determine their value and the required value of the money wage bill. For example, in the autumn of 1976, the Bureau of Labor Statistics (BLS) estimated the annual cost of a "lower" consumption budget for a four-person family in the urban United States at $8,162. If $8,162 represented the cultural subsistence requirements for an average family in the urban United States, the wage bill paid to the household had to be at least $8,162.[2]

[1]Canterbery (1980a, pp. 306–308) took this position several years ago.

[2]The content of the BLS budgets is based upon the manner of living and actual consumer choices in the 1960s. The nutritional and health standards, as determined by scientists and nutritionists, are used for the food-at-home and housing components. Sraffa's abstraction that has real (relative) prices and output determined separately at any point in time still is relevant and so is the provision that the wage rate is not based upon the marginal product of labor. Canterbery (1979b) arrives at the same point via a different route. The "demand" for labor is the loci of money wage rates and "marginal revenue products" from given technologies and product prices. However, since the labor supply is a function of expected wage rates, a selection of technology that just clears the labor market at any moment in time is very improbable. This idea is expanded in Canterbery (1980b). Nonetheless, at full employment across all labor markets, *money* wages can be bid up by Keynesian excess demand.

Although it cannot be denied that there are many American households that exist at the biological subsistence level, Galbraith's affluent society is indisputably an economy of surpluses. The estimate for the "higher" consumption budget for a four-person family in the urban United States in 1976 was $17,048, more than twice the lower budget. In an affluent economy, we need to identify the hierarchy of absolute physical necessities and "wants." Society imposes a rank order, because the satisfaction of a greater number of wants is usually associated with "higher standards of living."

There is a certain regularity in the way that most households allocate expenditures on food, clothing, transportation, and other items. The poor, for example, spend their incomes primarily on physiological necessities. After these same needs are met by the nonpoor, the discretionary income remaining meets "needs" or wants that are difficult to pigeonhole. The uncertainty increases as we shift focus away from specific needs, such as the need to be clothed, toward the particular way these needs and wants are met, such as attempts to be fashionably dressed. Although households tend to eat more (and sometimes better) as income increases, there is a limit to the amount of extra money that people spend on food as incomes rise. That is, beyond the income level that meets basic nutritional needs, food expenditure as a share of the household budget grows slowly. This general behavior pattern was first identified as Engel's law.

Engel's law is as successful in suppressing the role of consumption prices as is Sraffa. What turns out to be important to households is the ability to meet needs and wants with their real income levels, given their budget shares. The cost of a need or want is a weighted price index for a bundle of necessary production inputs, not a single price. It is more meaningful to speak of budget shares allocated to bundles of consumer inputs than to individual consumer products (Canterbery, 1979a). Such a relation among product-service groups, money incomes, and average group prices means that, once we have identified the household's income level, we also have come close to identifying the share of the household budget that goes to meet particular needs and therefore to necessary bundles of inputs.

Discretionary income is to consumption what physical surplus (over-capacity) is to production. Both are sources of instability in the advanced economy. Budget shares in Galbraith's system are to consumption what production prices are to production in Sraffa's system. Budget shares lead to an understanding of nonprice competition that is lost when disputes are confined to market pricing. Snob appeal takes on concrete meaning in the face of the one-to-two ratio of the subsistence to the "higher" consumption budget. The large gap between the lowest and highest incomes inspires the corporate structure to transcend the role of simple producer of goods and services. Although the difference between the consumer's physiological necessities budget and the higher income budget could in theory be devoted entirely to savings, the corporation tries to divert these household dollars toward consumer goods and services. The producers create many of the wants they seek to satisfy, an economic phenomenon Galbraith (1958) calls the *dependence effect*. Not surprisingly, in such an economy, a large share of the GNP subsidizes salespeople, marketing efforts, and advertising. Only in the affluent society can wants be created in a Galbraithian manner. As Galbraith (1967, p. 207) notes, "Mass communication was not necessary when the wants of the masses were anchored primarily in physical need. The masses could not then be persuaded as to their spending—this went for basic foods and shelter."

The mark-up and supra-surplus capitalism: Kalecki to Galbraith

Kalecki is primarily responsible for the introduction of imperfect competition into macroeconomic theory in Europe, a role performed by Sidney Weintraub (1959) in America. Galbraith's conception of the New Industrial State is consistent with both notions of pricing behavior. Kalecki's and Weintraub's vision of pricing in the manufacturing sector can be dramatized in one word: *mark-up*.[3] The mark-up plays a strategic role in supra-surplus capitalism.

According to Galbraith (1967, 1973), firms in the manufacturing sector have sufficient market power to pass on to the consumer most cost increases as well as price increases required by investment needs. Somewhere between 75 and 90 percent of gross (including replacement investment) fixed capital investment in the United States is financed from retained profits, the discretionary income of corporations. The giant firm has the power to select a percentage mark-up over production costs (mostly wages) that is sufficient to complete its investment plans most of the time without going hat in hand to a banker. This configuration serves the same purpose as Kalecki's capitalist plowing

[3]Whereas Kalecki's mark-up applies only to manufacturing, Weintraub's is more general and applies to all industries, including those that are nearly competitive.

all profits back into the firm, but the capitalist is replaced by the technostructure.

Capacity utilization may move up and down with the demand for products, but the corporation will stick with the mark-up that will provide its target level of retained profits. This target depends upon its dividend payout ratio to stockholders, its amount of debt relative to its equity, and, most importantly, its perceived investment needs.[4] As long as the firm's capacity is sufficient to meet demand for its products and as long as production costs do not vary greatly from expectations, the firm will cling to the price derived from its careful planning. The margin of prices over current costs already reflects the market power of the giant corporation.

Kalecki's measure of the "degree-of- monopoly" of the firm conforms neatly with Galbraithian power. The essence of the degree-of-monopoly formula is that a firm can raise its own price in proportion to its increase in production costs, if other firms in the industry do likewise. Non-price forms of competition displace price competition so that supply-side economics cannot remain simply the theory of price.

The mark-up and investment plans are inexorably linked. Because of the degree-of-monopoly factor, actual prices charged by the industrial firms do not reflect current demand conditions; they more closely mirror the funds requirements for the planned investment expenditures the technostructure deems sufficient to increase capacity (plant size or number of machines) to meet *expected future* demand. Such a mark-up serves the technostructure's affirmative purpose of growth. When costs of production rise, the firm protects its profits-for-investment flow by raising prices according to its established mark-up over costs. A fixed mark-up serves the technostructure's protective purpose. At times the capacity accumulated with these retained profits will be in excess of that needed to meet current demand, but this situation is no problem for an oligopoly. Supra-surplus capitalism also enjoys supra-surplus capacity. The technostructure savors bureaucratic advantage and hence power.

In the updated world of Galbraith and other contemporary Post

[4]The motivation for investment "needs" has been variously attributed to market share, growth, and power goals. These explanations have been put forward, respectively, by Alfred S. Eichner (1976); Robin Marris (1964); and John Kenneth Galbraith. A further exposition on this issue appears in James Galbraith's article in this symposium.

Keynesians, money income does arise from a whole spectrum of sources. If money wages are administered by union-management agreements, the balance of income is provided by the mark-up over wages, most of which will be retained profits (profits plus depreciation) and dividend payouts. If this mark-up remains constant throughout the economy and productivity remains unchanged, any cost increase from a boost in average wages will be reflected as an increase in the price level.

If prices are set with a constant or even a variable mark-up over wage costs, money wages become central to the price level. The money wages are inflexible downward (as Keynes argued for a different reason) because to reduce money wages violates the labor contract. In the short run, therefore, market prices must adjust to money wages and the cost of production rather than vice versa. There is a revised sequence in which the price level and the rate of inflation are resolved *after* the money wage rates and increases are determined. Money wages, exogeneous in Sraffa, are endogenous in Galbraith but determined by social-political conditions, not by the technology of production.

At this juncture, if Galbraith did not exist, Post Keynesians would have to invent him. The potential paradigm requires the establishment of a connection among personal incomes, demand, and production. In Galbraith (1958, 1967, 1973), demand is, for the most part, *managed* by the corporation and the industry. Nonetheless, when demand shifts up or down, since the neoclassical response of rising and falling prices is absent, adjustments made by the firm are in output levels. If GM is not selling its inventory of cars at the current prices (based upon mark-up over unit costs), GM produces fewer Chevrolets next month and eventually may even lay off production workers. Rather than responding to lower demand by reducing prices, giant producers reduce production levels.

Where corporate and union powers exist in supra-surplus capitalism and are symbiotic (Galbraith's term), *physiological* subsistence for the labor class must expand into *cultural* subsistence. The notion of cultural subsistence brings the personal income distribution in line with a Galbraithian estate of consumption. The technology of production and the prevailing level of production capacity still decide the total potential output of two types of goods: now culturally "necessary" consumption goods and the requisite investment goods. However, realized output depends upon effective demand and the income distribution. We, of course, do not have to be content with Sraffa's "given" level of output.

The distribution of income between workers and "capitalists" re-enters the picture, but in a more complex way than Kalecki would lead us to believe. There are *two* tugs-of-war between the manufacturers and the consumers–workers; producers seem unaware of one of them and workers of the other. Displaying the instincts attributed to corporate management by Galbraith, corporations create and stimulate new demand for their goods and services. However, in the planning system, the wherewithal to fulfill both the manufacturers' and the workers' dreams is decided at the labor-management bargaining table. Only in the guise of consumers are there any losers: Goodbye Adam Smith, in which consumers wear crowns.

The planning system has succeeded all too well in convincing consumers that they should expand the number of goods and services they consider necessary. In response to these culturally determined desires, the giant labor union demands higher wages so that the workers can pay for the newly defined standard of living. The corporation capitulates, knowing that the higher cost of production from a larger wage can be passed on to consumers. The illusion that a higher wage is always a good thing—a money illusion—is enjoyed by the workers, who don't quite sense the fallacy of composition in their dual role as both laborers and consumers. These increases merely cover the "cost of living." As Galbraith suggests, it is not mere historical accident that the highest paid workers reside in the protected part of the economy, the planning system.

If the process stopped at this point, the working class would increase its share of the national income, at least in money terms, but the defensive power instrument of the manufacturers is the mark-up. The concentrated industries can use the mark-up, augmented by ready access to the largest banks and the lowest rates of interest, to generate funds for investment purposes. Throughout the history of capitalism, the idea that workers have to be employed in order to purchase the producers' goods has always eluded manufacturers. Though it is in the interest of any single producer to minimize his total wage bill, if all producers succeed in that calculus they will find there is no outlet for their products.

Given the strength of the industrial labor union, industry's ability to pay the demanded wage is enhanced by its ability to impose price mark-ups upon the consumer.[5] The industrial union's power tool is the wage rate rather than the labor supply. This means that, in the short run, employment is not related to the wage rate, and the wage rate is related to employment only if full employment extends across all labor. Therefore, a high wage can be associated with a high unemployment rate, because employment is decided by technology and effective demand rather than by the marginal product of labor. This process is so deeply imbedded in the economic system that it took a four-year global depression (1979–1982) to slow wage (and price) inflation in the United States.

In the unskilled, nonorganized labor market, there is little incentive or ability to substitute capital goods for labor. Expected wage rates are low, and unskilled workers cannot operate complex machines. The long-run supply of unskilled workers is determined by nonwage elements. Few individuals actively strive to achieve characteristics that would yield low wages. Indeed, the unskilled might be viewed as failures, so their long-term supply is a kind of residual unrelated to wage rates. An unused supply of unskilled labor is a characteristic of recent experience in the industrialized countries. The wage differentials between the union-certified skilled and the unskilled is the consequence of (at least) dual labor markets that reflect the duality between the planning system and the competitive system.

Technological change—unpredictable and not widely understood—plays a major role in these theories. Its impact is readily seen once we accept the wage settlement as largely a political solution based upon the relative power of organized labor and organized production. It is precisely the more advanced secondary or planning sector of the economy that, in the long run, shifts toward more and more complex, automated ways of delivering its product. However, there is no guarantee that productivity will grow steadily faster than the wage rate. Moreover, we cannot expect the slow productivity growth in services to offset any such tendency. Stagflation is the secular consequence.

Even though the primary sector may contain competitive industries, the planning system of the advanced economy is in charge, wielding its power in the marketplace to control production and pass on rising costs (including money wage increases) to all of us. Its symbiotic relationship with big labor and big government gives giant business an almost

[5]In the remaining paragraphs Canterbery's vita theory (1979b, 1980b) is used to amend Galbraith. Piore's (1979) dual labor market perspective is also relevant to this discussion.

inexhaustible supply of funds for investment. The usually benign countervailing power of an earlier Galbraith (1952) gives way to (as JKG admits) non-benign compensatory power (1983). The well-funded investments in new technology that replace workers have the effect of redistributing income away from the working class, particularly away from the least skilled. Although the working class receives a share of profits, most ''non-earned'' income from high technology is accumulated by the entrepreneurial, managerial, and professional classes.

Technological progress alters the demand for a particular labor type in two ways. First, it can change the technical coefficients and thus labor-quantity requirements. Though capital goods and labor services complement each other in the short run (two workers may be needed for each new machine), they can become substitutes for each other in the longer run. The long-run trend of wages in the planning sector is known to be upward, and it is hardly surprising that the main purpose of new equipment in industrialized economies is to reduce labor requirements. Technological change also exerts a more indirect effect on labor demand. A new, more complex technology can cause a shift to labor of a different type altogether. Workers who once combined the ingredients for frozen cakes may be unqualified to monitor the automated machines that now perform this task, and unemployment of these workers results.

We have no assurance that displaced labor will be hired elsewhere. The rehiring of such labor requires the coincidence of new products and new industries emerging quickly enough to absorb the labor reserve. Even then, it is the more skilled reserve that is needed. Meanwhile, the life plans of the more advantaged workers move inexorably toward collectively increasing their numbers and the skilled labor supply. From the viewpoint of those who wish to have the highest possible personal income, this collective response is unfavorable. Rather than ''rationality'' being a way out of poverty or a low-income predicament, it can be a way in.

The requisites of technology rearrange the demands for different qualities of labor. The consequent arrangement of incomes is the stage upon which demand plays. The cultural generation of wants, though not entirely separate from technology, plays out much of its destiny within this dimly lit area at the interface between the wants of labor and those of corporate management. Within that gray area, Galbraith can tell us more than Sraffa or Kalecki can.

Whether all this is good or bad depends upon the institutionalized length of the workweek and the income distribution policies of the government. After all, the motivation behind the Industrial Revolution was to reduce physical labor in the process of creating production surpluses. One important measure of the output success of industrialization is the magnitude of unemployment that industry generates in the secondary sector. What we do with the freed effort we have so diligently sought depends upon the ethics of society and collective decisions regarding alternatives to physical work effort as a source of both pleasure and income. In this regard, Galbraith finds an unevenness in development between the private and public sector.

Conclusions

In order to fill the vacuum left by Sraffa and Kalecki, a theory of demand that relates production to a hierarchy of wants and a theory of the income distribution that relates incomes to job markets as well as to other elements are required. If labor is treated as a basic service, demand can be introduced into Sraffa's model. When hierarchical demand is considered, the true nature and importance of necessities, compared with luxuries in an advanced economy producing surpluses beyond physiological subsistence, is revealed. Income earners are then viewed as allocating expenditures among goods on the basis of a budget. In this view, the personal income distribution is dominant, and we are thus able to suppress orthodox price theory.

There is a connection among income distribution, consumer budget shares, production technology, and inflation that has not been widely appreciated. In Galbraith's planning system, we find a round robin of events in which giant business firms separate the affluent from their money by stimulating new wants. There is a kind of poetic justice in this, for the organized workers in the concentrated manufacturing industries demand higher wages to indulge their whetted appetites. The Post Keynesian price mark-up enables producers to pay the wages required to purchase the products the workers have been persuaded they truly need. In this process, the basic cost of remaining in the economic system keeps going up as both what is believed necessary expands and the prices of these "necessities" rise. As such wage settlements are "political," we cannot expect them to be related to productivity.

Moving from short-run variations in economic activity to economic growth, we still find technology and the income distribution to be the deciding forces. Traditionally, investment has been a source of volatility in industrial capacity; switching to new production processes is even less predictable. Moreover, the determinants of the personal income distribution add extra uncertainty, because the quality of the labor force at any time is unlikely to match exactly the new technological requirements. Finally, where labor services and capital goods are not substituted for each other in response to short-run relative price changes, we have to look to innovations and the birth of new industries to keep supra-surplus capitalism growing. The consumers' sovereignty—lost in the decline of the market—can be regained only through political sovereignty, which is itself in jeopardy at the hand of the same groups that felled the market. Galbraith noted the former in *The Affluent Society* and appraised the alternative sources of power in *The Anatomy of Power*. This appraisal of supra-surplus capitalism returns us, ironically, to concerns of the old political economists (e.g., Ricardo, Malthus, and Marx), who saw a close connection between state policy and the economy, thus clothing economics with real-world issues. Their world, the real world, is Galbraith's.

REFERENCES

Canterbery, E. Ray. "Inflation, Necessities, and Distributive Efficiency." In *Essays in Post-Keynesian Inflation*. Ed. by J. H. Gapinski and C. E. Rockwood. Cambridge, Mass.: Balinger, 1979a.

__________. "A Vita Theory of Personal Income Distribution." *Southern Economic Journal*, July 1979b, 46.

__________. *The Making of Economics*. 2nd ed. Belmont, CA.: Wadsworth Publishing Company, 1980a.

__________. "Welfare Economics and the Vita Theory." *The Eastern Economic Journal*, January 1980b, 6.

Eichner, Alfred S. *The Megacorp and Oligopoly: Micro Foundations of Macro Dynamics*. Cambridge, England: Cambridge University Press, 1976.

Galbraith, John Kenneth. *American Capitalism: The Concept of Countervailing Power*. Boston: Houghton, Mifflin Co., 1952.

__________. *The Affluent Society*. 2d ed. rev. Boston: Houghton Mifflin Co., 1958.

__________. *The New Industrial State*. Boston: Houghton Mifflin Co., 1967.

__________. *Economics and the Public Purpose*. Boston: Houghton Mifflin Co., 1973.

__________. *The Anatomy of Power*. Boston: Houghton Mifflin Co., 1983.

Kalecki, Michal. *Selected Essays on the Dynamics of the Capitalistic Economy*. Cambridge, England: Cambridge University Press, 1971.

Marris, Robin. *The Economic Theory of "Managerial" Capitalism*. New York: Basic Books, 1964.

Piore, Michael J., ed. *Unemployment and Inflation: Institutionalist and Structuralist Views*. Armonk, N.Y.: M. E. Sharpe, Inc., 1979.

Sraffa, Piero. *Production of Commodities by Means of Commodities*. Cambridge, England: Cambridge University Press, 1960.

Weintraub, Sidney. *A General Theory of the Price Level, Output, Income Distribution and Economic Growth*. Philadelphia: Chilton, 1959.

[11]

LILIANA BASILE and NERI SALVADORI

Kalecki's pricing theory

1. Introduction

Despite the recent interest in Kalecki's pricing theory (Eichner, 1976, 1979, 1981; Feiwel, 1975; Harcourt and Kenyon, 1976; Levine, 1981; Weintraub, 1979), assessments of Kalecki's own writings on this topic are rare (but see Riach, 1971; Harris, 1974; Asimakopulos, 1975 a,b,c; Reynolds, 1983).

Kalecki's work on pricing theory was concentrated in three periods: the late 1930s–early 1940s (Kalecki, 1939-40, 1941, 1943), the mid-1950s (Kalecki, 1954), and the late 1960s (Kalecki, 1971a).

This paper will demonstrate that both Kalecki's initial pricing theory, linked to Robinson's and Chamberlain's theory of imperfect competition, and his last formulation, associated with full cost theory, are the same as the simplified version he presented in 1954. This point has not been recognized in the literature on the topic. Indeed, some authors assert that Kalecki presented several approaches to pricing theory. For instance, Kaldor (1955–56) considers Kalecki's early treatment of pricing a theory (although basically neoclassical) while the 1954 treatment was simply a tautology (cf. Davidson, 1960, pp. 52–54; and Nuti, 1970). Asimakopulos (1975a) asserts that Kalecki's later work (1971a) had a "tautological nature" (p. 318), while the 1954 treatment had "very limited explanatory power" and some "technical problems" (p. 317). More recently Reynolds (1983) has stated that in 1954 "Kalecki

Liliana Basile is Ricercatore Confermato at the University of Naples, Italy, and Neri Salvadori is Professore Incaricato at the University of Catania, Italy, and Associate Professor at the University of Denver. They thank Jan Kregel and an anonymous referee for helpful comments. L. Basile thanks the C.N.R. (Italian Research Council) and both authors thank the M.P.I. (Italian Ministry of Public Education) for financial support. Usual caveats apply.

set out *for the first time* a meaningful, internally consistent theory to explain how firms set prices'' (p. 494, italics added).

Our analysis also allows us to explore Kalecki's general pricing theory and to extend to the general case Kalecki's statement of the conditions which allow a solution with positive prices for the simplified version of his theory (1954). Finally, we comment on the relation between pricing and the controversial notion of ''degree of monopoly'' with reference to Kalecki's (1938, 1943) papers which expound his theory of income distribution as determined by the ''degree of monopoly.''

2. The early writings

In Kalecki's 1938 *Econometrica* analysis of distribution there was no reference to the theory of pricing. This appeared a year later in the *Review of Economic Studies* (Kalecki, 1939–40), and again in 1941 in the *Oxford Economic Papers*. Kalecki's (1943) re-elaboration of his theory of distribution employed his pricing theory in support of some of the analysis.

Kalecki's 1939–40 and 1941 publications elaborate the following equation (Kalecki, 1941, p. 34; see also 1939–40, p. 99):

$$\frac{m_k}{p_k} = g_k\left(\frac{p_k}{\bar{p}}\right) \tag{1}$$

where m_k and p_k are the marginal cost and the price of the product of firm k respectively, and $\bar{p}$ is industry price (a weighted average of firms' prices).

The function $g_k(\cdot)$ is introduced in two stages (see especially Kalecki, 1939–40). In the first, referring to Robinson (1933) and Chamberlain (1933) and called *pure imperfect competition*, the number of firms is assumed ''so great that the problem of oligopoly does not come into the picture'' and the entrepreneurs are assumed to know both the demand curve for their product and their marginal cost curves (Kalecki, 1939–40, p. 91). In this case $g_k(\cdot)$ is the ratio of the marginal revenue to the price of firm k as a function of the ratio of the firm's price (p_k) to industry price ($\bar{p}$). Such a function can be obtained from the demand curve of firm k. More precisely

$$g_k\left(\frac{p_k}{\bar{p}}\right) \equiv 1 - \frac{1}{\epsilon_k\left(\frac{p_k}{\bar{p}}\right)}$$

where $\epsilon_k(p_k/\bar{p})$ is the elasticity of demand for the product of firm k as a function of $p_k/\bar{p}$. The shape of the function $\epsilon_k(\cdot)$ represents what Kalecki calls "the state of market imperfection" (Kalecki, 1939-40, p. 91).

In the second stage, Kalecki relaxes the assumption of pure imperfect competition, asserting that the function $g_k(\cdot)$ cannot be determined by the demand function alone since "the entrepreneur does not equate his marginal revenue . . . to his marginal cost . . . but fixes his price at a certain point where the former is greater than the latter." As a consequence

$$g_k\left(\frac{p_k}{\bar{p}}\right) = \left[\frac{1 - \dfrac{1}{\epsilon_k\left(\dfrac{p_k}{\bar{p}}\right)}}{\alpha_k}\right]$$

where α_k is what Kalecki calls "the degree of oligopoly."[1] (Kalecki, 1939–40, p. 98); obviously $\alpha_k > 1$.

Kalecki makes two important observations on this formulation (Kalecki, 1939-40, pp. 98–99). First, since the entrepreneur has only a vague idea of the demand function, the actual demand function cannot be used to determine the function $g_k(\cdot)$; rather the entrepreneur's *estimated* demand function[2] should be used:

$$g_k\left(\frac{p_k}{\bar{p}}\right) = \left[\frac{1 - \dfrac{1}{\omega_k\left(\dfrac{p_k}{\bar{p}}\right)}}{\alpha_k}\right]$$

where $\omega_k(\cdot)$ is the entrepreneur's estimate of $\epsilon_k(\cdot)$.

Second, since the entrepreneur does not know the precise nature of his marginal cost function and usually makes his decisions on "a crude notion such as the average cost of manual labour and raw materials at a 'normal' output," Kalecki suggests that m_k in eq. (1) should not be interpreted as actual marginal cost, but, instead, as "what the entrepre-

[1]The "degree of oligopoly" should not be confused with the "degree of monopoly."

[2]The concept of the estimated demand function used by Kalecki appears to be the same as Kaldor's (1934, pp. 59–61; 1935, p. 69n) *imagined demand curve*. Kaldor (1934) introduced it, in a review of J. Robinson's (1933) book, to similar purpose. See also Weintraub (1942).

neur considers it to be," i.e., what Kalecki will call "direct prime cost" in his subsequent writings[3] (1954, 1971).

To sum up, Kalecki's pricing theory expresses a relationship between m_k/p_k and $p_k/\bar{p}$ which is obtained from a set of conditions that are not fully explored except for the case of "pure imperfect competition." Therefore, the function $g_k(\cdot)$ appears as a theoretical construction which has a theoretical status similar to that of the individual demand curve. The difference is that the demand curve is obtained quite clearly from a well-defined data set (preference orderings) while the function $g_k(\cdot)$, except in a special case, is not. Hence, even if Kalecki's pricing theory is not complete, it cannot be considered tautological (see also Riach, 1971), as Machlup (1952) and others have asserted. Moreover, the link between Kalecki's pricing theory and Robinson's and Chamberlain's theory of imperfect competition appears to be very weak. It would seem that Kalecki only introduced "pure imperfect competition" in order to provide a special case of his theory which could be related to an already well-established theory.

3. *The Theory of Dynamics* (1954)

Let us quote Kalecki himself:

> In fixing the price the firm takes into consideration its average prime costs and the prices of other firms producing similar products. The firm must make sure that the price does not become too high in relation to prices of other firms, for this would drastically reduce sales, and that the price does not become too low in relation to its average prime cost, for this would drastically reduce the profit margin. Thus when the price p is determined by the firm in relation to unit prime cost u, care is taken that the ratio of p to the weighted average price of all firms, $\bar{p}$ ["weighted by the respective outputs and inclusive of the firm in question"—added in a footnote] does not become too high. . . . If u increases, p can be increased proportionately only if $\bar{p}$ rises proportionately as well. But if $\bar{p}$ increases less than u, the firm's price p will also be raised less than u. (Kalecki, 1954, pp. 44–45).

[3]A third, less important, remark is on page 99. If selling costs are to be considered, and if β_k is the ratio between selling cost and price, then

$$g_k\left(\frac{p_k}{\bar{p}}\right) \equiv \left[\frac{1 - \dfrac{1}{\omega_k\left(\dfrac{p_k}{\bar{p}}\right)}}{\alpha_k}\right] - \beta_k .$$

The above quotation suggests that the firm's price p is a function (increasing with respect to both variables) of the firm's prime cost u and the price of the industry $\bar{p}$; i.e.,

(2) $$p = F(u, \bar{p})$$

(3) $$\frac{\partial F}{\partial u} > 0, \quad \frac{\partial F}{\partial \bar{p}} > 0.$$

It also suggests[4] that:

(4) $$\text{if } \Delta u/u = \Delta\bar{p}/\bar{p} \quad \text{then} \quad \Delta p/p = \Delta u/u = \Delta\bar{p}/\bar{p}.$$

Suppose, now, that:

$$\Delta u/u = \Delta\bar{p}/\bar{p} = \Delta p/p = \alpha.$$

Since

$$\frac{\Delta p}{p} = \frac{F(u + \Delta u, \bar{p} + \Delta\bar{p}) - F(u, \bar{p})}{F(u, \bar{p})}$$

we get:

(5) $$\lambda F(u, \bar{p}) = F(\lambda u, \lambda\bar{p})$$

where $\lambda = 1 + \alpha$; i.e., the function $F(\cdot,\cdot)$ is homogeneous of degree one. Hence, statement (4) is not really an assumption, since it results from the fact that capitalists' pricing decisions do not depend on the choice of units of measure of commodities.

From (5) and (2), setting $\lambda = 1/p$, we get:

(6) $$1 = F(u/p, \bar{p}/p).$$

Since $F(\cdot,\cdot)$ is an increasing function with respect to both variables, eq. (6) implicitly defines u/p as a decreasing function of $(\bar{p}/p)$. Assume that:

(7) $$\frac{u}{p} = \phi\left(\frac{\bar{p}}{p}\right)$$

[4]Indeed, it also suggests that if $\Delta u/u > \Delta\bar{p}/p$ then $\Delta p/p < \Delta u/u$; but this statement is included within statement (4), because of inequalities (3).

is such a function, and define $g(\cdot)$ as

$$g(x) \equiv \phi(1/x).$$

Hence eq. (2) is recognized to be equivalent to eq. (1), since the marginal cost (m) may be interpreted as the prime cost (u) with the support of the second of Kalecki's remarks referred to in the previous section. It can thus be clearly seen that the theory set out by Kalecki in 1954 is the same as the theory in his early writings. The main differences appear[5] to be (i) the disappearance of any reference to the theory of imperfect competition, (ii) the greater emphasis on the behavior of the entrepreneurs in defining the function $g(\cdot)$, and (iii) the emphasis on the fact that function $g(\cdot)$ is increasing—note that $(\partial\omega/\partial(p_k/\bar{p})) > 0$ if the demand curve is assumed to be well behaved.

Kalecki (1954) does not extend the theory just reviewed; rather he analyzes a particular case, i.e., the case of a linerar $F(\cdot,\cdot)$ in the form

$$p = mu + n\bar{p} \tag{8}$$

where $m > 0$, $0 < n < 1$. The conditions $m > 0$, $n > 0$ have an obvious rationale. The condition $n < 1$ is sufficient for all prices to be defined and positive. (Since the similar condition for the general case has never been given, it will be provided in the next section.)

Asimakopulos (1975a) has criticized these conditions, arguing that $n < 1$ (and $m > 0$) could not be true for every firm. "In situations where price is set by a price leader and followed by others," he says, "n would be equal to one for the price followers and thus m would be equal to zero. . . . For the price leader, on the other hand," he continues, "n would be equal to zero and the value of m would depend on many (interdependent) factors, . . ." (p. 317).

However, a solution[6] to this objection exists in replacing the assumption of

$$0 < n < 1, m > 0$$

with

$$0 \leq n \leq 1, m \geq 0, 0 < \bar{n} < 1, \bar{m} > 0,$$

where $\bar{n}$ is the average of all n's weighted by the respective outputs, and $\bar{m}$ is the average of all m's weighted by the respective prime costs. In fact, these latter assumptions require that $n < 1$ and $m > 0$ at least for

[5]Kalecki himself stated that in his 1954 treatment he tried to remove the misunderstandings generated by his earlier treatment (cf. Kalecki, 1968, p. 168).

[6]This point is discussed more fully in Basile (1980).

some firms, which is true if we want, as Kalecki does, to analyze a system that differs from the case of "perfect competition" (where all firms are price-takers; i.e., $n = 1$, $m = 0$ for every firm) or "pure monopoly" (where all firms are price-makers; i.e., $n = 0$, $m > 1$ for every firm). Moreover, the assumptions $0 < \bar{n} < 1$, $\bar{m} > 0$ (jointly with $n \geq 0$, $m \geq 0$, $u > 0$) are necessary and sufficient to prove the existence of a positive solution for the price system.[7] Under these conditions all Kalecki's main conclusions remain valid.

4. The late paper

Kalecki reconsidered his pricing theory in a paper published posthumously in 1971. Each firm in an industry is presented as arriving at the price of his product p by "marking up" its prime cost u in order to cover overheads and profits. This "markup" is an increasing function of the ratio between the industry price, $\bar{p}$, and the firm price, p, because it is considered to be dependent on "competition." Thus,

$$p = u\left[1 + f\left(\frac{\bar{p}}{p}\right)\right] \tag{9}$$

To see that eq. (9) is equivalent to eq. (1) and to eq. (2) it is sufficient to define

$$f\left(\frac{\bar{p}}{p}\right) = \frac{1}{\phi\left(\frac{\bar{p}}{p}\right)} - 1$$

where $\phi(\cdot)$ is defined by eq. (7). This also proves that function $f(\cdot)$ is increasing.[8]

Hence Kalecki's 1971 treatment is formally identical to previous versions. The difference is in emphasis. Now the full-cost theory is presented as a particular case, i.e., the case of a constant $f(\cdot)$. Again

[7]We obtain from eq. (8) that p is defined and positive as u and $\bar{p}$ are defined and positive; u is given at a positive level; since $\bar{p} = \bar{u}\bar{m}/(1 - \bar{n})$ ($\bar{u}$ being the average of all u's weighted by the respective outputs; this formula is obtained as follows: $\bar{p} = \Sigma q_i p_i = \Sigma q_i m_i u_i + \Sigma q_i n_i \bar{p} = \bar{m}\bar{u} + \bar{n}\bar{p}$; q_i being the market share of firm i), $\bar{p}$ is defined if and only if $\bar{n} \neq 1$ and $\bar{p} > 0$ if and only if $\bar{m} > 0$ and $\bar{n} < 1$.

[8]Asimakopulos (1975a), referring to eq. (9), argues that the function $f(\cdot)$ cannot be

Kalecki provides an example[9] of his theory which can be related to a contemporary theory.

In recent years some authors (e.g., Harris, 1974; Asimakopulos, 1975b,c) have reviewed Kalecki's pricing theory without reference to analysis at firm level, concentrating their analysis on the industry. The industry price is obtained by marking up the average prime cost of the industry with a constant markup:

$$\bar{p} = (1 + \mu)\bar{u};$$

Kalecki's pricing theory is thus interpreted as equivalent to a full-cost theory at industry level, even if it is not at the firm level. This procedure may be justified by Kalecki's writings only if the effects of the structure of market shares, and of prime costs, are neglected.[10] Indeed, Kalecki (1943) himself seemed to think that the effect of the latter "upon the average percentage gross margin μ is most probably relatively small" (p. 14).

In Kalecki (1971a) the problem of the existence of solutions for the price equations is introduced (cf. p. 160). Unfortunately it is resolved by the unsatisfactory procedure of counting unknowns and equations. In the simplified (1954) case, it is also necessary to assume that $\bar{n} \neq 1$ (cf. note 7). Moreover, no attempt is made to assure that the solution is positive ($0 < \bar{n} < 1$, $\bar{m} > 0$, in the simplified case). This problem could be resolved by introducing the following assumptions about the function $f(\cdot,\cdot)$ defined by eq. (2):

$$F(0,0) \geq 0, \tag{10}$$

$$\frac{\partial^2 F}{\partial \bar{p}^2} \leq 0. \tag{11}$$

The rationale of assumption (10) is obvious. The rationale of assump-

an increasing function: "For the firm in a given situation both u and $\bar{p}$ are given . . . and therefore the higher the mark-up, the higher p, and the lower $\bar{p}/p$. Contrary to Kalecki's statement the function f appears to be a decreasing function!" (p. 318). Asimakopulos would be right if the function $f(\cdot)$ were defined implicitly by eq. (9), assuming u and $\bar{p}$ are given; but, as we have seen, the function $f(\cdot)$ defines the price-fixing policy of the firm and is determined independently of eq. (9).

[9]Kalecki has been clear on this point at least since Kalecki (1954, e.g., p. 51). Some critical remarks on full-cost theory are also to be found in Kalecki (1943, p. 27).

[10]It can be immediately seen (from eq. (A.7) of the Appendix) that if all u's are multiplied by λ the solution of eq. (A.7), p^*, will be multiplied by λ, because the functions $F_k(\cdot,\cdot)$ are homogeneous of degree 1.

tion (11) is the following: for successive increments in $\bar{p}$ (u being unchanged), the firm raises its price, p, more and more slowly to increase its market share. Since $F(\cdot,\cdot)$ is homogeneous of degree 1, inequality (11) is equivalent to each of the following inequalities:

$$\frac{\partial^2 F}{\partial u^2} \leq 0, \qquad \frac{\partial^2 F}{\partial u \partial \bar{p}} \geq 0.$$

The proof of existence (and unicity) of positive prices under assumptions (10) and (11) will be given in the appendix.

5. Degree of monopoly

Up to now we have not mentioned the *degree of monopoly*. Indeed, we have not needed this concept to reconstruct Kalecki's theory. This section attempts to clarify the relation between pricing and the degree of monopoly, which has been widely debated in the literature.

It appears that Kalecki introduced the notion of "degree of monopoly," giving a definition similar to that introduced by A. Lerner (1934) for the first time in Kalecki (1938):

$$\mu = \frac{p - m}{\bar{p}}$$

where μ is the degree of monopoly, p is the price, and m is the marginal cost. The paper was devoted to a statistical and analytical investigation of the determinants of the relative share of manual labor in national income. Kalecki concluded that "the relative shares of gross capitalist income and salaries in the aggregate turnover is with great approximation equal to the average degree of monopoly" (Kalecki, 1938, p. 102).[11]

In this analysis, however, Kalecki considers prices as givens. If we introduce his price theory into this analysis we discover that the degree of monopoly is not constant, but a function of $p_k/\bar{p}$:[12]

[11]It was sufficient to assume constant the average degree of monopoly to provide an answer to Keynes's question on the origin of the constancy of income shares (cf. Keynes, 1939, p. 49).

[12]In the case of "pure imperfect competition," the function $\mu_k(p_k/\bar{p})$ coincides with the function of the inverse of elasticity of the demand curve of firm k. Many authors (e.g., Davidson, 1960) have considered this case as the only one treated by Kalecki in his early writings. As we have tried to argue in this paper, the case of pure imperfect competition is considered by Kalecki only in an attempt to clarify the relation between his theory and the theory of imperfect competition.

$$\mu_k = \mu_k \left(\frac{p_k}{\bar{p}} \right) \equiv 1 - g_k \left(\frac{p_k}{\bar{p}} \right) .$$

The appearance of the function $g_k(\cdot)$ is equivalent to making the degree of monopoly a *function*.

Thus, Kalecki clarified the link between pricing and income distribution by means of a concept—degree of monopoly—which can be considered *either* as an auxiliary concept with no real explanatory power, *or* as a determinant of the analytical process, since it really determines the pricing functions. Kalecki (1938) follows the latter alternative.

Some years later, Kalecki (1943) was more accurate in using the ratios

$$\frac{p_k - m_k}{p_k}$$

In this essay, the previous ratios are not referred to as ''degrees of monopoly,'' but as ''percentage gross margins.'' Kalecki (1943) argued that ''in the movement of the average percentage gross margin μ [using as weights the respective values of sales] are mainly reflected changes in the degree of market imperfection and oligopoly, changes in the rates of prime selling costs, and bottlenecks in available manufacturing capacities'' (p. 16). Therefore, if prime selling costs are constant and firms are all working up to capacity, then μ ''reflects'' the degree of market imperfection and oligopoly of the industry. Besides, μ is equal to the ratio of profits plus overheads, to sales; in this way Kalecki reconfirmed the link between income distribution and the state of market imperfection that lies behind the link between income distribution and pricing functions.

In the *Theory of Economic Dynamics* (1954) Kalecki again used the term ''degree of monopoly'' without giving a precise definition or a clear measure, at least at the firm level. The degree of monopoly facing the firm is only mentioned in sentences such as the following: ''The coefficients m and n characterizing the price-fixing policy of the firm reflect what may be called the degree of monopoly of the firm's position'' (Kalecki 1954, p. 45). The degree of monopoly for an industry is considered an increasing function of $\bar{m}/(1 - \bar{n})$, i.e., the industry price/industry prime cost ratio (cf. pp. 49 and 59).

Finally, in his posthumously published paper (Kalecki, 1971a), the degree of monopoly is replaced by the assertion that the pricing functions reflect ''semi monopolistic influences . . . resulting from imperfect competition or oligopoly. The more intensive are these factors, the higher $f(\bar{p}/p)$ corresponding to a given relation $\bar{p}/p$" (Kalecki, 1971a, p. 169).[13]

Kalecki's concept of degree of monopoly thus started with a clear definition which soon encountered objection. Attempts to meet the objections made the definition progressively less clear, until it was finally abandoned. Thus the concept of "degree of monopoly," which had started as a statistically observable index of market imperfection, became a synthetic name given to the various forces protecting the firm's competitive position[14] which was ultimately considered unnecessary. This evolution does not however imply any change in Kalecki's pricing theory. If the pricing functions are initially taken as given, no reference to the degree of monopoly is necessary.[15] This seems to have been Kalecki's final position in his posthumously published paper.

6. Concluding remarks

We can thus see the continuity of Kalecki's thought with respect to pricing. Throughout his writings each firm is supposed to set its price with reference to its unit prime cost and the average price of the industry. The determination of the price function is not directly investigated, but it is presumed to depend on the various forces which protect the firm's competitive position which Kalecki collected in the term "degree of monopoly." Finally we have seen that the existence and positiveness of prices can be proven under assumptions compatible with the theory.

[13]Three years before Kalecki had recognized that "it is this term ['degree of monopoly'], I think, that facilitated the dismissal of the theory as being tautological" (Kalecki, 1968, p. 168).

[14]Feiwel (1975) also notes that the degree of monopoly was used by Kalecki as a synthetic name given to the "semi monopolistic and monopolistic influences resulting from imperfect competition and oligopoly" (p. 96).

[15]Reynolds (1983, p. 495), who agrees that the full appreciation of Kalecki's theory is not helped by his use of the term "degree of monopoly," also notes (pp. 497–499) that another source of misunderstanding is Kalecki's statistical analysis, which cannot be considered an empirical verification of his theory, but simply as a rationalization of observed movements in the time series.

APPENDIX

There exist n firms. Each firm k fixes its price p_k according to the following rule:

$$p_k = F_k(u_k, \bar{p}) \qquad (k = 1, 2, \ldots, n) \tag{A.1}$$

with

(A.2) $$F_k(0, 0) \geq 0$$

(A.3) $$\frac{\partial F_k}{\partial u_k} \geq 0, \qquad \frac{\partial F_k}{\partial \bar{p}} \geq 0,$$

(A.4) $$\frac{\partial^2 F}{\partial u^2{}_k} \leq 0, \qquad \frac{\partial^2 F}{\partial u_k \partial \bar{p}} \geq 0, \qquad \frac{\partial^2 F}{\partial \bar{p}^2} \leq 0,$$

there exist i and j such that

(A.5) $$\frac{\partial F_i}{\partial u_i} > 0, \qquad \frac{\partial F_j}{\partial \bar{p}} > 0,$$

where $F(\cdot,\cdot)$ is homogeneous of degree 1, u_k is the prime cost of firm k, and

(A.6) $$\bar{p} = \sum_{k=1}^{n} q_k p_k,$$

where q_k is the market share of firm k; of course $0 < q_k < 1$, $\Sigma q_k = 1$.

Since (A.2) and (A.3) hold, if u_k and $\bar{p}$ are defined and positive, then p_k is defined and positive. Since u_k is given at a positive level, we just have to prove that $\bar{p}$ is defined and positive. By substituting we obtain from eqs. (A.1) and (A.6) that:

(A.7) $$\bar{p} = \sum_{k=1}^{n} q_k F_k(u_k,\bar{p}),$$

which is one equation with one unknown since $u_1, u_2, \ldots, u_n$ are given. Let

$$G(\bar{p}) \equiv \sum_{k=1}^{n} q_k F_k,(u_k,\bar{p});$$

then eq. (A.7) is equivalent to

(A.8) $$\bar{p} = G(\bar{p}).$$

To prove that equation (A.8) has a positive solution we need to assume:

(A.9) There exists a non-negative real number θ such that

$$G'(\theta) < 1.$$

In fact, if $F_k(\cdot,\cdot)$ is homogeneous of degree 1, $u_k > 0, \bar{p} > 0$, and the first of inequalities (A.3) holds, then

$$\frac{\partial F_k}{\partial \bar{p}} \leq \frac{P_k}{\bar{p}}, \qquad \frac{\partial F_i}{\partial \bar{p}} < \frac{P_i}{\bar{p}};$$

as a consequence, if eq. (A.8) has a solution, then statement (A.9) holds. (The reader has probably noted that statement (A.9) is equivalent to $\bar{n} < 1$ in the simplified, 1954, version of Kalecki's pricing theory.)

Since

$$G(0) > 0 \tag{A.10}$$

we can choose θ so low that

$$G(\theta) > \theta. \tag{A.11}$$

Because of (A.4)

$$G(\bar{p}) \leq G(\theta) + G'(\theta)(\bar{p} - \theta). \tag{A.12}$$

Let

$$\delta = \frac{G(\theta) - \theta G'(\theta)}{1 - G'(\theta)}.$$

Since (A.9) and (A.11) hold, δ is defined and greater than θ. Moreover

$$G(\delta) \leq \delta \tag{A.13}$$

because of (A.12).

Finally, since (A.11) and (A.13) hold and function $G(\cdot)$ is continuous there exists $\bar{p}^*$, $\theta < \bar{p}^* \leq \delta$, which satisfies eq. (A.8). This proves existence and positiveness; to prove uniqueness it is sufficient to remark that the function $\bar{p} - G(\bar{p})$ is negative for $0 \leq \bar{p} \leq \theta$—because of (A.10), (A.11), and (A.4)— and is strictly increasing for $\bar{p} > \theta$—because of (A.9) and (A.4).

REFERENCES

Asimakopulos, A. "A Kaleckian Theory of Income Distribution." *Canadian Journal of Economics*, August 1975a, *8*, 313–333.

————. "The Price Policy of Firms, Employment and Distribution: A Comment." *Australian Economic Papers*, December 1975b, *14*, 261–262.

————. "Profits and Investment: A Kaleckian Approach." In *The Microeconomic Foundation of Macroeconomics*. Ed. by G. C. Harcourt and E. A. G. Robinson. London: Macmillan, 1975c, 328–353.

Basile, Liliana. "Prezzi e distribuzione in Michal Kalecki." *Studi Economici*, 1980, *35*, 27–56.

Chamberlain, E. H. *The Theory of Monopolistic Competition*. Cambridge, Mass.: Harvard University Press, 1933.

Davidson, Paul. *Theories of Aggregate Income Distribution*. New Brunswick, N.J.: Rutgers University Press, 1960.

Eichner, Alfred S. *The Megacorp and Oligopoly*. Cambridge: Cambridge University Press, 1976.

————. "A Post Keynesian Short Period Model." *Journal of Post Keynesian Economics*, Summer 1979, *1*(4), 38–63.

———. "Symposium: Price Formation Theory: Introduction." *Journal of Post Keynesian Economics*, Fall 1981, *5*(1), 81–116.

Feiwel, George R. *The Intellectual Capital of Michal Kalecki*. Knoxville: University of Tennessee Press, 1975.

Harcourt, G. C., and Kenyon, Peter. "Pricing and the Investment Decision." *Kyklos*, 1976, *29*, 449-477.

Harris, Donald J. "The Price Policy of Firms: The Level of Employment and Distribution of Income in the Short Run." *Australian Economic Papers*, June 1974, *13*, 144–151.

Kaldor, Nicholas. "Mrs. Robinson's 'Economics of Imperfect Competition.' " *Economica*, August 1934, *1*, 335–341. References are to the reprint in Kaldor 1960.

———. "Market Imperfection and Excess Capacity." *Economica*, February 1935, *2*, 33-50. References are to the reprint in Kaldor 1960.

———."Alternative Theories of Distribution." *Review of Economic Studies*, 1955-56, *23*, 83-100.

———. *Essay on Value and Distribution*. London: Duckworth, 1960.

Kalecki, Michal. "The Determinants of Distribution of the National Income." *Econometrica*, 1938, *6*, 97–112.

———."The Supply Curve of an Industry under Imperfect Competition." *Review of Economic Studies*, 1939-40, *9*, 91–112.

———."A Theory of Long-Run Distribution of the Product of Industry." *Oxford Economic Papers*, 1941, 31–41.

———. *Studies in Economic Dynamics*. London: Allen and Unwin, 1943.

———. *Theory of Economic Dynamics*. London: Allen and Unwin, 1954. References are to reprint of chapter "Costs and Prices" in Kalecki 1971b.

———. "Trend and the Business Cycle Reconsidered." *Economic Journal*, June 1968, *78*, 263-276. References are to reprint in Kalecki 1971b.

———. "Class Struggle and the Distribution of National Income." *Kyklos*, 1971a, *24*, 1-9. References are to reprint in Kalecki 1971b.

———. *Selected Essays on the Dynamics of the Capitalist Economy*. Cambridge: Cambridge University Press, 1971b.

Keynes, John M. "Relative Movements of Real Wages and Output." *Economic Journal*, March 1939, *49*, 34–51.

Lerner, Abba P. "The Concept of Monopoly and the Measurement of Monopoly Power." *Review of Economic Studies*, June 1934, *3*, 157–175.

Machlup, F. *The Political Economy of Monopoly*. Baltimore: Johns Hopkins, 1952.

Nuti, Domenico M. "Vulgar Economy in the Theory of Income Distribution." *De Economist*, 1970, *4*, 363–369.

Reynolds, Peter J. "Kalecki's Degree of Monopoly." *Journal of Post Keynesian Economics*, Spring 1983, *5*(3), 493–503.

Riach, P. A. "Kalecki's 'Degree of Monopoly' Reconsidered." *Australian Economic Papers*, June 1971, *10*, 50–60.

Robinson, Joan. *Economics of Imperfect Competition*. London: Macmillan, 1933.

Weintraub, Sidney. "Monopoly Equilibrium and Anticipated Demand." *Journal of Political Economy*, June 1942, *50*, 427–434.

———. "Generalizing Kalecki and Simplifying Macroeconomics." *Journal of Post Keynesian Economics*, Spring 1979, *1*(3), 101–106.

[12]

Cambridge Journal of Economics 1983, 7, 221–233

Kalečki and Keynes on finance, investment and saving

A. Asimakopulos

For both Kalečki and Keynes the key element in the determination of the level of economic activity in any short period in a capitalistic economy is the rate of investment that firms have decided to implement. Kalečki, with his concentration on profits (which are positively related to the level of economic activity), expressed this dependence in the following way:

> Thus capitalists, as a whole, determine their own profits by the extent of their investment and personal consumption. In a way they are 'masters of their fate'; but how they 'master' it is determined by objective factors, so that fluctuations of profits appear after all to be unavoidable (Kalečki, 1971, p. 13).

Keynes's own summary of his theory in the *Quarterly Journal of Economics* in 1937 when he responded to some reviews of The *General Theory* is

> . . . the level of output and employment as a whole depends on the amount of investment. I put it in this way, not because this is the only factor on which aggregate output depends, but because it is usual in a complex system to regard as the *causa causans* that factor which is most prone to sudden and wide fluctuation. More comprehensively, aggregate output depends on the propensity to hoard, on the policy of the monetary authority as it affects the quantity of money, on the state of confidence concerning the prospective yield of capital assets, on the propensity to spend and on the social factors which influence the level of the money wage. But of these several factors it is those which determine the rate of investment which are most unreliable, since it is they which are influenced by our views of the future about which we know so little (Keynes, 1973, p. 121).

These similarities have led Joan Robinson, among others, to claim that Kalečki 'had already published some articles in Polish (the first in 1933) outlining the main points of what afterwards became known as Keynes' theory . . .' (Robinson, 1973, p. 87). Kalečki himself had noted in his 1936 review of The *General Theory* for a Polish periodical that his 1933 study of the business cycle had emphasised the important role of investment in determining total output in a manner similar to that of Keynes. An early reference to this similarity, in English, is to be found in a footnote to his 1942 paper on 'A Theory of Profits' where he writes 'The theory of profits presented here is closely allied to Mr. Keynes' theory of saving and investment. It has been, however, developed independently of Mr. Keynes in [reference is made to Kalečki 1935A and B]' (Kalečki 1942, p. 258 n.1). A more forthright claim is made in the introduction to his *Selected Essays on the Dynamics of the*

*McGill University. I am grateful to L. G. Ascah and J. C. Weldon for comments on an earlier draft, but they are not responsible for any errors nor for the interpretation of writings in this paper.

0309–166X/83/030221 + 13 $03.00/0 © 1983 Academic Press Inc. (London) Limited

Capitalist Economy 1933–1970; 'The first part includes three papers published in 1933, 1934 and 1935 in Polish before Keynes' *General Theory* appeared, and containing, I believe, its essentials . . .' (Kalečki, 1971, vii). This claim has not gone without challenge, and Patinkin (1982) in his latest book has concluded that the General Theory was not an example of multiple discovery, in part because of his view of the 'central message' of the General Theory—the possibility of unemployment equilibrium—as contrasted with Kalečki's emphasis on the business cycle. What appears to have been overlooked in this literature is the extent to which Keynes's treatment of the finance required for an increase in investment was foreshadowed in Kalečki's 1935 papers, the first of which was published in French (1935A), and the second in English (1935B). Keynes's reference to the 'revolving fund' nature of finance, when he came to consider this question in his 1937 *Economic Journal* papers, is similar to Kalečki's image of 'the circle [of finance] will close itself' (Kalečki, 1935B, p. 343).

The availability of finance for firms was seen as an important precondition for both Kalečki and Keynes for the independence of investment from saving, an independence that was at the centre of their visions of the factors determining the levels of output and employment. In Joan Robinson's words, it is '. . . the central thesis of the *General Theory*, that firms are free, within wide limits, to accumulate as they please, and that the rate of saving of the economy as a whole accommodates itself to the rate of investment that they decree' (Robinson, 1962, pp. 82–83). Their treatments of finance should thus be seen as integral parts of their theories of the factors that can change effective demand, even though Keynes did not write on this question in connection with his theory of effective demand before 1937. Both Keynes and Kalečki emphasised that it was investment, through its effects on income (and for Kalečki in particular, the distribution of income) that resulted in the equality between planned investment and saving that was in the desired relation to income. As we shall see below, neither writer paid sufficient attention to the time required for this equality to be achieved, that is, for the full multiplier effects of a higher level of investment to be worked out. Keynes even appeared at times to confuse the definitional equality between saving and investment with the equilibrium relation between the two.

Keynes's justification for the use of the adjective *general* in the title of his book was that it dealt with the general case of possible short-period equilibrium positions for the economy. As a result of the investment decisions of firms and the propensities to save, these positions could often be accompanied by involuntary unemployment. While 'the postulates of the classical theory are applicable to a special case only and not to the general case, the situation which it assumes being a limiting point [a position of full employment] of the possible positions of equilibrium' (Keynes, 1936, p. 3). Our examination of Keynes's treatment of finance, which shows it to be based on 'special' conditions, does not in any way limit the 'generality' of his theory in so far as it refers to the possibility of the economy becoming 'stuck' in situations with less than full employment. What it does is to indicate that the complete independence of investment from saving, assumed by Keynes and Kalečki, may be related to the economic conditions at the time of writing of *The General Theory,* thus limiting the 'generality' of this aspect of their theories, and the policy prescriptions to be derived from them.

Kalečki on finance and investment

Kalečki was the first to write on the relation between finance and investment in connection with the theory of effective demand,[1] but it is not clear from the written evidence (in English), when he first presented his views on this relation. In the Foreword to *Studies in the Theory of Business Cycles 1933–39,* which contained translations of his pathbreaking 1933, 1934 and 1935 papers, Kalečki noted that he supplemented the first paper 'by a short passage concerning the problem of the money market taken from [Kalečki, 1935A], (Kalečki, 1966, p. 1). He did not make any reference there to his paper presented at the Econometric Society meeting in Leyden on October 1933, which in its published form (Kalečki, 1935B) also contained a section on finance. Three of the five paragraphs in that section (which will serve as the main source for our examination of Kalečki on this subject) are translations of the material in Kalečki, 1935A. There is no indication in the final version that these paragraphs were added after the presentation of the paper at Leyden, but the discussion of Kalečki's paper at the Econometric Society meeting points to their absence in the original version.[2]

Kalečki points out that 'credit inflation'—by which he means an increase in the money supplied by the banking system—is required if there is to be an increase in investment and in economic activity. It is required both to provide funds to finance an increase in investment, and to meet the higher transactions demand resulting from the consequent increase in economic activity and prices. On the first requirement Kalečki writes: 'When giving an investment order, the entrepreneur has to provide some corresponding fund, out of which he will currently finance the filling of that order' (Kalečki, 1935B, p. 144). Because Kalečki assumes that the current level of investment activity ' "finances itself" ' (*ibid.*), that is, is reflected in realised profits that are available for repeated investment at that level, 'new' credit is only required for the increment in the value of investment decisions over the current level. On the second requirement Kalečki notes: 'Another reason for the inflation of credit is the circumstance that the increase in the production of capital goods or in the consumption of capitalists . . . calls forth a rise of the general level of production and prices. This has the effect of increasing the demand for means of payment under the form of cash or current accounts, and to meet that increased demand a credit inflation becomes necessary' (*ibid.*).

Kalečki argues that the finance or credit advanced to entrepreneurs for investment is part of a circular flow that not only returns to the banking system within a year, but that restores the banks' initial liquidity position. He writes,

> Imagine . . . that some capitalists . . . borrow that amount at the Central Bank, in order to invest it in construction of some additional equipment. In the course of the same year that amount will be received by other capitalists under the form of profits (since, according to our assumptions, workers do not save), and put again into a bank as a savings deposit or used to pay off a debt to the Central Bank. Thus, the circle will close itself (Kalečki, 1935B, p. 343).

[1] Keynes had previously mentioned the importance of credit facilities in making possible changes in investment in his *Treatise on Money.* For example, '. . . the pace, at which the innovating entrepreneurs will be able to carry their projects into execution at a cost in interest which is not deterrent to them, will depend on the degree of complaisance of those responsible for the banking system' (Keynes, 1930, p. 96). Wicksell (1965, pp. 74–75) had earlier emphasised the importance of bank credit in enabling entrepreneurs to carry out their investment plans.

[2] A comment by Fritz Machlup that is reported in the publication of the proceedings of this 1933 meeting makes sense only if Kalečki had neglected to draw attention to the requirements for finance. Kalečki is reported to have 'agreed with Fritz Machlup that a credit inflation was necessarily implied in his explanation of the business cycle' (Marschak, 1934, p. 194). This comment might have been the catalyst for the inclusion of an explicit reference to the need for finance in Kalečki's final version of the paper. I am grateful to Don Patinkin for drawing my attention to this discussion.

The model in Kalečki's 1935 *Econometrica* paper is the same as the one in his 1933 paper on the business cycle, reprinted in English translation in the first chapter of Kalečki (1971), and the notation employed in the latter will be used here (this model was also published in French in Kalečki, 1935A). In that model there is no workers' saving and the consumption of capitalists is given by $C = B_0 + \lambda P$, where B_0 is positive, λ is a small positive fraction, and P is the level of profits. The short-period equilibrium level of profits is given by the equation, $P = (B_0 + A)/(1 - \lambda)$ where A is the rate of actual (and planned) investment. Saving is, of course, equal to this rate of investment ($S = P - B_0 - \lambda P = A$), and Kalečki's position is that this saving is available to continue financing a rate of investment equal to A in subsequent periods. If firms want to make investment decisions I, that are greater than A, then an extension of credit by the banking system that is equal to $I - A(= \Delta I)$ is necessary in order to provide the required finance for this increase of planned investment. It will be assumed, in line with Kalečki's suggestion, that the finance required for an increase in investment is obtained from the Central Bank, but nothing essential in the argument would be changed if it were to be obtained from commercial banks.

At the beginning of the period (year) in which investment is to be increased, there is an increase in the assets of the Central Bank of ΔI (debt notes of financing firms), and an increase in liabilities of ΔI (the increase in the chequing accounts of the financing firms).[1] Kalečki's argument that the spending of this finance for investment will result in the restoration of the initial liquidity position of the banking system—'the circle will close itself'—requires that the increase in assets and liabilities (or the change in their composition) be reversed. If debts are paid off equal to ΔI then the initial position would certainly be restored. (In all this we are ignoring the increased demand for money due to the transactions motive.) This is what the reference to 'pay off a debt to the Central Bank' means in Kalečki's statement quoted above referring to the 'closing' of the circle of finance. Kalečki also referred to the possibility of the capitalists financing the increase of investment by drawing down their savings deposits. There would thus initially be a change in the liquidity position of capitalists as a group, and not in that of the banks (unless the required reserve ratios for savings and chequing accounts differed). The initial situation would once again be restored if saving increased by the amount of the increase in investment, and it was 'put again into a bank as a savings deposit . . .' (*ibid.*).

For it to be possible that debts equal to the value of ΔI be paid off, saving—*desired* saving—must be increased by this amount. This eventuality requires the full operation of the multiplier, that is, the achievement of short-period equilibrium with the new level of investment. Using Kalečki's notation, we find the short-period equilibrium difference in profits to be $\Delta P = \Delta I/(1 - \lambda)$. The desired increase in saving, ΔS, is equal to $(1 - \lambda)\Delta P$, which is equal to ΔI. Since Kalečki assumes that the increase in saving is equal to the increase in planned investment by the end of the year, he is assuming that the full multiplier effect is completed within that period. If this increase in saving is used to increase savings deposits, when the investment finance was obtained through an extension of bank credit, then there has not been a restoration of the banks' pre-increase in investment loan liquidity

[1]Commercial banks could have made the finance available by selling bills or bonds. If they are purchased by private entities, then there is no net change in the banking system's total assets and liabilities, there is a change only in their composition. The assets have become less liquid, with bank debts of the financing firms replacing the more liquid bills and bonds. If the bills or bonds are purchased by the central bank then there will be a net increase in the banking system's assets and liabilities equal to the increase in investment. Again, the system is less 'liquid' than it was before this increase in finance.

position. The payback of bank debt is essential for this. In order for Kalečki's 'circle' to 'close itself', when investment finance is obtained through bank credit, it is thus necessary for both the operation of the full multiplier *and* the retirement of bank debt equal to the initiating credit to have occurred.

Kalečki's analysis dealt with a comparison of positions of short-period equilibrium, and he did not pay sufficient attention to the time required for the operation of the full multiplier in order to 'restore' the liquidity position of the banking system. In his statement of the multiplier he noted that it attains its full value 'eventually', even though he provided no analytical justification for the use of this adverb. *'The general level of production and prices must rise, eventually, so as to provide for an increment of the real profit equal to the increment of the production of capital goods and of the consumption of capitalists'* (Kalečki, 1935B, p. 343, emphasis in the original). In other contexts, however, he tended to forget the need for the time lapse. For example, in discussing the effects of an imposition of an increase in tax on capitalists' income in 1937 he writes 'the immediate result of an increased income tax is a rise of gross profit ... by the amount of the increment [in taxation]' (Kalečki, 1971, p. 39). This is *not* the immediate result, but the new short-period equilibrium position that would be reached after the multiplier had worked itself out.[1]

Kalečki's treatment of finance, investment and saving was also flawed because of his neglect of the need for long-term financing. Investing capitalists should replace their bank loans by long-term bonds that are a better 'match' for the expected life of the capital assets that they have acquired. Borrowing 'short' to invest 'long' can be very dangerous for a business enterprise. A reference to bonds in relation to financing investment is found only in a 1954 publication in a chapter on 'The Determinants of Profits'. 'If additional investment is financed by bank credit, the spending of the amounts in question will cause equal amounts of saved profits to accumulate as bank deposits. The investing capitalists will thus find it possible to float bonds to the same extent and thus to repay the bank credits' (Kalečki, 1954, p. 50). An earlier version of this chapter was published in the *Economic Journal* (Kalečki, 1942), and there is no reference there to the use of bonds to obtain the funds to repay bank loans.

Keynes on finance and investment

Keynes did not mention the finance requirements of an increase in investment decisions in his *General Theory*. He returned to this topic[2] in a June 1937 paper on 'Alternative Theories of the Rate of Interest' in response to comments by Ohlin (1937) and Robertson (1936). Keynes noted that he had not previously given sufficient emphasis to the fact 'that an investment *decision* (Professor Ohlin's investment *ex ante*) may sometimes involve a temporary demand for money before it is carried out, quite distinct from the demand for active balances which will arise as a result of the investment activity whilst it is going on'

[1]In his 1937 paper 'A Theory of the Business Cycle'—a paper to which Keynes made reference in his June 1937 article on finance and investment—Kalečki implicitly assumed that the full multiplier effect was worked out within a short period, a period he gave as being 'equal to a few months' (Kalečki, 1937, p. 82). In that paper Kalečki's emphasis was on the liquidity position of the investing capitalists, with their exposure to risk growing with the level of their planned investments. It was this increase in risk that limited (neglecting possible credit restraints from the banking system) the value of investment decisions in any short period, even though the prospective rate of profit exceeded the rate of interest. New investment decisions were, however, seen as being made in the succeeding short period because the saving in that period, which is equal to the value of the investment decisions currently planned, restores the liquidity position of capitalists as a group. Here again is the completion of the full multiplier effect within the short period, this time of a few months duration rather than a year.

[2]See reference in footnote 1, p. 217, to statements in his *Treatise of Money*.

(Keynes, 1973, p. 207, emphasis in the original). Keynes thus makes explicit reference to the two reasons Kalečki gave for the need for an increase in bank finance if investment is to be increased.

Keynes goes on to note that 'unless the banking system is prepared to augment the supply of money, lack of finance may prove an important obstacle to more than a certain amount of investment decisions being on the tapis at a certain time' (*ibid.*, p. 209). He sees this possible restraint on investment as being divorced from saving, since he argues that ' "finance" has nothing to do with saving' (*ibid.*). Keynes then continues in a way that is also reminiscent of Kalečki. 'It is to an important extent, the "financial" facilities which regulate the *pace* of new investment.... But if the banking system chooses to make the finance available and the investment projected by the new issues actually takes place, the appropriate level of incomes will be generated out of which there will necessarily remain over an amount of saving exactly sufficient to take care of the new investment' (*ibid.*, p. 210). That is, Keynes introduces investment finance into his system while still maintaining 'that it is not the rate of interest, but the level of incomes which ensures equality between saving and investment' (*ibid.*, p. 212).

Comments on this article by Ohlin, Robertson and Hawtrey appeared in the *Economic Journal* for September 1937, and Keynes replied in the December 1937 issue in an article entitled 'The "Ex Ante" Theory of the Rate of Interest'. In this paper he restricted himself to the matters raised by Ohlin because he appeared to recognise the crucial nature of 'finance' for his analysis. He wrote of Ohlin: 'He has compelled me to attend to an important link in the causal chain which I had previously overlooked, and has enabled me to make an important improvement in my analysis' (*ibid.*, pp. 215–216). Keynes emphasised the key role of 'finance' in investment decisions, and even provided a definition of this term ['In what follows I use the term "finance" to mean the credit required in the interval between planning and execution' (Keynes, 1973, p. 216n)], but he kept repeating that this finance is independent of planned saving. For example, 'Surely nothing is more certain than that the credit or "finance" required by *ex ante* investment is not mainly supplied by *ex ante* saving' (*ibid.*, p. 217). He also recognises that the availability of short-term finance is not sufficient for a favourable investment decision. 'The entrepreneur when he decides to invest has to be satisfied on two points: firstly, that he can obtain sufficient short-term finance during the period of producing the investment; and secondly, that he can eventually fund his short-term obligations by a long-term issue on satisfactory conditions' (*ibid.*). But apart from noting parenthetically in the following paragraph that 'the terms of supply of the finance required by *ex ante* investment' include 'some element of forecast on the part of the entrepreneur as to the terms on which he can fund his finance when the time comes' he then concentrates only on short-term finance. His general position is: 'Broadly speaking, therefore, the rate of interest relevant to *ex ante* investment is the rate of interest determined by the *current* stock of money and the *current* state of liquidity preferences, at the date when the finance required by the investment decisions has to be arranged' (*ibid.*, pp. 217–218). The rate of interest he is referring to—and the only one to which reference is made in the rest of his article—is the rate paid for bank loans, that is, the short-term interest rate. Since, as he noted, the terms on which long-term finance is expected to be available is also relevant to investment decisions, his analysis is based on the implicit assumption that the term-structure of interest rates is unchanged by the decisions contemplated.

In the remainder of the paper Keynes is concerned with maintaining his liquidity preference theory of the determination of the rate of interest as opposed to one that sees it as determined by saving and investment. He uses a simile that recalls Kalečki's 'circle' of finance by referring to 'a revolving fund of liquid finance', but this 'revolution' now takes place in an 'interim period' that is much shorter than Kalečki's 'year'. 'For "finance" is essentially a revolving fund. It employs no savings. It is, for the community as a whole, only a book-keeping transaction. As soon as it is "used" in the sense of being expended, the lack of liquidity is automatically made good and the readiness to become temporarily unliquid is available to be used over again. Finance covering the interregnum is, to use a phrase employed by bankers in a more limited context, necessarily "self-liquidating" for the community taken as a whole at the end of the interim period' (*ibid.*, p. 219). From this perspective Keynes argues (as did Kalečki) that a flow of new finance is only required when the rate of investment is to be increased since the current rate of investment is releasing finance equal in value to itself. This leads to what Keynes terms 'the most fundamental of my conclusions within this field'.

> ... in general, the banks hold the key position in the transition from a lower to a higher scale of activity. If they relax, the growing congestion of the short-term loan market or of the new issue market, as the case may be, will inhibit the improvement, no matter how thrifty the public purpose to be out of their future incomes. On the other hand, there will always be *exactly* enough *ex post* saving to take up the *ex post* investment and so release the finance which the latter has been previously employing. The investment market can become congested through shortage of cash. It can never become congested through shortage of saving. This is the most fundamental of my conclusions within this field' (*ibid.*, p. 222, emphasis in the original).

Our examination of Kalečki's treatment of the relations between finance, investment and saving shows that Keynes's position is based on very special assumptions, assumptions that are even more extreme than those made by Kalečki. In stating that 'the lack of liquidity is automatically made good' as soon as the investment expenditure is made, Keynes is assuming implicitly that the full multiplier operates instantaneously, with a new situation of short-period equilibrium being attained as soon as the investment expenditure is made. Such a situation is a necessary, even though not a sufficient, condition for the initial liquidity position to be restored. It is not enough to have *ex post* saving equal to *ex post* investment (this equality holds, of course, at all times as a result of the national accounts identities) in order for saving to be potentially available to repay the bank loans which made possible the increase in investment. To illustrate this, let us consider situations where investment has increased and short-period equilibrium has not yet been achieved.

(i) The increase in actual investment (ΔA) is less than the increase in planned investment (ΔI), due to mistaken short-term expectations that result in inventories that are lower than expected, as a result, for example, of unexpectedly high sales. Therefore, the increase in saving (ΔS) is less than the initiating increase in bank finance. (We have $\Delta S = \Delta A$, but $\Delta S < \Delta I$ since $\Delta A < \Delta I$.) It is thus insufficient to retire the full increase in bank loans. The firms whose inventories have been unexpectedly drawn down by the higher sales have more cash (including bank deposits), but they will use this unexpected increase in liquidity to replenish inventories in order to carry on with their businesses, and not to repay bank loans. The initial liquidity position of the banks is thus not 'automatically made good' even if the total increase in saving is directed to repaying bank debt.

(ii) $\Delta A = \Delta I$, but saving is not in the desired relation to income because consumption has not caught up with the increase in income (the full multiplier effect has not yet been achieved). This increase in saving (even though $\Delta S = \Delta I$) is not *all* available to pay back debts, since some of this saving is temporary (or 'disequilibrium' saving) which individuals intend to use as soon as possible for consumption purposes.

The definitional equality between saving and investment can thus provide no support for Keynes's position that 'there will always be *exactly* enough *ex post* saving to take up the *ex post* investment and so release the finance . . .' (Keynes, 1973, p. 222, emphasis in the original). The position he takes might indicate a confusion between the equality of *ex post* investment and saving and the conditions for short-period equilibrium.[1]

Finance, investment, speculation and saving

The examination of the similar treatments by Kalečki and Keynes of the relation between finance, investment and saving, has made clear that they underestimated the time required before it would be possible for the banks' liquidity position to be restored (abstracting from the increase in credit required to satisfy a higher transactions demand for money) after an increase in bank loans to finance an increase in investment. Keynes's position on this point was even more extreme than Kalečki's since he stated that the investment expenditure itself would be sufficient to release the finance tied up by the increase in investment decisions.[2] As we have seen, such a 'release' requires that there be an increase in desired saving equal to planned investment, and this saving must be used, directly or indirectly, to retire bank debt. The achievement of a higher level of investment thus requires the banking system to become less liquid (to increase its current account liabilities, balanced by IOU's from investing firms) and to maintain a less liquid position at least until the full multiplier has operated, and the increase in desired saving has caught up with the increase

[1]It is interesting to note Robertson's warning on this point, born of experience in controversies concerning saving, investment and the rate of interest. 'In any position other than one of static equilibrium, confusion between a concept of saving in which it is definitionally identical with investment and a concept in which it is functionally related to income will give rise to trouble.' (Robertson, 1951–52, p. 105). Another possible reason for Keynes's error is his presentation in *The General Theory* of the 'logical theory of the multiplier, which holds good continuously, without time-lag, at all moments of time' (Keynes, 1936, p. 122). In developing this approach he defines the 'marginal propensity to consume' without reference to a consumption function. It is defined to be equal to the ratio of the actual increment in consumption, to the actual increment in income, that occur during any time period (*ibid.*, 115). As we have seen, it is not enough for the increase in saving to be equal to the increase in investment for the finance to be 'released'. The full multiplier must have worked itself out, with the increase in saving being in the desired relation to income, and being used, directly or indirectly, to repay bank loans.

[2]In connection with this stand taken by Keynes, Robertson wrote to Keynes in a letter dated 31 December 1937 (see also Robertson, 1938, p. 315): 'I cannot see that any revolving fund is released, any willingness to undergo illiquidity set free for further employment, by the act of the borrowing entrepreneur in spending his loan. The bank has become a debtor to other entrepreneurs, work people, etc., instead of to the borrowing entrepreneur, that is all. The borrowing entrepreneur remains a debtor to the bank and the bank's assets have not been altered either in amount or in liquidity' (printed in Keynes, 1973, pp. 228–229).

Keynes's answer to Robertson appeared in the *Economic Journal* for June 1938 following Robertson (1938), and is reprinted in Keynes (1973, pp. 229–233). Keynes tried to evade the issues raised by Robertson by changing the questions. He stated that he used the term 'finance' to mean 'cash'. 'A large part of the outstanding confusion is due, I think, to Mr. Robertson's thinking of "finance" as consisting in bank loans; whereas in the article under discussion I introduced this term to mean *cash* temporarily held by entrepreneurs to provide against the outgoings in respect of an impending new activity' (*ibid.*, p. 229, emphasis in the original). This statement contradicts what he had written in the article discussed by Robertson where we find: 'In what follows I use the term "finance" to mean the credit required in the interval between planning and execution' (*ibid.*, p. 216, n. 1). Keynes also switched his position on the meaning to be attached to the significance of the expenditure of 'finance'. From 'As soon as it ["finance"] is "used" in the sense of being expended, the lack of liquidity is automatically made good and the readiness to become temporarily unliquid is available to be used over again' (*ibid.*, p. 219); it became 'the demand for cash, due to the requirements of "finance", is automatically at an end as soon as the finance is expended' (*ibid.*, p. 230). His retreat into this triviality is an implicit admission of the indefensibility of his earlier position.

in planned investment. A constant rate of increase in the level of investment over time will require banks to continue expanding their current liabilities, even if the resulting increases in desired saving are used to retire bank debts.

There is the further, complementary, point about the long-term financing required by firms to match their long-term commitments in their investment projects. These firms must be assured about the availability of long-term, as well as short-term, finance before committing themselves to investment decisions. There is scope here for the activities of intermediaries ('speculators') who are prepared to adjust their relative holdings of long and short-term securities. They could thus provide the investing firms with long-term finance *before* the full multiplier effects of the increase in investment have been completed by purchasing their long-term bonds with the proceeds of short-term loans from the banks. Such activity does not, of course, restore the initial liquidity position of the banks since one set of loans is replaced by another, but it does permit the investing firms to go ahead with their investment plans. After the full multiplier has operated, following a maintained increase in the rate of investment, there is an increase in desired saving that can, if directed to the purchase of long-term securities, relieve the pressure on these intermediaries (speculators) to support this higher rate of investment. In such a case banks will then no longer be required to keep increasing their loans. There is, however, the question of the terms at which speculators, and eventually those whose savings increase, would be willing to purchase long-term securities. Is the spread between the short- and long-term rates that they require sufficiently small so as not to discourage investment?

Kaldor, in his important 1939 paper on 'Speculation and Economic Stability', pointed out that Keynes's General Theory 'in so far as it concerns his theory of the rate of interest and the theory of the multiplier, is rather in the nature of a "special case"' (reprinted in Kaldor, 1960, p. 52), since it depends on the stabilising influence of speculation on the price of long-term bonds being infinite. By this he meant that it was based on the implicit assumption that speculators would absorb the new issues of long-term securities (obtaining the necessary funds by borrowing at short term) until the increased saving became available for this purpose, without any noticeable change in the term structure of interest rates. Kaldor illustrates the role of speculative activity by means of a numerical example in which the increase in investment is financed by the sale of long-term securities. The increase in desired saving is assumed to flow, directly or indirectly, to the purchase of long-term securities, but since it is not increased until *after* the investment has been made, the securities making possible the higher rate of investment are purchased by those who are prepared to increase their speculative commitments. Kaldor assumes that there is a one-'week' lag in the consumption function, i.e., $C_t = C(Y_{t-1})$, and a marginal propensity to save of one-quarter. In order to make possible a £1 million increase in the 'weekly' rate of investment, speculative resources must absorb an increase in long-term securities of £4 million. The formula showing the relation between the required total increase in long-term securities purchased out of speculative resources and the propensity to save (s) and the increase in investment per 'week' (ΔI), is $\Delta I/s$. (In the first week the total increase in investment (ΔI) must be financed by speculators. In the second week the increase in desired saving is $(1 - c)\Delta I$, where c is the marginal propensity to consume, and thus speculators are only required to absorb $c\Delta I$. In the third week, the increase in desired saving over its initial level is equal to $(1 - c^2)\Delta I$, and speculators are required to absorb additional securities equal in value to $c^2\Delta I$. The total amount that they must absorb until the full multiplier effect is completed is thus equal to $\Delta I(1 + c + c^2 + \ldots)$, or $\Delta I/1 - c = \Delta I/s$.) This amount is also the total increase in their bank loans.

The increase in speculative commitments (and the corresponding increase in bank loans) thus ceases once the full multiplier effect of a maintained increase in the rate of investment is completed. Kaldor concludes

> ... the contribution which the speculative resources of the market have to make is limited. Provided that the total required increase in the size of speculative stocks is not too large relatively to the resources of the market (i.e., provided it does not impair the degree of price stabilising influence) there will be no pressure on the price of securities (i.e. no tendency for the rate of interest to rise) either in the long run, or in the short run' (Kaldor, 1960, p. 50).

Kaldor introduces an important exception to this conclusion when he considers an open economy, as we shall see below, but his conclusion for a closed economy is more 'special' than he allows. He writes

> ... if we abstract from the case of foreign exchange under a gold standard or quasi-gold-standard regime, it is true that the degree of price-stabilising influence, though not perhaps infinite, is very much larger in the case of long-term bonds than for any other commodity; and this means that the Keynesian theory, though a 'special case', gives, nevertheless, a fair approximation to reality' (*ibid.*, p. 52).

Kaldor's judgement here reflects economic conditions ('reality') at the time at which his article was written. There was then still considerable unemployment, idle productive capacity, ample stocks of raw materials, and stable prices and money-wage rates. But in situations where prices have been increasing, and there are fears of further increases, there may very well be downward pressures on the prices of long-term securities even if the banks are prepared to increase their short-term loans, because savers find that other assets become more attractive to hold. The possible constraints on the ability of firms to increase their rates of investment under such circumstances should be recognised in a 'general' theory. An increase in the propensity to save in this case might make it more likely that an increase in investment could be accommodated without an increase in prices, and this could facilitate the financing of that investment by affecting expectations about future long-term interest rates. Such an increase in the propensity to save would also, if directed to long-term securities, relieve some of the pressures placed on speculators to facilitate an increase in investment since, as we have seen, the amount of long-term securities that speculators are called on to absorb when investment is increased is inversely related to the marginal propensity to save. The independence of investment, and the finance that makes investment possible, from saving is not as robust as Keynes stated. The investment market *can* become 'congested through shortage of saving' even in a closed economy.

An open economy

Consideration of an open economy strengthens the position that the treatments of finance by Kalečki and Keynes are based on conditions that are more special that is indicated by their statements. In an open economy the increase in imports following an increase in investment dampens the subsequent increase in income, and thus limits the increase in desired saving. The increase in domestic saving, even in short-period equilibrium, would be smaller than the increase in investment, with the decrease being substituted for by foreign saving. Only if the latter is directed to domestic long-term securities, at an unchanged term structure of interest rates, would we be in a situation similar to that of short-period equilibrium in a closed economy when the increase in desired saving is used to purchase such securities. If the increased deficit is financed by accommodating short-term loans (or by a decrease in the holdings of gold or foreign currencies), then the term structure would have to change to allow the increase in long-term debt to be absorbed by speculators. Such an increase in long-term interest rates could have an adverse effect on investment. The necessity for an increase in long-term rates under these conditions, and its import for casting doubt on Keynes's assertion that 'the investment market can be congested on account of a shortage of cash. It can never be congested on account of a shortage of savings' (Keynes, 1973, p. 222), was pointed out by Kaldor. 'The long-term rate rises *relatively* to the short-term rate simply because, owing to a shortage of savings, speculators are required to expand continuously the size of their commitments; and there are limits to the extent to which this is possible' (Kaldor, 1960, p. 51, emphasis in the original). He went on to note that 'Temporarily, the banks might prevent the long-term rate from rising by *reducing* the short-term rate; but however much they inundate the system with cash, sooner or later the long rate must rise' (*ibid.*, p. 52n, emphasis in the original).

Government expenditure and taxation

The introduction of government expenditure and taxation into the model of a closed economy has some formal similarities to the opening of an economy to foreign trade, since the condition for short-period equilibrium in a model with government activity is that desired saving be equal to the sum of planned investment and the government deficit. If the structure of government expenditure and taxation is such that the government deficit is a decreasing function of the level of income in the economy, then the increase in saving generated by an increase in investment will be less than this increase in investment. The consequent decrease in the government deficit dampens the multiplier effects of the increase in investment in a manner similar to the increase in imports in an open economy. In this case, however, the increase in domestic saving potentially available to fund the short-term credits financing the increase in investment is equal, at the conclusion of the multiplier process, to that increase, because less is required to finance the government deficit.

Large government deficits, and the fear of possibly increasing deficits, may increase apprehensions about future long-term interest rates. In such circumstances, firms might be reluctant to increase investment, even if short-term finance could be obtained, because of concern over being able to fund these credits at reasonable interest rates. Speculators might be unwilling to absorb additional long-term securities without substantial increases in long-term rates.[1] In such an environment an increase in the propensity to save—although

[1] The ability to obtain long-term finance for investment at rates not much above short-term rates, depends very much on economic conditions in the present and in the recent past, because of their effects on expectations. For example, concern has been expressed in the United States that the Federal Reserve Board might be unable to bring down long-term rates sufficiently to stimulate investment. It was reported in the *New York Times* of 23 December 1982, that:

At the Federal Reserve Board, which has nervously tried to push down interest rates to get a recovery started, the chairman, Paul A. Volcker, is still worried that record deficits in 1984 and beyond could get in the way of a recovery at the beginning, by forcing interest rates up again.

Mr. Volcker, in an appearance in Mayfield, Ky., last week even wondered if the Fed's current policy was not already running into trouble. He noted that long-term interest rates, which reflect inflationary expectations, inched up slightly in the days following the latest cut in the Fed's discount rate to 8½ percent.

taken by itself it would have adverse effects on effective demand—would lessen the depressing effects on financial markets of any given level of the government deficit. It might thus make it easier for firms to proceed with plans to increase investment.

Conclusion

Both Kalečki and Keynes emphasised the importance of an increase in bank loans in permitting firms to increase the rate of investment. For both it was the subsequent changes in income (as well as the distribution of income for Kalečki) that brought desired saving into equality with the increase in investment. They both underestimated the time required before the initial liquidity position of the banking system could be restored after banks increased their loans to finance an increase in investment (the position of Keynes in this regard is susceptible to even more criticism than is Kalečki's). There was also insufficient attention given to the requirement for long-term finance (or at least confidence about its availability) in order for firms to proceed with their investment plans (and in this case it is Kalečki's position that is weaker than Keynes's).

Keynes concluded his 1937 *Quarterly Journal of Economics* paper by drawing a distinction between the general nature of his 'diagnosis' of the factors affecting the level of output and employment and his 'suggestions for a cure'. The latter, he noted, 'avowedly, are not worked out completely, are on a different plane from the diagnosis. They are not meant to be definitive; they are subject to all sorts of special assumptions and are necessarily related to the particular conditions of the time' (Keynes, 1973, pp. 121–122). We have seen, however, that an important aspect of his diagnosis, his view of the general independence of investment from the propensity to save and the 'revolving nature of finance', can be shown not to be definitive but to be based on special assumptions, some of which are '... related to the particular conditions of the time' of composition of *The General Theory*.

None of these criticisms affect the conclusions of Kalečki and Keynes on the critical role of the rate of investment in determining effective demand, on the possibility of equilibrium with involuntary unemployment, and on the possibly large fluctuations in the rate of investment because of changing views concerning a future about which there is a great deal of uncertainty. What they do is to indicate that there may be limits, related in some way to the propensity to save, to the extent to which firms are in a position to increase their rate of investment even if short-term credit is available to finance such an increase.

Bibliography

Kaldor, N. 1960. Speculation and economic stability, *The Review of Economic Studies*, vol. 6, October 1939, 1–27; reprinted in Kaldor, N. *Essays in Economic Stability and Growth*, London, Duckworth

Kalečki, M. 1935A. Essai d'une théorie du mouvement cyclique des affaires, *Revue d'Economie Politique*, vol. 49

Kalečki, M. 1935B. A macrodynamic theory of business cycles, *Econometrica*, vol. 3, July.

Kalečki, M. 1937. A theory of the business cycle, *The Review of Economic Studies*, vol. 4, February

Kalečki, M. 1942. A theory of profits, *Economic Journal*, vol. 52, June–September

Kalečki, M. 1954. *Theory of Economic Dynamics*, London, George Allen and Unwin

Kalečki, M. 1966. *Studies in the Theory of Business Cycles 1933–39*, New York, Augustus M. Kelley

Kalečki, M. 1971. *Selected Essays on the Dynamics of the Capitalist Economy, 1933–1970* Cambridge, CUP

Keynes, J. M. 1930. *A Treatise on Money*, vol. II, London, Macmillan

Keynes, J. M. 1936. *The General Theory of Employment, Interest and Money*, London, Macmillan

Keynes, J. M. 1973. The General Theory and After: Part II defence and development, *The Collected Writings of John Maynard Keynes, vol. XIV*, London, Macmillan for the Royal Economic Society
Marschak, J. 1934. Report on the meeting of the Econometric Society in Leyden, *Econometrica*, vol. 2, April
Ohlin, B. 1937. Some notes on the Stockholm theory of saving and investment, *Economic Journal* vol. 47, March and June
Patinkin, D. 1982. *Anticipations of the General Theory? And Other Essays on Keynes*, Chicago, University of Chicago Press
Robertson, D. H. 1936. Some notes on Mr Keynes' General Theory of Employment, *Quarterly Journal of Economics*, vol. 51, November
Robertson, D. H. 1938. Mr. Keynes on 'Finance', *Economic Journal* vol. 48, June
Robertson, D. H. 1940. *Essays in Monetary Theory*, London, Staples Press
Robertson, D. H. 1951–52. Comments on Mr. Johnson's Notes, *The Review of Economic Studies*, vol. 19
Robinson, J. 1962. *Essays in the Theory of Economic Growth*, London, Macmillan
Robinson, J. 1973. *Collected Economic Papers*, vol. IV, Oxford, Basil Blackwell
Wicksell, K. 1965. *Interest and Prices*, New York, Augustus M. Kelley

[13]

Cambridge Journal of Economics 1986, **10**, 333–353

Michal Kalecki's contribution to the theory and practice of socialist planning

D. M. Nuti*

1. Introduction

Michal Kalecki's contributions to the economics of socialism—less widely known but no less important than his pioneering contributions to the economics of capitalism—span the period 1946–1970 and are affected by the development and performance of the Polish system, as well as coloured by his views on capitalist dynamics. They consist of a coherent model of the socialist economy and its functioning, characterised by centralised economic planning and political decentralisation with a limited role for markets; a well-developed theory of socialist dynamics, emphasising exogenous constraints to growth and accumulation policy, which were neglected by Polish leaders with dramatic consequences; and a number of planning procedures and guidelines of practical use, for the selection of investment projects, consumption planning and the construction of long-term plans.

2. Kalecki's model of the democratic planned economy

By 1942, in connection with British discussions on economic planning, Kalecki had already sketched the main features of his approach to economic planning: nationalisation of the most important enterprises (financial, industrial and public utilities); coordination and direction of their activity by a central institution of economic planning, responsible to Parliament; full public control over the banking and financial system, investment and foreign trade as well as, if possible, allocation of the main materials and products. Private enterprise would still play an important role in industrial sectors of secondary importance, in the production of consumption goods, and in the distributive services. Central planning of investment would ensure full employment of labour; Workers' Councils, representing workers, technical personnel and managers of each enterprise, now freed from the threat of unemployment, would maintain support for economic planning and exercise control over the development of their enterprises. Public control from below, together with the initiatives of a socialist government from above, would protect the system from regressing towards monopoly capitalism (Kalecki, 1942).

Kalecki's international reputation and his known socialist sympathies gave him instant access to the new rulers of People's Poland: in 1946 he was already—in a brief visit and from a distance—giving advice to the Polish Minister of Reconstruction on rationing

* European University Institute, Florence. Paper presented at the Conference on Michal Kalecki's economics, held by the Economics Department of Perugia University, 22–24 April 1986. I am grateful to Alberto Chilosi, Jerzy Osiatynski, Ferdinando Targetti and, in particular, to the discussant Lynn Mainwaring for useful comments.

(which he regarded as equivalent to but, practically, slightly superior to income subsidies), on monetary circulation and on the 1946–47 financial plans, which he analysed at great length (see respectively Kalecki, 1946A, B, C, first published in Kalecki, 1982, and editorial comments on pp. 308–310), checking the consistency of real and financial flows and using the budget as the primary instrument of macroeconomic planning. Kalecki's return to Poland in early 1955, as adviser to the Prime Minister, marked the beginning of a ten-year-long involvement in the shaping of the Polish economic system and policies: as a Vice-Chairman of the Economic Council advising the Council of Ministers from 1957 to its disbanding in 1963, and as head of the perspective plan division of the Central Planning Commission, in charge of drawing up the 1961–75 plan, until increasing disagreement with the government put an end to his advisory activity in 1964. Meanwhile, and until the end of his life, he continued to make important intellectual contributions to the economics of socialism; his papers on the organisation and functioning of the socialist economy, however, are concentrated in the period 1955–58.

Kalecki's socialist model retains, next to a dominant centrally-planned state sector, a liberalised cooperative sector and private handicrafts, as well as state small-scale production operating on similar principles: purely indicative plans in value terms, contractual cooperation with state industry and distribution network (though contracting can be made compulsory); free purchases and sales of non-contracted output in the market (though sales to the state not contracted in advance ought to take place below the market price); profit sharing (oddly enough, only applicable to technical personnel and managers and not to workers in the case of cooperatives); investment self-finance except for small-scale state enterprises where investment is also funded by local authorities; employment limits for artisans (e.g., five workers excluding apprentices); local controls. Kalecki recognises the practical difficulties and the disproportionate administrative effort of attempting to control production in small-scale units characterised by highly diversified and rapidly changing composition, and the counterproductive nature of price and other control (Kalecki, 1956A; there is no mention of agriculture in that paper, produced for the Polish Prime Minister and first published in Kalecki, 1982).

Large-scale state enterprises, on the contrary, in Kalecki's view should be given physical targets for both total employment and the larger investments in new capacity, as well as targets for the net value of production, its main composition, the wage fund and distribution of main inputs; they should also be subject to price controls for both their purchases and sales (1956B, 1957C, D, 1958A, B). With respect to employment the model is centrally planned more tightly than the traditional Soviet-type model: against strong opposition from most of his colleagues Kalecki was adamant that enterprises should not be free to set the level of employment; he knew only too well how enterprise autonomy and labour unemployment went hand-in-hand in the capitalist economy and was not prepared to leave state enterprises any discretion in this matter. 'In England for so many years they paid me to liquidate unemployment, and here you want to pay me to generate it'—was his cry at the suggestion that enterprises should only be subject to a limit on their total wage fund, at a memorable session of a special Committee on enterprise organisation set up by the Council of Ministers (see editorial notes, Kalecki 1982, p. 324). In other respects, however, Kalecki's model of socialism is more 'liberal' than the conventional Soviet-type model (to which the Polish actual model has adhered broadly to date).

First, Kalecki laid emphasis on the *net* value of output (1957D; this notion was actually implemented in Poland in the 1974 reform; see Nuti, 1977) and neither on the physical nor the gross value indicators of Soviet-type planning.

Second, he also envisaged, next to centralised investment, some decentralised investments out of own funds and interest-bearing but non-returnable loans, both to allow for enterprise initiative and to reduce the pro-investment bias associated with free investment funds (1957D).

Third, Kalecki strongly recommended the restructuring of industrial organisation along vertical lines (1957B): large-scale associations of vertically integrated enterprises largely, though not fully, self-sufficient (along the lines later adopted by the GDR: see Granick, 1970; Melzer, 1981) would cooperate in the reciprocal supply of semi-finished products and in the distribution of essential materials. Enterprises would retain autonomy as members of the association, so that each *koncern* would be responsible for a given finished product (or group of similar products) without introducing monopolistic tendencies. Central authorities would be concerned only with the group performance in the supply of finished goods without interfering in their internal organisation. Mutual interest of member enterprises in the overall performance of the group would secure their cooperation; actual orders and incentives regulating enterprise activity would be decentralised to *koncern* level and the central authorities would only have to deal with a small number of agencies, simplifying and de-bureaucratising economic administration, especially in the distribution of centrally-allocated materials. (Large-scale industrial associations were revamped in Poland in the 1974 reform but member enterprises were more tightly merged than envisaged by Kalecki, and the element of vertical integration was the exception, not the norm, which emphasised horizontal concentration; see Nuti, 1977).

Fourth, Kalecki envisaged in his model—in place of economic decentralisation—generalised political decentralisation under the guise of Workers' Councils which, in every enterprise, would take decisions about the organisation of production (work conditions, overtime pay, etc.), oppose the excessive bureaucratisation and centralisation tendencies which appear when the enterprise director answers only to central powers, and exercise initiative under the stimulus of material incentives (Kalecki, 1956B). At the time Oskar Lange regarded enterprise autonomy extending to prices and investment as a precondition of workers' self-management: without greater enterprise independence Workers' Councils—wrote Lange in the same issue of the Party monthly *Nowe Drogi*—'. . . would be a fiction, since they would not have anything to decide . . .' (Lange, 1956). But Kalecki was much too concerned with the maintenance of full employment to push enterprise autonomy further, and regarded Workers' Councils as a political countervailing power holding central government in check.

Kalecki's distrust of the market and his reliance on planning have perhaps been underplayed in subsequent literature. Brus, for instance, writes: 'He did not . . . oppose the idea of utilising the market-mechanism, but considered it a subordinate element in the running of an economy which should be planned centrally as far as the main lines of development were concerned' (Brus, 1977; also quoted by Sawyer, 1985). I believe the example of inter-war Poland, the experience of capitalism as he knew it and his overall theoretical background led Kalecki to hold stronger views. Under no circumstances should firms be allowed to set prices, except local small-scale enterprises (see Kalecki, 1958B, with the significant title 'Centralised price formation as an essential feature of the socialist economy'). Reliance on market signals leads to economic stagnation, whereas the fully-employed socialist economy needs to grow *via* investment; purely indicative planning can lead to even worse mistakes than detailed centralised planning; profit is a synthetic indicator of performance but this is a disadvantage as well as an advantage, because there is no point in raising profits at the cost of unemployment (1956B, 1957A, C, D and editorial comments on the account of a March 1957 discussion within the Economic Model Commission, Kalecki, 1982, pp. 336–339). How, then, should the time honoured question of price determination be solved in the socialist economy? Just as under capitalism, by charging a mark-up on current costs, except that the mark-up should be related to the needs of investment finance (1958B; also making allowances for import-intensity, Kalecki and Polaczek, 1957A, B). Full costs should provide a basis also for intra-CMEA trade (Kalecki, 1962). Markets are left to determine quantities, rather than prices, and in the event of disequilibrium the adjustment process takes place through planned quantity adjustment rather than through prices. Kalecki simply did not believe in short-term substitutability in either production or consumption and this set him apart from the neoclassical tradition, even if Marxist-inspired (e.g. Oskar Lange), and from the whole tradition of 'market-socialism'.

In brief, Michal Kalecki's model of the socialist economy is a cross between the GDR (vertical groupings subject to central planning, a liberalised private sector) and Yugoslavia (cooperative sector, self-management) but with roles for markets, plans and self-management intermediate between the two. It is a very topical model, corresponding to what IMF officials today call 'the modified centrally planned economy' (Wolf, 1985), no longer corresponding to the classical Soviet-type model but still a far cry from full-fledged market socialism. It is also the furthest Gorbachev's reform can go in the USSR if it succeeds, at any rate within the foreseeable future. Kalecki was aware that the model he outlined was far from ideal, but he knew also that there is no point in replicating capitalist markets and capitalist plans—a lesson which most East European reformers less acquainted than Kalecki with 'realised capitalism' still have to learn. Between piecemeal improvements and general change of principles, Kalecki favoured the first (1958A, in 1982, p. 88). He was aware that his proposed improvements would not put an end to the conflictual aspects of socialism: he was prepared to pay for Workers' Councils the price of possible disruption and growth deceleration, and only too aware, prophetically, of the strength of central opposition to their effective operation. Referring to his proposed 'synthesis of central planning and workers' councils' he wrote:

> We should not delude ourselves that such a system is free of contradictions and easy to steer. There is no doubt that always there will exist tendencies towards the erosion of the prerogatives of Workers' Councils through greater centralisation, as well as towards the weakening of central plan discipline through Workers' Councils. On the one hand there will be the danger of weakening Workers' Councils and bureaucratising the whole system of management, on the other hand Workers' Councils, through their pressure, can lead to situations where it is necessary to reduce the pace of growth or to become dependent on foreign aid, or where after a period of chaos 'order is restored', returning to the system of bureaucratic centralism (Kalecki, 1956C, in Kalecki 1982, p. 99; my translation).

An important element of Kalecki's approach to the formulation of a model of viable socialism, finally, is the strong weight given to actual *economic policies*, as well as to systemic questions; indeed one of his 1957 articles bears the significant title 'The role of the model should not be overestimated' (1957A)—a message which should be repeated *ad nauseam* for the benefit of all East European reformers and counter-reformers alike.

3. Investment and growth policies

A high and rising share of capital accumulation in national income has been the policy adopted by the Soviet Union since the inception of its First Five Year Plan (1928) and imitated by the other countries where a Soviet-type system was introduced after the war.

This policy, raised to the status of official dogma as a 'law of faster development of department I' (producing production goods in Marx's reproduction schemes) or priority for heavy industry or for 'group A', was plausible in a country like the Soviet Union in the late twenties: rural, industrially undeveloped, labour-abundant, capital-constrained and practically closed yet wishing to accelerate growth. Its soundness has been well theorised by the Soviet economist Feldman (1928, 1929) under precisely these assumptions. These were not, however, the conditions of the European countries which joined the Soviet bloc, with the exception perhaps of Bulgaria and Romania. Michal Kalecki was the first outspoken opponent of this official dogma; his criticism, originally raised in a paper presented to the Second Congress of Polish economists (1956C, in Kalecki, 1984) was further developed (see for instance 1958C) and became the main theme of his 'Theory of growth of the socialist economy', devoted precisely to the study of exogenous constraints limiting the feasibility and plausibility of ambitious investment policies (1963A).

In Kalecki's approach the economic growth of a full-employment economy above its 'natural' growth rate (determined by the growth of the labour force and technical progress) has increasing costs in terms of a lower share of consumption. These costs are lowered by international trade but reassert themselves because of the necessity of balancing foreign trade over time and set an upper limit to the share of investment that can be gainfully undertaken. Within this limit, which is seen as a maximum, set not by political but by technical considerations, central powers can exercise their political discretion according to the strength of their political concern for current consumption and careful consideration of the actual trade-off between the share of consumption and faster growth—a trade-off which worsens with the acceleration of growth.

Kalecki's notion of maximum investment share is best analysed with the help of a simple model (similar to that of Kalecki, 1963A). Consider a socialist economy where all savings are invested or, rather, savings are generated *via* financial planning to match planned investment; labour is fully employed and labour reserves (e.g. agricultural underemployment) have been exhausted. There is a range of alternative production techniques whereby output is produced by labour and capital, and technology is embodied in capital equipment of constant productivity and uniform lifetime. Provisionally assume that technical progress does not occur. The economy is closed (or, which is the same, foreign trade is balanced at a given level). The following symbols are introduced:

Y = national income	C = total consumption
L = labour force	n = growth rate of L
g_n = natural growth rate of income = n	g = actual growth rate of income
K = capital stock	y = labour productivity Y/L
k = capital per man K/L	v = capital/output ratio K/Y
s = share of investment in national income	
t = lifetime of equipment	

The following identities hold:

$$v \equiv K/Y = (K/L)/(Y/L) = k/y \tag{3.1}$$

$$s \equiv g.v \tag{3.2}$$

$$C \equiv (1-s)Y \tag{3.3}$$

At time 0 let the labour force be L_0. For a given technical choice that has prevailed for the previous t years, corresponding to given values of k_0, y_0, the three identities above identify also v_0, s_0 (since $g=g_n$ is also known) and C_0. For an unchanged technical choice after t years income Y_t and consumption C_t would be given by:

$$Y_t = Y_0(1+g_n)^t \tag{3.4}$$

$$C_t=(1-s_0)Y_0(1+g_n)^t. \tag{3.5}$$

Suppose planners considered switching to a more capital intensive technique with parameters k_1 and y_1. Of course since $k_1 > k_0$ there must be also $y_1 > y_0$, otherwise the new technique is absolutely inferior and should not be considered at all; and $v_1 > v_0$ otherwise the original technique is absolutely inferior and should have not been chosen in the first place. Define

$$p \equiv (y_1 - y_0)/y_0 \tag{3.6}$$

If the economy switched to technique 1, after t years the whole capital stock would be of the new kind and the values of Y_t and C_t would be given not by 3.4 and 3.5 but by 3.4′ and 3.5′:

$$Y_t = Y_0(1+g_n)^t(1+p) \tag{3.4′}$$

$$C_t=(1-s_1)Y_0(1+g_n)^t(1+p) \tag{3.5′}$$

At time t income with the newly adopted technique 1 would be greater than with former technique 0 by a factor of $(1+p)$ but the share of investment would also be higher for the more capital intensive technique because of 3.2 and the fact that $v_1 > v_2$; hence $(1-s_1)<(1-s_0)$ and C_t is not necessarily higher than with the previous technique. For consumption to be higher after the switch the condition must be satisfied (from 3.5 and 3.5′):

$$(1-s_1)(1+p)>(1-s_0). \tag{3.7}$$

Otherwise, consumption is sacrificed not only throughout the transition to the new technique for t years but ever after if the new technique is maintained. While other writers (for instance Horvat, 1958) had stressed the existence of a limit to the economy's absorption capacity of investment from the viewpoint of income, beyond which investment would not raise *income*, Kalecki introduces a stricter limit, beyond which investment does not raise *maintainable consumption* levels.

Kalecki's condition 3.7 appears as a kind of golden rule of accumulation; in fact it can be proven that *it is the same thing as the golden rule of accumulation* familiar from Western literature on the theory of economic growth (Hahn and Matthews, 1964), except that it is a rule about *maximum* and not about desirable accumulation. For two techniques to be equally eligible from the viewpoint of the maximum sustainable consumption per head, the inequality (3.7) should turn into an equality, or

$$(1-s_1)(1+p)-(1-s_0)=0 \tag{3.8}$$

from which, substituting for the values of s from 3.2,

$$g_n = p/(v_1 + v_1 . p - v_0) \text{ is obtained.} \tag{3.9}$$

For any given wage rate, the profit rate on the switch to the more capital intensive technique—regardless of whether such a profit rate is actually monitored, calculated (which Kalecki does not) or is even a concept ideologically allowed—is

$$r=(y_1-y_0)/(k_1-k_0) \tag{3.10}$$

from which, substituting from 3.1 and 3.6, we have:

$$r=p/(v_1+v_1.p-v_0)=g_n, \text{ Q.E.D.} \tag{3.11}$$

This proposition [which can be obtained from Kalecki's model but was not fully drawn out by him beyond the expression of (3.7)] holds also when there is technical progress, as long as this is *neutral* in Kalecki's sense of the rate of progress being uniform regardless of capital intensity of output (therefore identical to Harrod-neutrality, whereby progress is uniform regardless of capital/output ratios; see Chilosi, 1971). If progress was faster the higher the capital intensity of output (Kalecki's capital-intensity-encouraging progress) it might pay to invest beyond the limits indicated by (3.7), because the benefits of higher capital intensity are underestimated by p, whereas if productivity growth and capital intensity of output were inversely related condition (3.7) would hold *a fortiori*. Foreign trade does not alter the approach, though it may shift temporarily the investment costs of growth acceleration at full employment and, therefore, the attractiveness of alternative rates of accumulation.

In fact Kalecki's notion of a maximum limit to the share of accumulation should not necessarily be approached, let alone met. Kalecki introduces a supply function of savings on the part of the planners, which he calls the planners' 'decisional curve' (to stress its non-technical nature) but which is simply a special form of 'objective function': instead of expressing preferences about dated consumption levels, per man or overall, Kalecki's planners compare the falling growth acceleration dg/ds obtained by higher investment shares at higher levels of growth rate g, with the increasing growth acceleration which they would require to induce them to squeeze consumption further at higher growth rates. A balance is struck when the sacrifices demanded for acceleration (by the economy as a whole) are equal to the price that planners are willing to pay (see Fig. 1). The objective

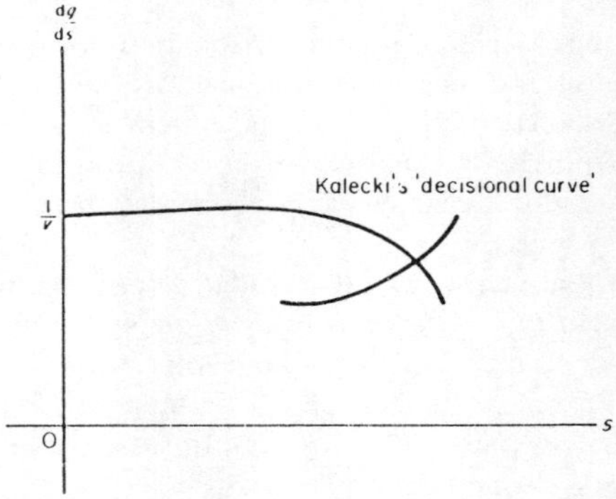

Fig. 1. *v, marginal capital/output ratio; g, growth rate of income; s, share of investment in national income*

lesson of this exercise is not optimisation *per se*, which Kalecki stresses is a pure pedagogical device, but the notion that planners' investment policy should not only stay within the golden rule limit but also demand a greater acceleration of income for every percentage sacrifice in the share of consumption associated with it.

This lesson was quickly absorbed, popularised and developed by Kalecki's pupils (in particular, Laski, 1965; Jozefiak, 1971; and many others) but was coldly received in most other circles. Polish leaders had already reacted in 1964 to Kalecki's theories and his application of those theories to Polish long-term planning by dismissing him from his advisory role. Accumulation policies throughout the sixties (and well into the seventies) remained as much based on high and rising investment shares as ever before, throughout Eastern Europe. In the Soviet Union, the book (Kalecki, 1963A) was published with a misleading and patronising introduction by Academician Khatchaturov (Polish translation in Kalecki, 1984), who praised the mathematical approach while lamenting the neglect of socio-political factors (what could have been more socio-political than Kalecki's concern for the plausibility and the intelligent use of people's sacrifices?). The Polish academic establishment at first appeared to accept, or at least not to reject, Kalecki's approach, which found its way into textbooks on the economics of socialism. But in 1968 an attack was launched by party hacks in writings and at two meetings at the Central School of the Party and at the Central School of Planning and Statistics (SGPiS). Kalecki was accused of being a 'prisoner of capital fetishism' (by W. Iskra), of 'smuggling bourgeois economics' (by B. Rudowicz), of organising a 'cult of his theory and personality' among his followers (by D. Sokolow), of plagiarism of Harrod and Domar (though Kalecki had long acknowledged the connection and stressed the differences), of excessive formalism, neglect of the human factor and other inanities (by J. Gorski, who in earlier writings had expressed appreciation). Kalecki replied and, later, resigned (see Osiatynski's account of those meetings in Kalecki, 1984); official condemnation did not prevent Kalecki's critics from continuing to use his work in their texts, but deleting the source (see Nuti, 1973).

In truth, *Kalecki's contentions about either the golden rule limit or the planners' increasing supply price of savings have no general validity; yet he was right in the specific conditions* of Eastern Europe at the time and with reference to the policies followed there by socialist leaders, and he was proven right, with a vengeance, by the recurring Polish crises (from 1970 to 1980 through intermediate stages), the generalised decline to date and the policy reversal of the early 1980s.

The adoption of more capital-intensive techniques than those which satisfy condition (3.7) cannot be regarded as *necessarily* mistaken: in principle—as long as the new technique is not absolutely inferior, which has been ruled out in the analysis above—that policy can always be reversed and will lead to higher consumption than with the less capital-intensive technique throughout the period of transition back to that technique. This gain in consumption may be considered as insufficient to compensate for the sacrifices incurred during the transition to the more capital-intensive technique and before the policy is reversed; but this is a political judgement, not a technical one as Kalecki would have us believe. His neglect of potential gain from policy reversal is something of a sleight of hand; we know from optimum saving theory that golden rule growth is a crude benchmark against which to assess accumulation policy and that maximisation of maintainable consumption per head is not necessarily the best course. Yet if, in principle, it cannot be said that East European planners were inefficient simply because of their disregard of golden rules, it is right to put on them the burden of proof: what conceivable reason might there have been to shift consumption from today to tomorrow, if tomorrow's gain can only be a temporary blip? Speeding up the achievement of full communism is not a good enough answer, since nobody ever said that communist bliss had to be prepaid. No other possible reasons—as far as I know—have been given. In practical terms, therefore, Kalecki stood on firm ground.

Theoretical weakness and practical strength is a characteristic also of Kalecki's 'decisional curve'. The notion that planners should require faster acceleration of growth to be induced to invest higher shares of national income may seem harmless enough. This is, for instance, how the level of expenditure (and therefore its share in a given income) behaves with respect to quantity demanded for any demand function whose price elasticity falls with the quantity demanded, as happens, for instance, for any downward sloping linear demand function for any commodity. But suppose that demand is, at some point, fairly inelastic to price increases and elastic to price decreases: total revenue beyond that point will be rising with quantity at an *increasing* rate; hence, progressively *smaller* increases in quantity will be required to induce the consumer to raise the share of that good in his total expenditure beyond that point. The economic meaning is that there is a target minimum quantity below which a commodity's demand price rises steeply. Is there any reason to exclude, in principle, the possibility that growth-minded planners might likewise price additional growth more highly, in terms of consumption forsaken, at lower than at higher growth rates, at least over a certain range? This time the burden of proof is on Kalecki, and there is nothing in his work, or in the theory of demand or of optimum saving, to justify the need for a monotonically rising 'decisional curve' as a *general* case. Yet the notion that at some point demand for growth becomes less elastic down to unity or less must be correct since some current income must be consumed even if growth becomes inordinately cheap; i.e., there will be maximum share of accumulation and *in its neighbourhood* the decisional curve must be rising as Kalecki supposed. If it is accepted that golden rule growth sets a maximum limit to the accumulation share, why should planners choose a minimum growth close to that limit? When the economy is close enough to the limit of sustainable consumption, Kalecki's argument applies. The question becomes one of fact: in the 1960s were Polish planners overstepping the limits of people's forebearance in their trading off of current for future consumption, or the (related) limits of the planners' own ability to deliver the consumption goods promised with the payment of wages? If they had not been, the Polish crises would have been averted. That Kalecki was right is shown by Gomulka's fall (within months of Kalecki's death), by the mounting excess demand for consumption goods at official prices and the inability of authorities to make price increases acceptable to the population, by the greater emphasis on consumption in the plans for the 1970s, the mounting external debt and deteriorating performance. The consumption sacrifices opposed by Kalecki were not worth undertaking. The lesson should not be lost on the rest of the socialist bloc where repeatedly investment policies have neglected the constraints of full employment, natural resources and foreign balance, and have often generated not higher income, let alone higher consumption, nor sufficiently higher consumption with respect to *some* preference system, but only excess capacity. Kalecki was fighting a dogma and could not afford to dilute his case with too many qualifications; that he glossed over some of them does not mean that he was unaware of their existence.

4. Shadow interest rates and technical choice

The choice of techniques was investigated by Kalecki not only in a macroeconomic context (as seen in the previous section) but also at the micro-level, in the selection of investment projects. There is a link between his macro-analysis and his micro-findings, which were co-authored with Mieczyslaw Rakowski, an officer of the Polish Planning Commission. Their joint efforts (Kalecki and Rakowski, 1959) became almost verbatim the official handbook on project selection (KPpRM, 1962).

Since the mid fifties in Poland the choice between alternative projects had been following informally the Soviet practice: (i) the scope of selection was limited to alternative ways of producing the same kind of capacity (decided by the centre or by enterprise associations), and not extended to the choice between plants producing alternative products; (ii) investment funds were made available to enterprises from the government budget at no cost; (iii) investing enterprises confronted with alternative ways of producing identical capacity were instructed to choose a more investment-intensive alternative only if it led to operating costs economies sufficient to recover the associated *additional* investment cost within a maximum number of years, a statutory 'standard recoupment period' fixed by the centre. The codification of this informal practice in 1962 was profoundly influenced by the work of Kalecki on his own and with Rakowski.

The basic rule adopted by the Polish Planning Commission in their 1962 *Instrukcja Ogolna* (General Instruction) issued to all industrial enterprises required investors to aggregate costs into investment and yearly operating costs, reject inferior alternatives (costlier in both investment and operation) and minimise the sum of operating costs and a fraction of investment costs given by the inverse of the standard recoupment period:

$$C + \frac{1}{T}I = \text{minimum} \tag{4.1}$$

where C now stands for yearly operating costs, I for the investment costs associated with C, and T is the standard recoupment period. In the Polish practice T was fixed at six years for new plants and five years for modernisation investment; these rates were uniform throughout the economy. Clearly the recommended procedure is tantamount to a shadow capital charge of $1/T$; in a market economy, where an interest rate r prevails and capital is competitively rented, equipment of expected lifetime t would command a capital charge equal to a fraction $r(1+r)^t/((1+r)^t-1)$ of its purchasing price (here we abstract from the complications of inflation accounting, because there was price stability in that decade in Poland and because in any case inflation should not affect competitive rentals other than through its impact on the nominal interest rate r). Hence there is an implied relation between T and an *implicit* interest rate, i.e.

$$T = \frac{(1+r)^t - 1}{r.(1+r)^t.} \tag{4.2}$$

For $T=6$ and an investment lifetime of 20 years (regarded in the *Instrukcja* as the average lifetime of equipment in Poland at the time of issue) there was an implicit interest rate of about 15·7%, which is rather high in view of price stability. The same rate applied to investment in modernisation, which was shorter-lived and required a shorter standard recoupment period: five years was an approximation.

Polish practice here differed from that of the Soviet Union and Czechoslovakia, where the standard recoupment period was different in different sectors (ranging from 3 to 10 years according to the ranking of each sector in national policy; the more favoured, the longer the period over which additional investment could be recouped) and straight-line amortisation was added to $1/T$ to calculate the shadow investment charge. This departure had been advocated by Kalecki on the grounds of efficiency: seeing that these calculations affected not capacity expansion but only its form there was no reason to favour capital intensity in favoured sectors (Kalecki, 1965), while durability differences between plants could be accounted for in other ways than through amortisation (Kalecki, 1958D; see below, this section).

There are three main innovations introduced into this practice by Kalecki and Rakowski: (i) a link between the uniform standard recoupment period in the economy and labour-saving investment opportunities in modernisation; (ii) the compounding of output losses due to the 'freezing' of investment resources in incomplete projects during their gestation period; (iii) the correction of investment and operating costs to account for differences in expected lifetime of projects, based on the hypothetical comparison of steady-state balanced stocks of those projects (for a more detailed discussion, see Nuti, 1971).

The rationale behind the value of T recommended by Kalecki and Rakowski for the Polish economy (in other East European countries following the same practice no rationale is given) is concern over the possibility of a labour shortage. Given full employment of labour, new plants would be operated by a number of workers equal to the natural increase of the labour force, plus workers formerly attached to equipment now come to the end of its lifetime, plus workers freed by investment in modernisation. The lower the standard recoupment period, the higher the labour requirements of new plants (labour forming the bulk of operating costs) and the lower the investment in modernisation and therefore the lower the number of workers freed from scrapped plants. Given the non-regulatory nature of wages policy with respect to the relative scarcity of labour, and the lack of actual investment charges, the shadow capital charge implicit in the value of T is used to prevent labour shortage. Kalecki and Rakowski had estimated that there existed ample labour-saving opportunities in the Polish economy through modernisation investment which could be recouped in five or six years. Hence, as long as labour could be drawn from this source, it would be wasteful to undertake more investment-intensive projects unless their additional cost could be recovered in less than the same period (the differential T adopted in the end for new investment and modernisation is a rough way of accounting for the longer expected life of new versus modernised plant; for a more formal analysis see Nuti, 1971). The high shadow charge therefore simply reflected the low technical level of Polish industry and the high profitability of investment in its modernisation. In view of this rationale, one would have expected the standard recoupment period to have varied over time; the shadow capital charge, however, proved just as rigid as actual prices and was not altered for as long as the *Instrukcja* remained in force, i.e. until 1969, when a specific shadow capital charge of 0·12 (corresponding to roughly $T=8$) replaced T.

Kalecki's keen eye for planning malpractices had identified the dangerous propensity to open a wide 'investment front', starting more projects than could be finished on schedule, and he alerted the planners to the social cost involved in locking up resources during the gestation period of projects. To favour quick-yielding projects and discourage the unnecessary prolongation of gestation periods, Kalecki introduced a 'coefficient of immobilisation' by which investment costs had to be compounded during the corresponding immobilisation period (Kalecki, 1958D). Kalecki and Rakowski assume that if one unit of investment were to be 'unfrozen' it would yield an amount of national product of an average pattern equal to $1/v$ where v is the gross capital/output ratio. Allowing for depreciation of fixed capital at a yearly rate d, the net product would be $(1/v-d)$ per annum. At full employment, in order to release the manpower necessary to man this unit of investment some additional investment must be undertaken elsewhere in the economy, given by $a.T$, where a is the labour cost of the production of one unit of gross output and T is the standard recoupment period. The yearly net product of one unfrozen unit of investment is then reckoned as:

$$q = \frac{1}{v + a.T} - d. \qquad (4.3)$$

It is difficult to see why the locking up of investment resources in the form of a longer gestation period should be treated any differently from the locking up of investment resources in the form of a higher investment intensity. Consistency would require $q = 1/T$, and it is no accident that the Soviet, Czechoslovak and Hungarian investment choice methodologies of the 1960s all use $1/T$ as the fraction of investment costs to be added to actual costs during gestation. As it happens, the value of the relevant parameters estimated by Kalecki and Rakowski for the Polish economy are $v = 2{\cdot}5$, $a = 0{\cdot}5$, $d = 0{\cdot}03$, which give a magnitude of q, subsequently codified in the *Instrukcja*, of 0·15, i.e. comfortably close to 0·157 (corresponding to $T = 6$). When I put this question to Michal Kalecki he insisted that $1/T$ and q were different concepts and could differ; the only way I could accept this was by looking at them respectively as linked to notional long term and short term interest rates. Kalecki insisted that their near-identity was a mere coincidence, but seeing that they were so close he saw no point in discussing the question further.

A third implicit interest rate, one moreover equal to the growth rate of investment (i.e. complying with the golden rule of the previous section), is implicit in Kalecki and Rakowski's treatment of plant lifetime. Instead of gearing the shadow capital charge to plant durability as in a competitive rental market, or adding straight line amortisation to $1/T$ as the Soviet and Czech planners, Kalecki and Rakowski proceeded from a detailed analysis of the costs and benefits of plant durability.

A longer-lived plant has the relative advantage of producing a given stream of output for a longer period, but also the disadvantage of being tied to a given technical form for a longer period, therefore remaining excluded from the benefit of technical progress of the embodied kind. The balance between the two effects in the comparison of two alternative lifetimes depends on the difference in durability, the rate at which operating costs decrease every year in the new plants, and the growth rate of investment in the production of the output considered. Suppose that investment in plants of durability of n years grows at a rate g per year, and the capital output v is constant over time. If investment at a time t is indicated by I, in the preceding year it was $I(1+g)^{-1}$ and $(i-1)$ years back it was $I(1+g)^{-(i-1)}$. The stock of fixed capital operating in a given year (expressed at historical cost at constant prices) is the sum of gross investment carried out in the last n years; since the flow of output per unit of investment is constant through time this gives a convenient index of output capacity, M_n:

$$M_n = \sum_{i=1}^{n} I\left(\frac{1}{1+g}\right)^{i-1} = I\left(1-\left(\frac{1}{1+g}\right)^n\right)(1+g)/g \tag{4.4}$$

Since the capital–output ratio is v, the output of this stock of capital is F_n, or

$$F_n = \frac{M_n}{v} = I\left(1-\left(\frac{1}{1+g}\right)^n\right)(1+g)/g.v. \tag{4.5}$$

In order to make this technical alternative comparable with that of plants of durability n_s, which is taken as 'standard', the same procedure is applied to a hypothetical stream of investment with identical I and g but with lifetime n_s and with investment/output ratio v_s. Other things being equal, the output flow of an investment process with parameters v, n, will be equal to that of an investment process of standard durability n_s and investment output ratio v_s if

$$v/v_s = \left(1-\left(\frac{1}{1+g}\right)^n\right)\bigg/\left(1-\left(\frac{1}{1+g}\right)^{n_s}\right) = z_n \tag{4.6}$$

Thus Kalecki and Rakowski and the Polish *Instrukcja* recommend that the comparison of projects should be made not minimising actual and shadow costs for the actual capacity, but the ratio between costs and z_n times actual capacity. For a standard durability $n_s=20$ and $g=7\%$, for instance, z_n is 0·86 for $n=15$ and 1·10 for $n=25$: in other words planners should prefer a 25-year-long project to a 20-year one, given $g=7\%$, if the investment-output ratio is less than 10% higher than for the 20-year-long project; while $n=15$ can be preferred to standard durability n_s if its investment output ratio is lower by more than 14%.

The effect of durability over the introduction of technical progress is accounted for in a similar way. It is assumed that, for investment growing at a rate g per year, total operating costs of production in the *new* investment increase at a rate $c<g$, because of technical progress advancing at a rate approximately equal to $g-c$. Following the same method used for output, the relation between total costs G_n for a stock of plants of durability n and total costs G_{ns} for a stock of plants of durability n_s is given by

$$y_n = G_n/G_{ns} = \left(1-\left(\frac{1}{1+c}\right)^n\right)\Big/\left(1-\left(\frac{1}{1+c}\right)^{n_s}\right). \qquad (4.7)$$

If we call C the operating costs in a stock of plants of durability n, the operating costs in an identical stock of plants of durability n_s would be y_nC, a longer lifetime of plant involving a flow of costs larger by a factor of y_n. For instance, for $g=7\%$ and $c=3\%$ (with technical progress advancing at a rate of 3·9%) and $n_s=20$ years, y_n will be 0·80 for $n=15$ and 1·17 for $n=25$. Instead of minimising the expression given in (4.1) above, investors are instructed to select projects so that:

$$E=\frac{\mathrm{I}(1/T)(1+q.z)+C.y_n}{\mathrm{X}.z_n}=\text{minimum} \qquad (4.8)$$

where z is the average period of freezing of investment resources during the gestation period and X is the capacity target.

A final refinement was introduced to take into account the possible differences between the rate at which labour costs and other costs (raw materials, semi-finished products, fuel, energy and capital maintenance) fall in time, but the basic approach remained unchanged: tables for alternative values of y_n and z_n were attached to the *Instrukcja* for the use of investors. Basically, for each project of given technical durability, first the lifetime for which the expression above reaches a minimum is found and this is taken as the optimum economic lifetime of the project; then the project is chosen for which that expression, taken for the optimum economic lifetime of each project, is lowest.

The comparison of projects with reference to the characteristics of hypothetical balanced stocks is very ingenious; it inspired my treatment of more complicated time patterns of input and outputs (Nuti, 1970); it is not, however, immune from criticism. The optimum economic lifetime of plants might vary with the reference durability n_s, which is arbitrary; the optimum lifetime of a plant should be assessed without reference to a standard durability. The treatment of durability differs from that of gestation, whereas gestation and durability are both aspects of the time profile of inputs and outputs and should be treated in the same way. If the growth rate of investment is slowing down, the advantage of a longer lifetime is higher than if the growth rate is constant, and the reverse is true for an accelerating growth rate; the opposite applies to the disadvantages of longer lifetimes. What is most interesting, however, is that in an economy where investing firms obtained funds free of charge from the state budget no less than *three* shadow rates were introduced, *implicit* in T, q and in the use of g to calculate y_n and z_n. Shadow rates were fairly close (15·7% for T, 15% for q, 7–15% for g) but the approach was untidy and messy. Why did Kalecki become so involved in it? Presumably the answer is that he would have liked to introduce an actual interest rate in investment selection (see section 2 above) but was operating within a system dominated by a Soviet practice (that of recoupment period) difficult to change; he also specifically did not want to introduce interest and profitability in the selection of the areas of capacity expansion (except in the long run); at the same time he wanted to improve the existing planning system, practice prevailing over theory in his concern.

5. The perspective plan

Kalecki's ideas about socialist planning reviewed in the previous sections are brought together in the procedure he devised for the construction of a perspective plan, i.e. a plan for the long-term development of a socialist economy (see Kalecki 1958E, 1963C, D). What follows is a generalisation and formalisation of Kalecki's procedure.

The perspective plan covers a time span of 15 to 20 years; the planning horizon is actually longer, in that investment expenditure in the last few years of the plan is laid down on the assumption that the broad lines of development of the economy outlined in the plan will also continue after the end of the plan period. It is a 'sliding' plan; the first five years become the starting point for drawing a medium-run plan for the economy, especially the investment plan and, as time goes by, the terminal date of the perspective plan period is shifted forward, say, by five years every five years, so that a picture of the perspective development of the economy is kept, brought up to date as past and current experience produces more accurate projections. The plan is drawn at constant prices and is, therefore, designed basically to check the consistency of physical flows, while financial flows and the price level are adjusted later, with the drawing up of short-run financial balances and balances of the income and expenditure of the population.

The first stage in the construction of the perspective plan is the choice of a preliminary target for the average growth rate during the period, which we can call $\bar{g}_0$. The main constraints on average growth are: (i) the expected growth rate of the active population and the growth rate of its average productivity (partly dependent on technical progress and, partly, on the rate of investment itself); (ii) the minimum growth rate of consumption of the population and the share of accumulation associated with it, constraining $\bar{g}_0$ for the preliminary coefficients, at the prices and the sectoral composition of the base period; (iii) the balance of foreign trade. These constraints can be summed up as:

$$\bar{g}_0 \leqslant n_0 + h_0 \tag{5.1}$$

$$\bar{g}_0 \leqslant s/v_0 \tag{5.2}$$

$$\bar{g}_0 \leqslant \frac{g_x}{e_m} \tag{5.3}$$

where $\bar{g}_0$ is the preliminary target for the average growth of income over the period, n_0 and h_0 are preliminary estimates of population growth and of average productivity growth; s is the maximum share of accumulation corresponding to the minimum consumption requirements of the population, and v_0 is a preliminary estimate of average investment intensity; g_x is the expected growth rate of the value of exports, and e_m is the estimate of the elasticity of imports with respect to income (given the planners' expectations about world demand and relative internal and international prices). Ideally, all these constraints should be simultaneously met so as to have the equality sign in equations (5.1–5.3); if one of the constraints bites first, to some extent it might be possible to ease whatever is the bottleneck by bringing the right side of the other equations closer to $\bar{g}_0$: for instance, to raise h_0 or lower e_m or raise g_x at the expense of raising v_0, but there might be limits to the possibility of trading off one constraint for another and the most stringent constraint will determine the highest $\bar{g}_0$ which is tentatively considered feasible. However, even if the tentatively chosen growth rate does not quite meet all constraints one might pass to the second stage of the calculations, since the purpose of this stage is only that of ruling out blatantly unrealistic variants of the plan checking the internal consistency of expectations. The estimates are aggregates of different sectors, and it is not granted that the subsequent breakdown of these variables will give aggregation weights consistent with the provisional calculations.

The second stage is a tentative estimate of the output structure of different sectors required for final uses in each year. The changes in the pattern of final private consumption are predicted (by means of calculations of consumption elasticities, the analysis of family budgets, available time series of consumption data, the pattern of consumption of countries at similar stages of development, etc.) or planned (on the basis of consumption norms). Public consumption of the product of each sector can be added directly, but the requirements of the net output of each sector for investment and exports will depend in turn on the targets for gross output expansion in the different sectors, so that only preliminary estimates can be inserted at this stage, to be checked later for consistency with data obtained at the next stage. These operations can be summarised as the drawing of a set of provisional vectors of final demands in each period,

$$\mathbf{y}_{t+j} = \mathbf{c}_{t+j} + \mathbf{u}_{t+j} + \mathbf{s}_{t+j} + \mathbf{f}_{t+j}, j = 0, 1, \ldots, 20; \tag{5.4}$$

where **y** is the vector of final demand, **c** is the vector of private and **u** of public consumption, **s** is the provisional investment vector estimate and **f** the export vector.

The third stage consists of the attempt to estimate the sectoral breakdown of demand for intermediate products corresponding, in each period during the plan, to the provisional estimate of final demand obtained in stage two. This is done by means of either input–output analysis, or the material balances of resources and uses usually drawn in planned economies for the main commodity groups. In either case allowance has to be made for technical progress so that *ex ante* planning matrices **A** of technological coefficients have to be used rather than *ex post* tables. An estimate of the gross output targets **x** consistent with the final output targets of the perspective plan is thus obtained:

$$\mathbf{x}_{t+j} = \mathbf{A}_{t+j}\mathbf{x}_{t+j} + \mathbf{y}_{t+j}, j = 0, 1, \ldots, 15\text{–}20. \tag{5.5}$$

The fourth stage consists of a reassessment of the provisional estimates, for investment and foreign trade, on the basis of the supply constraints on the growth of each sector. Productive activities are divided into two main categories, of 'supply determined' and 'demand determined' activities (Kalecki, 1963 and his Preface to Rakowski, 1963). The first category includes those activities which are subject to a ceiling for their long-run growth rate, for technical or organisational reasons, which cannot be removed even at the expense of higher capital expenditure. The technological and organisational limits are given by limited natural resources, or by the time necessary for the introduction of new technological processes, or for the training of workers or technicians of different skills, or by difficulties in recruiting manpower for certain trades (mining, for instance). Demand-determined industries are the industries which, within the relevant range of the growth rate of national income, are not subject to such ceilings in their growth rates. The comparison between the estimates of gross output requirements and the ceilings limiting the growth of supply-determined industries will give a first assessment of import requirements, to which non-competitive imports have to be added, to obtain total import requirements. In order to meet import requirements with exports, the targets for the final output of the industries which are not supply-determined has to be raised, following the indications of foreign trade agencies, as long as higher amounts of output marketed for exports are not counterbalanced by more unfavourable terms of trade. Once the net trade balance and the actual targets for the increase of gross output are known, a more accurate estimate of investment requirements can be obtained and checked against the provisional estimates adopted at stage two. If the divergence between the initial estimates of the net trade balance and investment requirements and the estimates obtained at stage four is not acceptable the process of plan construction will have to start again, from stage two, until the two estimates are sufficiently close and the relations hold:

$$\mathbf{x}_{t+j}+\mathbf{m}_{t+j}=\mathbf{A}_{t+j}\mathbf{x}_{t+j}+\mathbf{y}_{t+j}, j=0,1,\ldots,15\text{–}20; \tag{5.6}$$

$$\mathbf{x}_{t+j}\leqslant\tilde{\mathbf{x}}_{t+j} \tag{5.7}$$

$$\mathbf{s}_{t+j}=\mathbf{B}_{t+j}(\mathbf{x}_{t+j+1}-\mathbf{x}_{t+j}) \tag{5.8}$$

$$\mathbf{p}.\mathbf{f}_{t+j}=r.p_i.\mathbf{m}_{t+j} \tag{5.9}$$

where $\mathbf{m}$ is imports, $\tilde{\mathbf{x}}_{t+j}$ is the capacity constraint of x_{t+j}, $\mathbf{B}_{t+j}$ is the matrix of projected investment requirements on a sector-to-sector basis; p and p_i are internal and international prices and r the exchange rate.

The choice of the technical form of investment is undertaken at this stage. Whenever alternative ways of achieving given targets for output expansion in different sectors are available the procedure for technical choice is usually that of minimising the sum of perspective operation costs and a shadow charge for investment, according to the methods discussed in section 4 above. Alternative ways of earning foreign currency, and the alternative between import and domestic productions, are treated as any other technical choice, in the same way (Kalecki, 1971B).

After these stages are performed the disaggregated data can be aggregated to recompute the aggregate targets for the growth of national income, investment intensity and import requirements, in order to check them against the preliminary estimates. In case of inconsistency the plan is revised and a new variant is worked out through the stages described above.

> The variant finally adopted should be distinguished by the highest possible rate of growth at which there is a realistic possibility of balancing foreign trade and at which the relative share of productive investment plus the increase in inventories in the national income is considered tolerable by the authorities from the point of view of the impact upon consumption and unproductive investment in the short run (Kalecki, 1963).

This procedure proposed by Kalecki has a number of shortcomings. Computations undertaken at constant prices can at most ensure the *consistency* of plans in physical terms (as long as aggregation weights within sectors do not change too drastically) but there is nothing to ensure that the relative prices deriving *from the plan* should be consistent with the relative prices assumed *in the construction of the plan*. On the side of production goods, the relative scarcities of inputs caused in the very process of planning might diverge from initial relative prices and, if this divergence is neglected, opportunities for substitution among alternative inputs might be lost. For consumption goods, the relative long-run production costs of consumption goods over the plan period might diverge from the pattern of relative prices of consumption goods initially assumed for the purposes of forecasting consumption patterns over the period, inducing, therefore, the neglect of opportunities for substitution among alternative consumption goods. Finally, since the calculations for investment choice are carried out for given output expansion targets, the procedure implies that the quantity of material inputs in the operation of the plants after construction and the proportion in which material inputs are required to make the investment goods considered are not affected by the technique eventually chosen; technological choice, in other words, is assumed to take the form of the substitution between labour and an aggregate notion of investment measured at constant prices, instead of more complex alternatives.

These shortcomings can be summed up as the possible *inefficiency* resulting from the neglect of three main feedbacks of the plan on the system of prices (and hence, whenever alternative consumption and production choices are available, on the pattern of planned quantities). These feedbacks are: (i) the choice of the technical form of investment on the physical composition of the sectoral targets for output expansion; (ii) the feedback of the investment plan on the prices of investment goods to be used as basis of plan construction; (iii) the feedback of relative costs of consumption goods resulting from the plan on the relative prices to be used as the basis of the consumption plan. The extent of the divergence between the plan obtained following the stages outlined and an 'ideal' plan, which should be constructed taking into account also the feedbacks mentioned here, and the practical importance of this divergence, are questions open to discussion. According to Michal Kalecki the drawbacks of performing calculations to choose techniques measuring the value of investment (per unit of output or per labour employed) at constant prices are of the same nature as all index number problems and can be reduced, in the framework of investment planning, by using chain indexes of the volume of investment (Kalecki, 1963A, ch. 1). He recognises that the crude recoupment period approach and the other rules put forward for investment choice are only a first approximation to a complex problem (Kalecki, 1963C) but regards more sophisticated approaches as not necessarily representing an improvement, given the inaccuracy of initial data and the uncertainty about the future. The necessity of checking the consistency between the relative prices of consumption goods at which future consumption is being forecast and relative costs anticipated in the calculations of 'investment effectiveness' has been stressed by Kalecki himself, although his own treatment of the problem does not seem to provide a satisfactory solution.[1]

In handling these problems in Poland in the early 1960s Kalecki rose to the challenge of 'realised' socialism and favoured approximate procedures of practical use to rigorous solutions without application. Even with hindsight, nobody could say that he was wrong.

Summary and conclusion

Kalecki's contribution to the theory and practice of socialist planning—as distinguished from the wider aspects of socialist economy and society—are discussed in this paper under four headings:

[1] This question will be treated in a future paper.

(i) Kalecki's comprehensive and coherent picture of the organisation model of the socialist economy as an alternative to the Soviet-type model different from the 'market socialism' of Lange and other reformers. In Kalecki's model prices are fixed, as in his picture of the capitalist economy, by mark-up pricing, with the average mark-up on actual and shadow costs related to the requirements of investment finance; markets are used but market signals are quantity signals determining quantity adjustments in the use and expansion of capacity; firms performance is assessed using net value indicators but within wage guidelines and employment targets; investment is kept in check by interest payments deducted from performance indicators; but neither investment nor employment is guided by enterprise profitability considerations; central planning is made easier by grouping enterprises in vertically integrated sectoral associations. The countervailing power *vis-à-vis* central planners is not the market but Workers' Councils: in Kalecki's reform scheme therefore democratisation takes the place of marketisation.

(ii) Kalecki's approach to the external and political limits to the accumulation policy of central planners. Labour force growth and technical progress set a limit to the accumulation that can be usefully undertaken from the viewpoint of *maintainable* consumption growth (golden rule accumulation of Western texts being regarded not as an optimum but as a maximum accumulation policy). Within this maximum limit, planners' concern for short-term consumption *should* (following from a rationality postulate in Kalecki but really embodying a plausible but special preference system on the part of planners) stop well short of that maximum.

(iii) Kalecki's innovations in revamping the Soviet-type approach to investment project selection based on the notion of 'standard recoupment period' in place of interest rates. Kalecki and Rakowski linked this period to the marginal labour-saving opportunities in modernisation given the full employment constraint of the socialist economy, introduced an alternative implicit rate of interest in dealing with the immobilisation of resources during investment gestation, and used investment growth rates in discriminating between projects of different lifetimes. Theoretically the use of multiple implicit shadow rates of interest can be questioned; in practice their values were close and these improvements of current practice must have seemed to Kalecki as more easily acceptable to Polish leaders than actual interest rates, and more desirable than an unqualified use of actual interest rates for the choice of investment levels and structure instead of just technical choice.

(iv) Kalecki's procedure for the construction of a perspective plan of the development of the socialist economy, as a foundation for medium-run and investment planning. This brings together all the previous points and leads to a practical solution of plan formulation, which in theory can be regarded as possibly inefficient because it neglects a number of feedbacks in plan construction, but in practice is of considerable use especially if compared with the alternative Soviet-type methods using material balances alone.

This critical but positive assessment leads to some reconsideration of Kalecki's overall contribution to socialist economics. Accused of not being a Marxist he was more Leninist than his critics (with his emphasis on workers' control). Accused of neglecting social and political factors he had the most perceptive feeling for precisely these factors, with his emphasis on democratisation and on the political limits to investment policies and other work (not reviewed in this paper) on subjects ranging from economic criminality to peasant behaviour, from systemic influence on labour productivity to income distribution between manual and non-manual workers (see Kalecki, 1984, Part III). For a man revered as a great theoretician, his propositions often lack generality, though the qualifications are not significant in practice for Eastern Europe in the 1960s. In this Kalecki is in a position similar to that of Keynes, who also claimed generality for a theory deeply grounded in the time and place of his theorising, Britain in the 1930s, and requiring some practically plausible qualifications which reduce generality without reducing policy relevance. Keynes was really a high Tory believing in markets, as Kalecki was a high Socialist believing in planning, and the theoretical and political stance of both has been frequently misunderstood. The world is not in the best of possible states, not because of qualification required for the general validity of their theories, but because of the pursuit of pre-Keynesian and pre-Kaleckian policies in both West and East.

In one respect Kalecki's contribution to socialist economics has not yet been tested, i.e. the viability of his model of socialist organisation, since the combination of central planning and workers' control has not been realised anywhere. That model was more the product of Polish conditions in the 1960s than perhaps anything else produced by Kalecki; it may be no accident that he decided to include almost none of his papers on the subject in his *Selected Papers* on socialism (Kalecki, 1972), though pessimism on workers' powers, which was justified in 1968 Poland, might not be justified today, after the explosive effects of workers' discontent in 1980–81 Poland, and in the reform climate set up by Gorbachev. Kalecki's qualms about market prices, the risks of unemployment associated with decentralisation and the risks of central planning without workers' control, however, remain as valid and relevant today as ever.

Bibliography

Brus, W. 1977. Kalecki's economics of socialism, *Oxford Bulletin of Economics and Statistics*, vol. 39, no. 1, February (Michal Kalecki Memorial Issue)

Chilosi, A. 1971. The theory of growth of a socialist economy of M. Kalecki, *Economics of Planning*, vol. 11, no. 3

Feinstein, C. (ed.) 1967. *Socialism, Capitalism and Economic Growth, Essays in honour of Maurice Dobb*, Cambridge, CUP

Feldman, G. A. 1928. K teorii tempov narodnogo dokhoda (On the theory of growth rates of national income), *Planovoe Khoziaistvo*, no. 11 and 12, November and December; English translation from Russian in Spulber (1964)

Feldman, G. A. 1929. O limitakh industrializatsii (On limits to industrialisation), *Planovoe Khoziaistvo*, no. 2, February; English translation from Russian in Spulber (1964)

Granick, D. 1975. *Enterprise Guidance in Eastern Europe*, Princeton, Princeton University Press

Hahn, F. H. and Matthews, R. C. O. 1964. The theory of economic growth: a survey, *Economic Journal*, December

Horvat, B. 1958. The optimum rate of investment, *Economic Journal*, vol. LXVIII, no. 272, December

Jeffries, I. (ed.) 1981. *The Industrial Enterprise in Eastern Europe*, London, Praeger

Jozefiak, C. 1971. *Optimum techniczno-renowacjine w gospodarce socjalistycznej* (Optimum technical choice in the socialist economy), Warsaw, PWN

Kalecki, M. 1942. Basic preconditions for a democratic planned economy, *Labour Discussion Notes*, no. 35, September, The Socialist Clarity Group, London (Polish version in Kalecki, 1982)

Kalecki, M. 1946A. Uwagi o racjonowaniu i systemie cen (Observations on rationing and the price system), first published in Kalecki (1982)

Kalecki, M. 1946B. Uwagi o oszczednosciach i obiegu pienieznym w Polsce (Observations on savings and monetary circulation in Poland), first published in Kalecki (1982)

Kalecki, M. 1946C. Plany finansowe na II polrocze 1946 r. i na I polrocze 1947 r. (Financial plans for the second semester of 1946 and the first semester of 1947), first published in Kalecki (1982)

Kalecki, M. 1956A. Liberalizacja zarzadzania drobnym przemyslem (Liberalisation of management in small-scale industry), first published in Kalecki (1982)

Kalecki, M. 1956B. Rady robotnicze a centralne planowanie (Workers' councils and central planning), *Nowe Drogi*, no. 11–12, November–December; also in Kalecki (1982)

Kalecki, M. 1956C. Dynamika inwestycji i dochodu narodowego w gospodarcze socjalistycznej, *Ekonomista*, no. 5

Kalecki, M. 1957A. Nie przeceniac roli modelu (The role of the model should not be overestimated), *Trybuna Ludu*, no. 33, 3 February; also in Kalecki (1981)

Kalecki, M. 1957B. Koncern pionowy? *Polityka* no. 8, 17–23 April, Warsaw; also as, Koncern pionowy jako element nowego modelu gospodarczego (Vertically integrated enterprise groups as an element of the new economic model), in Kalecki (1982)

Kalecki, M. 1957C. Zmiany modelu gospodarczego w zakresie bodzcow ekonomicznych (Changes of the economic model in the area of economic incentives), first published in Kalecki (1982)

Kalecki, M. 1957D. Schemat nowego systemu bodzcow i nakazow (Scheme of the new system of incentives and orders), *Zycie Gospodarcze*, 21 July 1957, no. 29; also in Kalecki (1982)

Kalecki, M. 1957E. Uwagi o metodzie prac nad planem perspektywiczym (Notes on the perspective plan methodology), first published in Kalecki (1982)

Kalecki, M. 1958A. Bodzce zainteresowania materialnego w gospodarce socjalistycznej (Material incentives in the socialist economy), in the proceedings of a conference on the same subject in January 1956, *Szkice Ekonomiczne*, ZNE PAN, Warsaw; also in Kalecki (1982)

Kalecki, M. 1958B. Centralisticko odredivanje cena kao bitni elemenat socijalisticke economike (Centralised price formation as an essential element of the socialist economy), *Medzunarodni Problemi*, no. 3, Belgrade; Polish translation in Kalecki (1982)

Kalecki, M. 1958C. Czynniki okreslajace tempo wzrostu gospodarki socjalistycznej (Factors limiting the growth rate of a socialist economy), *Gospodarka Planowa*, no. 8

Kalecki, M. 1958D. O wspolczynniku zamrozenia (On the freezing coefficient), *Ekonomista*, no. 6

Kalecki, M. 1958E. Plan perspektiwyczny na lata 1961–75 (The perspective plan for 1961–75), *Nowe Drogi*, no. 8, August; English translation in *Polish Perspectives*, no. 3, 1959

Kalecki, M. 1962. Problemy wlasnej bazy cen krajow RWPG (Problems of the own price basis for CMEA countries), first published in Kalecki (1982)

Kalecki, M. 1963A. *Zarys teorii wzrostu gospodarki socjalistycznej* (Outline of a theory of growth of the socialist economy), Warsaw, PWN, English translation in Kalecki (1972)

Kalecki, M. 1963B. Zagadnienie optymalnej struktury spozycia (The problem of optimum consumption structure), *Gospodarka Planowa*, July, also in Kalecki, 1984; English translation in *Mathematical Studies in Economics and Statistics in the USSR and Eastern Europe*, vol. I, no. 4, 1966

Kalecki, M. 1963C. An outline of a method of constructing a perspective plan, in SGPiS, 1963

Kalecki, M. 1963D. O podstawowych zasadach planowania wieloletniego (On the general principles of long-term planning), *Zycie Gospodarcze*, no. 24; in Kalecki, 1982

Kalecki, M. 1965. Krzywa produkcji a rachunek efektywnosci inwestycji (Production curve and the evaluation of investment effectiveness), *Ekonomista*, no. 1; English translation in Feinstein (ed.), 1967

Kalecki, M. 1971A. *Selected Essays on the Dynamics of the Capitalist Economy*, Cambridge, CUP

Kalecki, M. 1971B. Zakres stosowania rachunku efektywnosci inwestycji w gospodarce socjalistycznej (The scope of the evaluation of investment efficiency in a socialist economy), *Gospodarka Planowa*, no. 5; English translation in Kalecki, 1972 .

Kalecki, M. 1972. *Selected Essays on the Economic Growth of the Socialist and the Mixed Economy*, Cambridge, CUP

Kalecki, M. 1982. *Dziela, tom 3: Socjalizm—Funkcjonowanie i wieloletnie planowanie*, (vol. 3 of Collected Works on 'Socialism—Functioning and Long-Term Planning', edited by J. Osiatynski), Warsaw, PWN

Kalecki, M. 1984. *Dziela, tom 4: Socjalism—Wzrost gospodarczy i efektywnosc inwestycji* (vol. 4 of Collected Works on 'Socialism—Economic Growth and Investment Effectiveness', edited by J. Osiatynski), Warsaw, PWN

Kalecki, M. and Polaczek, S. 1957A. Uwagi w sprawie metody ustalania cen surowcow podstawowych (Notes on a method for fixing the prices of basic raw materials), *Gospodarka Planowa* no. 4; also in Kalecki (1982)

Kalecki, M. and Polaczek, S. 1957B. Dyskusja o cenach surowcow podstawowych (The debate on the prices of basic raw materials), *Gospodarka Planowa*, no. 9; also in Kalecki (1982)

UWE, BRISTOL LIBRARY SERVICES

Kalecki, M. and Rakowski, M. 1959. Uogolnienie wzoru ekonomicznej efektywnosci inwestycji (A generalised formula of investment effectiveness), *Gospodarka Planowa*, no. 11; English translation in Nove and Zauberman (eds), (1964)

KPpRM-Komisia Planowania przy Radzie Ministrow 1962. *Instrukcja ogolna w sprawie metodyki badan ekonomicznej efektywnosci inwestycji* (General instruction on the methodology for determining the economic effectiveness of investment), Warsaw

Lange, O. 1956. Budowa nowego modelu gospodarczego musi oprzec sie na dynamice klasy robotniczej i socjalistycznej inteligencji (The construction of the new economic model must be based on the dynamics of the working class and the socialist intelligentzia), *Nowy Drogi*, no. 11–12

Laski, K. 1965. *Zarys teorii reprodukcji socjalistycznej* (Outline of a theory of socialist reproduction), Warsaw, PWN

Melzer, M. 1981. Combine formation and the role of the enterprise in East German industry', in Jeffries (ed.) 1981

Nove, A. and Zauberman, A. (eds) 1964. *Studies on the Theory of Reproduction and Prices*, Warsaw, PWN

Nuti, D. M. 1970. Capitalism, socialism and steady growth, *Economic Journal*, vol. LXXX, March

Nuti, D. M. 1971. The evolution of Polish investment planning, *Jahrbuch der Wirtschaft Osteuropas*, Band 3

Nuti, D. M. 1973. The political economy of socialism—orthodoxy and change in Polish texts, *Soviet Studies*, vol. XXV, October

Nuti, D. M. 1977. Large corporations and the reform of Polish industry, *Jahrbuch der Wirtschaft Osteuropas*, Band 7

Rakowski, M. (ed.) 1963. *Efektywnosc Inwestycji* (Investment efficiency), Warsaw, PWN, English translation 1966, Warsaw, PWN

Sawyer, M. C. 1985. *The Economics of Michal Kalecki*, London, Macmillan

SGPiS 1963. *Essays on Planning and Economic Development*, Teaching Materials, vol. 8, Warsaw

Spulber, N. (ed.) 1964. *Foundations of Soviet Strategy for Economic Growth—Selected Soviet Essays 1924–1930*, Bloomington,

Wolf, T. A. 1985. Economic stabilisation in planned economies, *IMF Staff Papers*, vol. 32, no. 1, March

[14]

PETER KRIESLER

Kalecki's pricing theory revisited

The paper looks at the development of Kalecki's pricing theory, arguing that there was substantial modification and change in the various formulations, and therefore it rejects any argument of continuity in that theoretical development. It considers the elements common to all versions of the theory before concentrating on the earliest formulation. Although, in this version, the analysis concentrated on the individual firm, this was broadened in later versions to incorporate industry-wide considerations; however Kalecki never adequately dealt with the problems of defining an industry. Kalecki's 1939–1942 work on price theory is seen as an unsuccessful attempt to widen the scope of the analysis by utilizing the tools of orthodox microeconomic theory. After the detour provided by these articles, Kalecki made various attempts to reformulate the theory, but did not appear to be satisfied with any of them.

Kalecki was ultimately unable to incorporate his basic insights with respect to the pricing decision in the manufacturing sector of capitalist economies into a formal model which was compatible with his analysis of the determination of distribution and the level of output. He modified and changed his pricing equation from his earliest English publication on that theme in 1938 until his posthumously published paper in 1971.

This theme stands in antithesis to that of Basile and Salvadori (1984–85, p. 259), where they argue for "the continuity of Kalecki's thought with respect to pricing"; that is:

The author is a member of the School of Economics, University of New South Wales.

He would like to thank the editor of this journal, Paul Davidson, for his detailed comments on an earlier draft of this paper.

> both Kalecki's initial pricing theory . . . and his last formulation . . . are the same as the simplified version he presented in 1954. (1984–5, p. 249)

This statement is true only at a very superficial level, and, in fact, Kalecki's analysis of pricing evolved through various versions as he attempted to solve certain problems inherent in each version. For Kalecki, prices in the manufacturing sector at less than full capacity utilization were determined by a markup on unit prime costs, which was itself determined by the degree of competitiveness. However, because the range of parameters considered by Kalecki varied greatly, this was reflected in substantial differences in the pricing equation in the development of Kalecki's work.

Before discussing the individual models, it is important to identify the common elements which run through all versions of Kalecki's pricing analysis.

1. Common elements

The analysis is concerned with advanced capitalist economies, which, for the sake of simplicity, are assumed to be closed with no government sector.

The starting point of Kalecki's analysis of pricing was the distinction between the industrial manufacturing sector and the raw materials sector. Kalecki concentrated on the imperfectly competitive manufacturing sector where excess capacity created elastic supply conditions so that prices were determined on the basis of costs. This was contrasted with the more competitive raw materials sector where short-period inelastic supply meant that prices were directly influenced by changes in demand. Kalecki noted (1954, p. 11): "It is clear that these two types of price formation arise out of different conditions of supply." In the raw materials sector, either increases in demand cannot wholly be met by increases in supply inducing predominantly price responses, or supply is subject to increasing costs so that both quantity supplied and price increase. Despite references to the competitiveness of this sector, this kind of competition should not be confused with the "perfect" competition of neoclassical theory. Rather, it is a reference to the fact that, in this sector, both supply and demand factors play a role in the determination of price. As a result, any market imperfection on the production side can influence price only by manipulating supply. For these reasons, prices of raw materials tend to "fluctuate much more strongly'' than other prices (1938, p. 110).

Kalecki's main concern, however, was with the imperfectly competitive manufacturing sector. Here Kalecki was an important originator of the use of reverse L-shaped cost curves, with marginal costs (and, therefore, average variable costs) constant up to the level of full capacity utilization. This, coupled with the postulate of general excess capacity as the norm, results in changes in demand being met by changes in supply, without any changes in costs or prices. As a result, Kalecki argued that prices in the manufacturing sector are determined as a markup on costs, with the markup being determined by ''semi-monopolistic and monopolistic'' factors which Kalecki labeled ''degree of monopoly'' (1968, p. 168).

2. ''The determinants of distribution of national income''

The chief concern of Kalecki (1938, slightly revised as the first chapter of Kalecki, 1939a) was with ''the determinants of distribution of national income.'' Nevertheless, there are important discussions both as to the nature of costs in the manufacturing sector and as to the determination of prices in that sector.

In his 1938 analysis of price, Kalecki uses Lerner's measure of the degree of monopoly (see Lerner, 1934):

$$\mu = (p - m)/p \tag{1}$$

where p is price, m is marginal cost, and μ is the measure of the degree of monopoly, that is, the markup.

In both Lerner's and Kalecki's formulation, price must be taken as referring to ''net price,'' which is ''the revenue per unit of product after the deduction of advertising costs, etc.'' (Kalecki, 1938, p. 100).[1] Similarly marginal costs were taken by them to include only production costs, thereby excluding selling costs, transport costs, and any other costs not directly arising from the production process.

From equation (1), it follows that:

> with a given degree of monopoly the relation of price to marginal cost is a constant $1/(1 - \mu)$. (Kalecki 1939, p. 27)

This is represented in Figure 1.

[1]It should be noted that advertising has two distinct components: the initial (capital) advertising expenditure of a firm attempting to break into a market, and the ''day-to-day'' advertising of established firms. It is the latter which is relevant here.

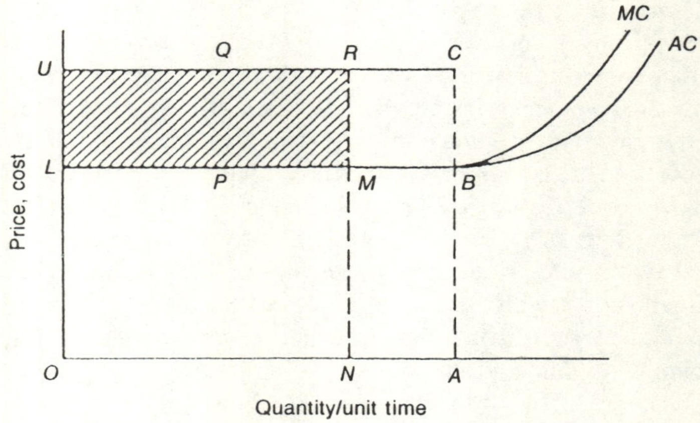

Figure 1

Cost curves of an enterprise in an imperfectly competitive market

The cost curves in Figure 1 are drawn on the assumption of constant marginal cost, up to the level of full capacity utilization, *OA*. Below this point, marginal cost is constant and equal to average variable cost, which is represented by the line *LPM*. The ratio of price to marginal cost, for a given "degree of monopoly" (i.e., for a given markup), is constant and equal to the reciprocal of one minus the markup. Therefore, from a given marginal cost curve, the "price curve" corresponding to it can be imputed from this proportional relationship, with a given "degree of monopoly." This is shown on the diagram as *UQRC*, which represents neither a demand curve nor an average revenue curve. Rather it is a "price" curve describing the price that results from a given average variable cost curve with given "degree of monopoly."

For this analysis to provide a coherent nontautologous theory of price, the markup must itself be determined. For Kalecki, the clue to the determination of the markup lies in the factors influencing the competitiveness of the industry, for example, the degree of concentration, the relation of transport costs to price, the degree of standardization of price, the organization of commodity exchange, and so on (Kalecki, 1939a, p. 82). These forces may be difficult to quantify with any degree of precision; nevertheless, as Riach has pointed out, they provide a coherent theory of pricing (1971, p. 52; see also Kriesler, 1987, Appendix).

This early version of Kalecki's analysis has been subjected both to the charge that it is a tautology and to the charge that the markup was equal to, and was solely determined by, the elasticity of demand for the output of the firm concerned. It can be shown that under neoclassical profit-maximizing assumptions, with marginal cost equal to marginal revenue, the markup is equal to the reciprocal of the elasticity of demand.[2] It should be noted that this inverse relationship between the markup and the elasticity of demand is applicable only in the absence of advertising. When enterprises engage in "day-to-day" advertising for a product, then the price which is relevant for the firms selling the product differs from the price used to estimate the elasticity of demand. For the former, the relevant price is net price, allowing for the deduction of (inter alia) advertising costs. However, the price which is important from the viewpoint of the consumer, and hence the price utilized to calculate demand elasticity, is the gross price, before any such deduction. The equality of the "markup" with the inverse of the elasticity of demand was derived on the basis of a uniform price. However, where the price paid by the consumer differs from the price relevant to the producer, then this relationship no longer holds. In fact, it may be contended that, even in the absence of advertising, the equality between the "markup" and the inverse of the demand elasticity is dubious. The argument holds because the derivation of the elasticity concepts relies on static equilibrium conditions, and certain shaped cost and revenue curves.

> If we are willing to admit that firms act as neoclassical profit maximizers, then and *only* then . . . [will] the degree of monopoly vary inversely with the elasticity of demand. (King and Regan, 1976, p. 53n)

For elasticity to play a role, it must be calculable, which requires knowledge of the individual firm's demand curve in order to determine marginal revenue. There are, however, insurmountable difficulties in oligopolistic industries for individual firms trying to identify or determine their demand curves. In some situations with, for example, high levels of interdependence of price and demand of the different firms in the market, no determinate demand curve can be considered for any

[2]See, for example, Kalecki (1938, p. 100), Kalecki (1939a, p. 19), and Sylos-Labini (1969, p. 96). See also Kalecki (1942, p. 123), where he utilized this relationship to argue for the importance of the "degree of monopoly" as a determinant of gross profit. But note that in the two original Kalecki references this relationship is referred to only in a footnote or in passing while in Kalecki (1942, p. 123; emphasis added) it holds only under "*pure* imperfect competition."

firm in isolation. Yet, the question of the determinacy of a firm's elasticity depends on the determinacy of the firm's demand curve and of its marginal revenue. The idea of elasticity is contingent on the theory of imperfect competition utilized. Hence, it is necessary to consider whether the relevant parameters are determinate in Kalecki's model. This is not an easy question to answer, as Kalecki does not explicitly expound a theory of imperfect competition. In "Money and Real Wages" (1939b, p. 52) Kalecki argues that in the imperfectly competitive (industrial) sector of the economy "establishments are in general not fully utilized since they maintain a monopolistic (cartels) or quasi-monopolistic imperfect competition position in the market." In Kalecki (1938, p. 111) and Kalecki (1939a, p. 35), an important role is assigned to cartels in the "slump" aspect of the trade cycle. Clearly, in the case of cartels, interdependence between firms is so strong as to render incoherent the notion of independent determinate demand curves for individual firms. Therefore, in such cases, the elasticity of demand is also not capable of being determined.

In the case of "quasi-monopolistic" or imperfect competition, Kalecki's views are much more difficult to perceive. In "Money and Real Wages" (1939b, p. 52n) he refers to Sraffa (1926), Chamberlin (1933), and Robinson (1933), while in Kalecki (1939a, p. 28) he refers to Harrod's "Doctrines of Imperfect Competition" (Harrod, 1934). Kalecki's position is ascertainable only by inference. In Kalecki (1938) and Kalecki (1939a) there is no mention either of the marginal revenue curve or of the demand curve. In fact, instead of utilizing a demand curve where it is appropriate, he derives a "price curve" which, although not the same, serves a very similar function. Given this relation, marginal revenue is not determined from the demand curve. Rather, it is represented by the "price line" (*QRC*), which is a line parallel to the constant marginal cost curve, with the distance between the lines determined by the markup, up to the current level of output, *ON*. If the firm wishes to increase output beyond this level, then demand and supply considerations both become important in determining price. In other words, due to the fact that the firms are not profit-maximizers in the static orthodox manner, marginal cost will not, in general, be equal to marginal revenue. However, it is only when these two are equal that the inverse relation between the markup and the elasticity of demand can be established.

Given that the concept of marginal revenue and in particular the demand curve had been established by the time of Kalecki's writing, and that he was probably familiar with it, there is a strong inference that his neglect was due to the fact that he did not feel that it had a role to play in his analysis. This inference is reinforced by his next major article on microdistribution (Kalecki, 1939–40). In this paper, Kalecki utilizes an entirely new approach, where marginal revenue and the elasticity of demand become important tools of the analysis. However, the use of the firm's elasticity of demand is suspect because it is applicable only in the absence of advertising and in a static equilibrium framework and, in addition, requires marginal revenue to be calculable. Yet Kalecki's earlier model does not require marginal revenue to be calculable and it does allow for the incorporation of selling costs.

In orthodox analysis, a profit-maximizing firm will produce at the level where marginal costs are equal to marginal revenues. In this static framework the markup is a dependent variable. For Kalecki, the markup is determined by the degree of monopoly, so that price becomes the dependent variable within a dynamic framework. This reverses the causality assumed in elasticity analysis which is derived under the assumption of static conditions and is, therefore, hardly relevant in a dynamic framework. Therefore, to postulate a strict equality between the "markup" and the inverse of the elasticity of demand is spurious. This is not to say that the elasticity of demand is not a determinant of the markup, but rather that it is not the sole determinant.[3]

The analysis of price in these early papers of Kalecki concentrates on the individual firm. Although wider considerations may enter into the

[3]Cf. Sylos-Labini (1969, pp. 90–93). Some economists have confused the role of elasticity in Kalecki's analysis. They see elasticity either as being the measure of the "degree of monopoly" or as being its sole determinant, rather than as only one determinant. For example, H. G. Johnson (1973, pp. 197–199) takes this confusion to its logical extreme with the argument that "the elasticity of demand is not determined by the capitalists in a particular industry since it is not a parameter of behaviour but a variable" (p. 198). This entirely misconstrues the role of elasticity in the analysis. Similarly, Kaldor concludes that "Kalecki built . . . a simplified theory of distribution, where the share of profits in output is shown to be determined by the elasticity of demand alone" (1968, p. 365). Following Kaldor, Nuti contended that either the "degree of monopoly" is a tautology or "the degree of monopoly is obtained from the demand curve from each firm and is equal to the inverse of the demand elasticity, given the hypothesis of profit maximization; the theory runs up against the same problems as neoclassical theory, namely the reliance upon microeconomic concepts (here the elasticity of demand) to explain a macroeconomic problem" (1972, p. 226). See also Rostow (1948, p. 226), Davidson (1959, pp. 53, 133n), Dobb (1975, p. 269), Hahn (1972, p. 37), Rowthorn (1981, p. 36n), and Reynolds (1983, p. 497). In all these cases the role of the elasticity of demand has been greatly overrated. As noted above, Kalecki referred to it very casually and it played no role in his theoretical construct.

determination of the markup, they are not institutionalized into the price equations, as they were in Kalecki's later works.[4]

3. Pricing, 1939–42

The early formulation of Kalecki's pricing analysis created problems for the analysis of distribution for which it was the foundation.[5] As a result, Kalecki attempted to reformulate the analysis in a manner which introduced wider elements, in particular oligopolistic interdependence, into the pricing equation, as well as providing a framework more susceptible to aggregation. "The Supply Curve of an Industry under Imperfect Competition" (1939–40) and "A Theory of Long-Run Distribution of the Product of Industry" (1941) represent his initial attempts at solving these dilemmas by providing the framework for an analysis of an industry in an imperfectly competitive market. These papers were Kalecki's first attempts to generalize some of the concepts of his earlier papers, as well as his endeavors to deal with the theory of oligopoly. Their lack of success is apparent from the fact that they are ignored by Kalecki, who does not mention them again in later writings.

In 1935, Kalecki left Poland, and, after spending some time in Sweden, he came to England. During this period, particularly due to his friendship with Joan Robinson, he came into contact with the new developments in the analysis of the theory of the firm, which he incorporated into the papers under discussion. Two particular instances of Kalecki's utilizing elements of the new theoretical developments are his use of the distinction between differing market situations and his use of concepts developed at the Oxford Institute of Statistics associated with the work of Hall and Hitch.

The stated purpose of Kalecki (1939–40, p. 91) is to shed "some

[4]Basile and Salvadori (1984–85, p. 257) mistakenly represent Kalecki's price equation in these papers as:

$$\mu = (p - m)/\bar{p}.$$

By introducing into the denominator average price $\bar{p}$, rather than just p, they have widened the analysis to incorporate elements not explicitly considered by Kalecki.

[5]The emphasis, in these early papers, on the individual firm meant that the pricing decision was analyzed independent of the economic environment in which the firm operated. More importantly, Kalecki experienced severe problems in aggregating from the level of the individual firm to that of the industrial sector as a whole, due to the problems caused by the possibility of changes in the composition of output. See Kriesler (1987, pp. 48–51).

light" on "the concept of the short-period supply curve of an industry under imperfect competition." It is clear, however, from the contents that Kalecki had other motives. The problems with deriving such a curve are documented in Robinson (1933, p. 86) and revolve around the inability to derive an industry demand curve independent of the general state of overall demand. To overcome this problem, Kalecki defines a given state of "market imperfection" determined by the elasticity of demand for the product of the firms in the industry and by the ratio of each firm's price to the industry's average price. Changes in "market imperfection" induce shifts in the industry supply curve.

The analysis initially considers "pure imperfect competition," which corresponds to "monopolistic competition" in modern terminology, and then allows for oligopoly.

For "pure imperfect competition," Kalecki (1939–40, p. 91–92) notes:

> The market imperfection is given if the elasticity of demand for the product of each firm e_k is a determinate function of the ratio of its price p_k to the average price $\bar{p}$ or:
>
> (2) $$e_k = \epsilon_k(p_k/\bar{p})$$
>
> the shape of the function ϵ_k representing the state of market imperfection.

If for a given $(p_k/\bar{p})$ elasticity rises, then market imperfection is said to fall.

From the definition of own-price point elasticity: $e_k = (do_k/dp_k) \cdot (p_k/o_k)$, and, integrating equation (2) for a given $\bar{p}$, we obtain the following:

(3) $$o_k = c_k f_k$$

where

$$\log f_k = \int \frac{d(p_k/\bar{p})}{(p_k/\bar{p})} \epsilon_k$$

and c_k is a constant of integration.

Therefore, f_k is determined by ϵ_k.

Equation (3) is the demand curve for the output of the k-th firm in terms of the ratio of its price to the industry average price. The term c_k will vary with variations in the general industry demand for the product.

At this stage it should be noted that, although Kalecki derives the demand curve for individual firms and the industry supply curve rather than the firm's pricing equation, the latter can be inferred from the analysis. In "pure imperfect competition" short-period equilibrium will require marginal cost (m_k) to be equated to marginal revenue (m_r). Under these conditions the latter will be equal to $(1 - 1/e_k)$. Therefore, for a profit-maximizing entrepreneur in short-period equilibrium (as it appears in Kalecki, 1939–40):

$$m_k = p_k(1 - 1/e_k). \tag{4}$$

From (4), the price equation can be derived:

$$p_k = m_k e_k/(e_k - 1). \tag{5}$$

The pricing equation underlying this analysis is similar to that referred to in the discussion of the conditions under which the markup is equal to the inverse of the firm's own-price point elasticity of demand. That is, the two pricing equations will coincide only in a static equilibrium framework where the firm knows (or can estimate) its demand curve and in the absence of advertising. This is the case only in Kalecki (1939–40), but not in his other works.

By equating short-period marginal costs with short-period marginal revenues, assuming that marginal cost curves are horizontal or increasing and that the coefficient c_k bears a definite relationship to the general level of demand for the industry's output, Kalecki derives the industry's supply curve. From this Kalecki (1939–40, p. 97) concludes that:

> (1) the supply curve is horizontal or increasing;
>
> (2) a rise in the prices of prime factors causes all ordinates of the supply curve to increase more or less in the same proportion as an appropriate index of these prices;
>
> (3) when market imperfection increases the supply curve usually shifts upwards.

In the case of oligopoly, Kalecki (1939–40, p. 97) argues that price is set in such a way that marginal revenue is greater than marginal cost:

> He does not reduce his price below this level because he assumes that this will induce his competitors to reduce their prices and so the average price, sufficiently to render his operation unprofitable. But neither does he raise the price above this level because he assumes that his competitors will not raise their prices sufficiently to make *this* operation profitable.

This argument, based on the model in Hall and Hitch (1951), has serious shortcomings related to the fact that at the relevant point marginal revenue is undefined, due to the kink in the demand curve at that point. If this were not the case, it is unclear why the price charged would not be at the point where marginal cost equalled marginal revenue, as this would be the profit-maximizing point for each firm.

The degree of oligopoly is defined by the ratio:

$$a_k = p_k/m_k(1 - 1/e_k) \qquad a_k > 1 \tag{6}$$

while the price is determined by:

$$p_k = m_k a_k(e_k/[e_k - 1]). \tag{7}$$

Kalecki points out that the entrepreneur will not know his actual elasticity of demand: "In fact, he has only a vague idea on this subject, which may diverge substantially from the actual position" (1939–40, p. 98). Therefore Kalecki advocates replacing e_k with w_k, which is the entrepreneur's estimate of the former (see Basile and Salvadori, 1984–85, p. 251), so we replace (7) with:

$$p_k = m_k a_k(w_k/[w_k - 1]). \tag{8}$$

Similarly, the entrepreneur will be "ignorant . . . as regards the precise nature of his marginal cost function" (Kalecki, 1939–40, pp. 98–99):

> It is obvious that for the purpose of the preceding argument we must attribute to the marginal cost *m* not its actual value but what the entrepreneur considers it to be; and that in consequence the relevant marginal cost curve is often horizontal up to the point of the full use of equipment.

Finally, Kalecki incorporates selling costs, not, as in his earlier papers, as a deduction from price, but now as an addition to marginal costs. This was probably due to the problems of analyzing price in terms of elasticity if selling costs are deducted from price.[6]

[6]The same analysis of pricing is used in Kalecki (1940—see pp. 34–37).

Kalecki concluded that (1939–40, p. 99):

> the supply curve shifts upward if there is an increase in market imperfection, in the degree of oligopoly or in the rate of prime selling costs. All other properties of this supply curve are . . . the same as deduced above.

The ''degree of oligopoly'' is determined by the ratio of marginal revenue to marginal cost, where marginal costs include ''marginal selling costs'' (Kalecki, 1939–40, pp. 97–99). In order to obtain empirical results, Kalecki simplifies the analysis, by introducing the ''reduced supply curve,'' which related reduced prices (''ratios of commodity price to the index of prime factor-prices'') and reduced outputs—which compares output with that produced by the equipment of the base year (p. 100). Kalecki then shows that this relation is very similar to the ratio of proceeds to prime costs. The ''quasi supply curve'' is defined as ''representing the functional connection between the ratio of proceeds to prime costs and reduced output'' (p. 103), and this was the proxy Kalecki utilized to investigate ''the reduced supply curve.'' These were the ratios, independent of the argument earlier in the text, which were used by Kalecki to determine aspects of distribution. At the end of the article, insights into distribution are reached, not from the basis of the theoretical discussion, but rather from the manipulation of ratios that have been simplified to yield empirical results.

In Kalecki (1939–40) and Kalecki (1941), an initial attempt was made to use the tools of ''orthodox'' microeconomic theory. Unfortunately, Kalecki's use of these tools is unsatisfactory as he makes numerous errors,[7] is ambiguous and inconsistent.[8] Some examples (all from Kalecki, 1939–40) are presented below.

[7]One example is Kalecki's use of marginal revenue in a situation in which marginal revenue is undefined.

[8]One inconsistency involves obtaining equation (2) (Kalecki, 1939–40, p. 92) from the positive definition of the elasticity of demand, namely:

$$e_k = do_k/dp_k \cdot p_k/o_k$$

where e is the elasticity of demand for the product of the k-th firm, and p and o are that firm's price and output, respectively.

On the other hand, equation (3) requires the ''negative'' definition of the elasticity of demand:

$$e_k = -do_k/dp_k \cdot p_k/o_k$$

to be used.

1. In the case of "pure imperfect competition" where there is a very large number of firms, it is legitimate to fix the average price of all firms ($\bar{p}$), while the price of one firm varies. But in the case of oligopoly, any variation in one firm's price will influence that average, especially due to the interrelationship of prices assumed by Kalecki. Therefore, in his analysis of oligopoly, Kalecki is incorrect in utilizing results obtained under the assumption of "pure imperfect competition," where that result depends on the average price being fixed while the individual price can vary.

2. Kalecki defines elasticity, in absolute terms, in the conventional way. That is:

$$e_k = do_k/dp_k \cdot p_k/o_k.$$

The elasticity referred to, however, is not the usual point elasticity of own-price demand; it is the elasticity with respect to the ratio of own-price to industry average price (own/industry elasticity). This creates problems. For example, if both own-price and the industry price change in the same proportion (so that there is no change in the ratio) with no change in the firm's output, then the own/industry elasticity will remain unchanged while the own-price elasticity will vary. Therefore Kalecki's use of elasticity concepts can be seen to be highly ambiguous.

3. The concept of "industry" is taken for granted. This may be reasonable if the industry under consideration consists of single product firms producing a homogeneous output. However, where the products of firms are differentiated in the eyes of consumers then problems with defining an industry become extremely complex.[9] Kalecki does not come to grips with these issues.

To show this, consider the definition of the marginal revenue (MR_k) of the k-th firm:

$$MR_k = d(p_k o_k)/do_k = p_k + o_k \cdot dp_k/do_k$$
$$= p_k\,(1 + o_k/p_k \cdot dp_k/do_k).$$

Substituting $e_k = -do_k/dp_k \cdot p_k/o_k$, we obtain the following:

$$MR_k = p_k(1 - 1/e_k)$$

which is the expression utilized by Kalecki to derive equation (3).

[9]The difficulty of defining either the industry or the commodity where there is product differentiation has been well documented (see Kriesler, 1987, pp. 11–13; 24–26).

In addition to these logical problems, Kalecki himself questions the usefulness of some of the concepts. He admits that the entrepreneur will only have a "vague idea" of "the actual elasticity of demand for his product in terms of the ratio of his price to average price" and of the "precise nature of his marginal cost function." Further, these vague ideas "may diverge substantially from the actual position" (1939–40, p. 98). In the case of marginal cost this does not represent a problem, as marginal cost can be assumed to be horizontal. But for marginal revenue, there is no such "easy" solution.

It may be that these errors were pointed out, or realized by Kalecki, and played some role in his "abandoning" of these articles. In any case, he did not make further reference to them. The use of the tools of "orthodox" microeconomic theory was not repeated in any of Kalecki's later works. In addition, the attempt by Kalecki, in these articles, to incorporate into his analysis the different market classifications defined by the contemporary literature was discarded. In his next major work on the subject (Kalecki, 1943) no distinction is made between the types of imperfect competition which are treated under the general head of "conditions of market imperfection and oligopoly." The distinction does not reappear in subsequent works where such situations are described as "semi-monopolistic" (see, for example, Kalecki, 1954, p. 13).

For all these reasons, then, it appears that Kalecki abandoned these early articles. They represent a digression that led nowhere and hence were discarded, having little influence on his subsequent analysis. The main theme, in terms of his pricing theory, is taken up again in 1943 with the publication of *Studies in Economic Dynamics*.

4. The analyses of price determination in Kalecki's later works

In the analyses of price determinations in Kalecki (1943), Kalecki (1954), and Kalecki (1971b), the "Kaleckian approximations" of constant average variable and marginal costs up to the level of full capacity, and of the existence of excess capacity as the general rule in the manufacturing sector, play important roles. The concept of industry which plays an important role in each of these is not adequately defined.[10] In

[10]Kalecki (1943) proposes a definition of industry based on the interdependence of both cost and price. Neither criteria separately gives an unambiguous definition of an industry; and, to a certain extent they are mutually exclusive. Kalecki (1954) simply talks about "firms producing similar products," while the issue is not discussed at all in Kalecki (1971a). See Kriesler (1987, pp. 60–64).

Kalecki (1943), "the firms fix the prices of their products, taking into consideration the mobility of customers (market imperfection) and the influence of their own prices on those of their rivals (oligopoly)" (p. 10); average variable costs also play a role in price determination through their influence on "gross margins" (profits and overheads). "In view of the uncertainties faced in the process of price fixing," Kalecki (1954, p. 12) explicitly states that he does not assume "that the firm attempts to maximize its profits in any precise sort of manner":[11]

> In fixing the price the firm takes into consideration its average prime costs and the prices of other firms producing similar products.

In Kalecki (1954) the mobility of customers arising from the heterogeneity of products was not seen as exerting an influence on the pricing decisions of entrepreneurs independently of the general interdependence among firms. In the explicit formulation of the pricing equation (equation 9), an important variable is $\bar{p}$, the average price of industry (p. 15), which only makes "sense" if the "industry" is adequately defined. This is reiterated in Kalecki (1971b, p. 160):

> Each firm in an industry arrives at the price of its product by "marking up" its direct cost consisting of average cost of wages *plus* raw materials in order to cover overheads and achieve profits. But this mark-up is dependent on "competition," i.e. on [the] relation of the ensuing price to the weighted average price of this product for the industry as a whole.

For Kalecki, average (prime) costs are the basis on which pricing decisions are made, and such decisions will reflect the competitiveness ("degree of monopoly") of the economic environment facing the decision maker. Kalecki reasons that the relationship between price and cost should reflect such factors. In Kalecki (1938) and Kalecki (1939a) this relationship was formalized as the "degree of monopoly." In Kalecki (1943), rigorous analysis results in a very similar formulation, with the title of "percentage gross margins."

One aspect of Kalecki's 1943 definition of an industry required that the changes in unit prime costs of the firms in an industry be similar. In an industry with n firms, the n prices charged by the firms for their product are denoted as $p_1, p_2, \ldots, p_r, \ldots, p_n$; and the average prime costs as $a_1, a_2, \ldots, a_r, \ldots, a_n$. For the k-th firm, the margin of

[11]This point seems to have been missed in Fine and Murfin (1984), who stress the importance of profit maximizing for the "Kaleckian tradition" (see, for example, p. 101).

profits plus overheads is equal to $(p_k - a_k)$, which Kalecki calls the "gross margins," while $[(p_k - a_k)/p_k]$, which corresponds to the measure of the degree of monopoly in Kalecki (1938, 1939a), is called the "percentage gross margins." Kalecki shows that if the average costs of all the firms in the industry change proportionately, prices will react in such a way that there will be no change in percentage gross margins. After examining the implications of a change in the conditions of market imperfection (transport costs), Kalecki concludes "that with a given relation of average costs within the industry, and on condition that no firm is working up to capacity, the percentage gross margins $[(p_k - a_k)/p_k]$ reflect changes in the state of market imperfection and oligopoly" (1943, p. 11). The concept of the percentage gross margins is then refined by Kalecki and used to analyze the determination of distributive shares.

In Kalecki (1954), the parameters defining the pricing decision of the firm are the firm's average prime costs and the interrelationship with the prices of other firms producing "similar products." This is embodied in the following equation from Kalecki (1954):

$$p = mu + n\bar{p} \tag{9}$$

where

p is the firm's price,
u is the firm's unit prime cost,
$\bar{p}$ is the weighted average price of all firms producing "similar" products, "weighted by the respective outputs and inclusive of the firm in question" (p. 12n), and
m, n are positive coefficients.

Clearly, for $\bar{p}$ to be at all meaningful the "industry" or relevant group must be adequately defined. If $n\bar{p}$ is interpreted as expressing the influence of the prices of other firms producing "similar products," then conceptual problems arise with Kalecki's method of weighting prices. The first problem results from consideration of what the most suitable weighting system would be. On the interpretation of $n\bar{p}$ stated above, the appropriate weights for the calculation of $\bar{p}$ for each firm would be related to the extent to which each firm is seen as a competitor. Firms which are "nearer" to the firm in question in terms cf competitiveness (cf. Kaldor, 1934) should have a higher weight than firms which are "farther." Only rarely will such a weighting system be equivalent to the one proposed by Kalecki, which required weighting on the basis primarily of output; this can only be regarded as a proxy. There is a further problem, however, with Kalecki's weighting system. The weighting of a firm's price by its output introduces bias into the calculation because output is not independent of price. This problem was emphasized by Sylos-Labini (1969), where the difference between large firms and small firms is qualitative as well as quantitative, resulting from technological discontinuities: "Only large firms can apply certain methods, both technical and organizational, and only large firms can realize certain economies of scale" (p. 35). Therefore a distinction can be drawn between the extremes of large, dominant firms with high output technologies operating at low cost and charging prices below the industry average, and small firms with lower output and hence higher costs and charging higher than average prices. It follows that bias, in the measure of the industry's average price, is introduced resulting from this correlation between a firm's price and the weight accorded it (i.e., output).

Finally, problems result from the inclusion, in the calculation of $\bar{p}$, of the "firm in question." It must be assumed that the firm's price used to calculate $\bar{p}$ is a datum, namely, the actual price charged by that firm, as opposed to p, which is a decision variable. Nevertheless, there is an incongruity because, according to equation (9), the price charged by a firm can further influence that firm's pricing decision. Consider, for example, the effects of a decline in the unit prime costs of a single firm—assuming this has no effect on other firms. By equation (9) this will lead to a reduction in that firm's price. This in turn will cause a reduction in the industry average price $\bar{p}$, causing a subsequent reduction in p. Again this reduces $\bar{p}$. This process continues until eventually it converges to a new equilibrium.[12] Movements along the equilibrium path are generated solely by changes in the firm's price and the influence of those changes on the industry average price. It is unlikely that the firm would take so long to adjust to changes in its own costs. Even if other firms react, so there are other influences on the industry average price, each firm will continue to be, at least partially, influenced by its own price. In an industry where all the firms' price equations are of the same type as (9), then any change in the price charged by one firm, because of its impact on the industry average price, will cause changes

[12]For proof of convergence to equilibrium, see Basile and Salvador (1984–85, Appendix).

in the price of all firms. This will continue with a long adjustment process converging to a new equilibrium. The problem with this scenario is that it does not conform to evidence (both empirical and theoretical) which suggests relative price stability in oligopolistic industries.

For equation (9), Kalecki ''postulates'' $n < 1$. To justify this, he considers a firm for which $p = \bar{p}$; then:

$$p = mu + np \tag{10}$$

$$(1 - n)p = mu$$

$$p = \frac{mu}{1 - n}.$$

Now, given: $mu > 0$ and $p > 0$, this means that, for that firm, n must lie between zero and one ($0 < n < 1$).

In the general price equation (9), m and n reflect different influences on price. The symbol m reflects the markup, which is an indication of those influences on price resulting from considerations of general competitiveness, with the important exception of the interdependence of the firms within the industry. The symbol n reflects the influence on price of the interdependence of the firms within the industry. It should be noted that it is mathematically possible for n to be greater than 1 for any firm whose price is greater than the industry average price ($\bar{p}$). However, economically this is unlikely as it implies that the firm under consideration is extremely influenced by the other firms—in which case it would be unlikely to charge so high a price.[13]

[13]Asimakopulos disputes Kalecki's assertion that $n < 1$. ''In situations where price is set by a price leader and followed by others, n would be equal to one for the price followers and thus m would be equal to zero'' (1975, p. 317). Because this relates to homogeneous oligopoly, it is not a criticism of Kalecki, who concentrated on differentiated oligopoly. However, a differentiated model is discussed in a footnote: ''This conclusion also holds when there is product differentiation. The price equation for a price follower would still have m equal to zero, with

$$p_F = p_L + d \quad \text{or} \quad p_F = (1 + d)p_L$$

where p_F and p_L represent the prices of the follower and the leader and d is the recognized price differential, expressed either in absolute terms, or as a ratio, whichever is appropriate'' (p. 317n). However, Asimakopulos' pricing model describes a different market situation from that envisaged by Kalecki, and the two can be reconciled if Kalecki's assumptions are replaced by: $0 \leq n \leq 1$, $m \geq 1$, $0 < \bar{n} < 1$ and $\bar{m} > 1$. See Basile and Salvadori (1984–85, pp. 254–255).

The important difference between the analysis of price determination in Kalecki (1943) and that in Kalecki (1954) is the explicit inclusion, in the price equations of the latter, of the term reflecting the interdependence of the firms within an industry. In order to calculate the industry's average price ($\bar{p}$), the industry must be clearly defined. This is not the case in the analysis of Kalecki (1954), where the definition of industry is not stated precisely.[14]

5. "Class Struggle and the Distribution of National Income"

Although the text of Kalecki (1954) was reprinted in a second edition in 1965 and in Kalecki (1971a), his dissatisfaction with this approach is apparent in the version of the analysis contained in his final paper on distribution (Kalecki, 1971b), where the measure reflecting the degree of monopoly in Kalecki (1954) is substantially modified. Firms determine their product's price (p) by "marking up" direct (or prime) costs (u). The markup $[(p - u)/u]$ is itself determined by the interdependence (or "competition") of the firms in the "industry," which is reflected in the ratio of the firm's price (p) to the weighted average price of the industry ($\bar{p}$), so:

(11)[15] $$(p - u)/u = f(\bar{p}/p)$$

By manipulating equation (11), Kalecki obtains:

$$p = u[1 + f(\bar{p}/p)].$$

[14]The analysis of price determination in these later papers is important as it provides the starting point for Kalecki's analysis of distribution. In addition, Kalecki's analysis of price determination has had an important impact on economic theory. Many important works have been significantly influenced by Kalecki's price analysis. For example, Baran and Sweezy (1966), Steindl (1952; 1979), Sylos-Labini (1969; 1974; 1979; 1979a), Robinson (1956), and Cowling (1983) have all acknowledged their debt to Kalecki's work on prices.

[15]This equation is a weak form of equation (10) and can be derived as follows:

(10) $$p = mu + n\bar{p}$$

$$1 = m(u/p) + n(\bar{p}/p)$$

$$u/p = 1/m[1 - n(\bar{p}/p)]$$

$$(p - u)/u = [n(\bar{p}/p) - (1 - m)]/[1 - n(\bar{p}/p)]$$

$$= f(\bar{p}/p).$$

I am indebted to A. Asimakopulos and R. Rowthorn for this point. See also Basile and Salvadori (1984–85, p. 255).

As Kalecki argues, "f is an increasing function: the lower is p in relation to $\bar{p}$, the higher will be fixed the mark up" (1971b, p. 160).[16]

The inadequacy of Kalecki's concept of industry is of importance as the values of $\bar{p}$ and f are strongly influenced by the exact dimensions of the particular industry being analyzed.

Kalecki argues that the function f will vary for the various firms in the industry and will reflect "semi-monopolistic" influences and that increases in these influences are reflected by a higher f. Variations in prices among the firms in an industry result from differences in direct costs and in the function f.

According to Kalecki, with function f constant, proportionate changes in all direct costs will lead to proportionate changes in all prices. This follows from equation (11), as $\bar{p}/p$ will not change. If, on the other hand, the direct cost of only one firm changes, then its price will change less than proportionately due to the change in the opposite direction of $\bar{p}/p$.

High profit levels,[17] if they accrue to only one firm, will increase the bargaining strength of trade unions for increased wages. If wage increases are granted, and there is no change in the function f, then by equation (11) prices will rise, providing the incentive for new wage demands. This is likely to continue, thereby eroding the competitiveness of the firm concerned. The only solution is the acceptance of a lower value for f and hence a lower markup.

It is important to note that in Kalecki (1971b) the basic analysis of distribution is conducted in terms of macroeconomic aggregates such as total profits, aggregate wages, and total output. The main role of the "microanalysis" is in determining the likely changes in price resulting from changes in these aggregates, in particular, of trade union pressure. In other words, from 1954, Kalecki made no new attempts at analyzing pricing or the relative distributive shares utilizing microeconomic concepts. The reasons for this are never given, but can be deduced from the arguments presented in this paper, as follows. First, Kalecki's earliest work on pricing theory did not adequately incorporate the economic environment facing firms, nor the influence of competing firms. Second, Kalecki was unable to provide an analytically

[16]It should be noted that f in this case is determined by the same factors as m and n and is not, therefore, determined solely by trade union activity, as Cowling (1982, p. 100) seems to suggest.

[17]The important variable is profit level, not markup, as a high markup is consistent with a low profit level if, for example, overheads are high.

adequate definition of industry, despite the importance of this for his later works on pricing and distribution. Finally, Kalecki's attempts to use the tools of orthodox analysis in his pricing equations, in Kalecki (1939–40, 1941), contained analytical problems which led to their being abandoned.

It can be seen that, although in all versions of Kalecki's pricing analysis the firm sets its price on the basis of unit prime costs, it is only in the later versions that industry average price enters as an independent variable. Further, contrary to the arguments of Basile and Salvadori, we have seen that Kalecki's pricing analysis underwent substantial modification and development.

REFERENCES

American Economic Association. *Readings in Price Theory*. London: George Allen and Unwin Ltd., 1953.

Asimakopulos, A. "A Kaleckian Theory of Income Distribution." *Canadian Journal of Economics*, 1975, *8*, 313–333.

———. *An Introduction to the Theory of Micro-economics*. Toronto: Oxford University Press, 1978.

Baran, P. A., and Sweezy, P. *Monopoly Capital*. England: Penguin Books, 1966. Reprinted 1970, 1973.

Basile, L., and Salvadori, N. "Kalecki's Pricing Theory." *Journal of Post Keynesian Economics*, Winter 1984-85, 7 (2), 249-262.

Breit, W., and Hochman, H. M., eds. *Readings in Microeconomics*. 2nd ed. New York: Holt, Rinehart & Winston Inc., 1971.

Chamberlin, E. H. *The Theory of Monopolistic Competition*. First published in 1933. 4th ed. Cambridge, Mass.: Harvard University Press, 1942.

Cowling, K. *Monopoly Capitalism*. London: The Macmillan Press Ltd., 1982.

Davidson, P. *Theories of Aggregate Income Distribution*. New Brunswick, N.J.: Rutgers University Press, 1959.

Dobb, M. *Theories of Value and Distribution since Adam Smith*. First published in 1973. Cambridge: Cambridge University Press, paperback edition, 1975.

Fine, B., and Murfin, A. *Macroeconomics and Monopoly Capitalism*. Sussex: Wheatsheaf Books Ltd., 1984.

Hahn, F. H. *The Share of Wages in National Income*. London: Weidenfeld and Nicolson, 1972.

Hall, R., and Hitch, C. J. "Price Theory and Business Behaviour." *Oxford Economic Papers*, 1939, *2*, 12–45. Reprinted in Wilson and Andrews (1951, pp. 107–136).

Harrod, R. F. "Doctrines of Imperfect Competition." *Quarterly Journal of Economics*, 1934, *48*, 442–470. Reprinted in Harrod (1952, pp. 111–138).

———. *Economic Essays*. London: Macmillan and Co., 1952.

Hunt, E. K., and Schwartz, J. G., eds. *A Critique of Economic Theory*. Middlesex: Penguin Books, 1972.

Johnson, H. G. *The Theory of Income Distribution*. London: Gray-Mills Publishing Ltd., 1973.

Kaldor, N. "Mrs. Robinson's *Economics of Imperfect Competition*." *Economica*, 1934, N.S. *1*, 335-341.

———. "Alternative Theories of Distribution." *Review of Economic Studies*, 1955, *23*, 83-100. Reprinted in McCormick and Smith (1968, pp. 349-379).

Kalecki, M. "A Macrodynamic Theory of Business Cycles." *Econometrica*, 1935, *3*, 327-344.

———. "The Determinants of Distribution of National Income." *Econometrica*, 1938, *6*, 97-112.

———. *Essays in the Theory of Economic Fluctuations*. London: George Allen & Unwin Ltd., 1939a.

———. "Money and Real Wages, Part I (Theory)." First published in 1939b. Trans. from the Polish in Kalecki (1969, pp. 40-59).

———. "The Supply Curve of an Industry under Imperfect Competition." *Review of Economic Studies*, 1939-40, *7*, 91-112.

———. "A Theory of Long-Run Distribution of the Product of Industry." *Oxford Economic Papers*, 1941, N.S. (5), 31-41.

———. "Mr Whitman on the Concept of 'Degree of Monopoly': A Comment." *Economic Journal*, 1942, *52*, 121-127.

———. *Studies in Economic Dynamics*. London: George Allen & Unwin, 1943.

———. *Theory of Economic Dynamics*. London: George Allen & Unwin, 1954.

———. "Trend and the Business Cycle." 1968. Reprinted in Kalecki (1971a, pp. 165-183).

———. *Studies in the Theory of Business Cycles: 1933-1939*. Oxford: Basil Blackwell, 1969.

———. *Selected Essays on the Dynamics of the Capitalist Economy (1933-70)*. Cambridge: Cambridge University Press, 1971a.

———. "Class Struggle and Distribution of National Income." *Kyklos*, 1971b, *24*, 1-9. Reprinted in Kalecki (1971a, pp. 156-164).

King, J., and Regan, P. *Relative Income Shares*. London: The Macmillan Press Ltd., 1976.

Kriesler, P. *Kalecki's Microanalysis*. Cambridge: Cambridge University Press, 1987.

Lerner, A. "The Concept of Monopoly and the Measurement of Monopoly Power." *Review of Economic Studies*, 1934, *1*, 157-175. Reprinted in Breit and Hochman (1971, pp. 207-223).

McCormick, B. J., and Smith, E. O., eds. *The Labour Market*. Middlesex: Penguin Books, 1968. Reprinted in 1971.

Nuti, D. M. " 'Vulgar Economy' in the Theory of Income Distribution." *De Economist*, 1970, *118*, 363-369. Reprinted in Hunt and Schwartz (1972, pp. 222-232).

Reynolds, P. "Kalecki's Degree of Monopoly." *Journal of Post Keynesian Economics*, Spring 1983, *5* (3), 493-503.

Riach, P. A. "Kalecki's 'Degree of Monopoly' Reconsidered." *Australian Economic Papers*, 1971, *10*, 50-60.

Robinson, J. *The Economics of Imperfect Competition*. London: Macmillan, 1933.

———. *The Accumulation of Capital*. London: Macmillan, 1956.

———. "A Further Note." *Review of Economic Studies*, 1969, *36*, 260-262.

———. "Michal Kalecki on the Economics of Capitalism." *Oxford Bulletin of Economics and Statistics*, 1977, *39*, 7–18.

Rostow, W. W. *British Economy of the Nineteenth Century*. Oxford at the Clarendon Press, 1948.

Rowthorn, B. "Demand, Real Wages and Economic Growth." *Thames Papers in Political Economy*, 1981.

Sraffa, P. "On the Relations between Cost and Quantity Produced." *Annali di Economia*, 1925, *2*.

———. "The Laws of Returns under Competitive Conditions." *Economic Journal*, 1926, *36*, 535–550. Reprinted in American Economic Association (1953, pp. 180–197).

Steindl, J. *Small and Big Business*. Oxford: Basil Blackwood, 1945.

———. *Maturity and Stagnation in American Capitalism*. Oxford: Basil Blackwood, 1952.

———. "Stagnation Theory and Stagnation Policy." *Cambridge Journal of Economics*, 1979, *3*, 1–14.

Sylos-Labini, P. *Oligopoly and Technical Progress*. Rev. ed. Cambridge, Mass.: Harvard University Press, 1969.

———. *Trade Unions, Inflation and Productivity*. Surrey: Unwin Brothers Ltd., 1974.

———. "Industrial Pricing in the United Kingdom." *Cambridge Journal of Economics*, 1979a, *3*, 153–164.

———. "Prices and Income Distribution in Manufacturing Industry." *Journal of Post Keynesian Economics*, Fall 1979b, 2 (1), 3–25.

———. "Rigid Prices, Flexible Prices and Inflation." *Banca Nazionale del Lavoro Quarterly Review*, 1982 (140).

Wilson, T., and Andrews, P. W. S., eds. *Oxford Studies in the Price Mechanism*. Oxford: Clarendon Press, 1951. Reprinted in 1952.

[15]

Bulletin of Economic Research 43:3, 1991, 0307-3378 $2.00

KEYNES, KALECKI, RICARDIAN EQUIVALENCE, AND THE REAL BALANCE EFFECT

Robert W. Dimand

A. C. Pigou (1943) used the real balance effect to argue that the classical assumption of wage and price flexibility ensures full employment equilibrium, even in the case of a liquidity trap combined with perfectly interest-inelastic saving and investment. A sufficiently low price would make the real value of nominal assets high enough and consumers wealthy enough so that aggregate demand would equal potential output. John R. Presley (1986) has shown that J. M. Keynes displayed a clear grasp of the real balance effect as early as 1925, when Keynes corresponded with D. H. Robertson about drafts of Robertson (1926). Keynes and Robertson had recognized in 1925 that a change in the absolute price level would affect consumption by altering the real value of wealth, and had used this 'induced lacking' in stability analysis. If Keynes understood the real balance effect, why then did Keynes (1936) hold that an unemployment equilibrium is possible even with flexible wages and prices?

Examination of other writings by Keynes shows that his neglect of the real balance effect reflected an awareness of the very narrow range of assets to which the effect applies, combined with a recognition of other channels through which a lower price level would reduce effective demand, rather than increase it.

Keynes's reaction to the Pigou effect appears in his correspondence as editor of the *Economic Journal* with Michal Kalecki about Kalecki's 1944 comment on Pigou (1943). This correspondence was first published in 1979 in Polish translation in Kalecki's *Works*, of which an English edition is forthcoming, and is printed in an appendix to Patinkin (1982). Patinkin (1982) and Asimakopulos (1990) concentrate on earlier correspondence between Keynes and Kalecki rather than on the 1944 exchange.

Kalecki (1944) pointed out that since the Pigou effect concerned changes in net wealth, only bank debts backed by gold or other outside money were relevant, not bank debt backed by the loan portfolios of the banks. Keynes and Kalecki also agreed, 30 years before Barro (1974), that changes in the real value of the national debt would not affect consumption. Kalecki's letter to Keynes on 28 February 1944, concluded with the parenthetical remark that 'If the interest on [National] Debt is financed by taxation its existence does not affect the aggregate disposable income' (Patinkin (1982), p. 103). As Keynes wrote to Kalecki on 8 March 1944:

> Assuming that interest is paid on this out of taxation, it cannot affect the wealth of the community one way or another. Thus, it seems to me that Pigou is in reality depending entirely on the increase in the value of gold.
>
> The whole thing, however, is really too fantastic for words and scarcely worth discussing (Patinkin (1982), p. 103).

The market value of the public debt is the present discounted value of the stream of payments to be made on the debt, both interest and repayment of principal. If these payments are financed by taxation, the market value of the public debt would equal the present discounted value of the taxes that would have to be levied to make those payments. By agreeing that the size of the public debt does not affect consumption as long as payments on the debt are financed by taxation, Keynes and Kalecki held that the value of the public debt to bondholders would be just offset by the anticipated liability of taxpayers. Keynes had noted in the *General Theory* that rates of consumption reflect foreseen changes in wealth, with only unforeseen changes in wealth causing changes in consumption: 'The consumption of the wealth-owning class may be extremely susceptible to unforeseen changes in the money-value of its wealth' (Keynes (1936), ch. 8, pp. 92–3). Debt neutrality was, however, mentioned only in correspondence between Keynes and Kalecki, not in Kalecki's published note.

Writing to Kalecki on 22 February 1944, Keynes noted that the falling price level, during the period of transition to a new lower level, would raise the real rate of interest, so that 'People would save more, and not less, as Pigou assumes' (Patinkin (1982), p. 102). Another reason for dismissing the Pigou effect as 'too fantastic for words' had been offered by Keynes in 1931, in his Harris Foundation lectures in Chicago, when he argued that a rise in the real value of inside debt due to a reduction in prices, such as was then advocated by O. M. W. Sprague, would not be neutral:

> all this financial structure would be deranged by the adoption of Dr Sprague's proposal. A widespread bankruptcy, default, and repudiation of bonds would necessarily ensue. Banks would be in jeopardy (Keynes (1931), p. 33; (1973), Vol. XIII, p. 361).

If the lower price level had not been anticipated when the nominal debts were contracted, the increased value of inside debt would depress aggregate demand. As the volume of inside debt far exceeds the amount of outside money, the Pigou effect would be swamped. Keynes has thus discussed in 1931 what James Tobin (1980, pp. 9–11) terms, in reference to Irving Fisher (1933), the Fisher effect. In the *General Theory*, Keynes (1936, ch. 19, p. 262) noted the transfer of wealth from entrepreneurs to rentiers due to lower prices could depress consumption.

Keynes (1936) has been criticized, from the standpoint of the permanent income and life cycle theories of consumption, for relating consumption to current income rather than to wealth. His discussion of the real balance effect shows that he recognized the link between wealth and consumption. This recognition also lay behind his wartime comment that 'A remission of taxation on which people could only rely for an indefinitely short period might have very limited effect in stimulating their consumption' (Keynes (1980), Vol. XXVII, p. 320).

The rejection of the real balance effect by Keynes and Kalecki was not based on any failure to understand the relationship of asset-holding to consumption. Their position reflected a distinction between inside and outside assets and an argument that government debt is not net wealth, as well as a concern by Keynes with the nonneutrality of unanticipated changes in the real value of inside debt.

Department of Economics, Brock University,
St Catherines, Ontario, Canada L2S 3A1

Received June 1990,
revision accepted
September 1990

REFERENCES

Asimakopulos, A. (1990). 'Kalecki and Keynes: Their Correspondence', *History of Political Economy*, Vol. XXII, No. 1, pp. 49–64.

Barro, R. J. (1974). 'Are Government Bonds Net Wealth?' *Journal of Political Economy*, Vol. LXXXII, No. 6, pp. 1095–118.

Fisher, I. (1933). 'The Debt-Deflation Theory of Great Depressions', *Econometrica*, Vol. I, No. 4, pp. 337–57.

Kalecki, M. (1944). 'Professor Pigou on "The Classical Stationary State": A Comment', *Economic Journal*, Vol. LIV, No. 1, pp. 131–2.

Kalecki, M. (forthcoming). *Works*, ed. Jerzy Osiatynski, Oxford University Press, Oxford, Vol. I.

Keynes, J. M. (1931). 'An Economic Analysis of Unemployment', in Wright, Q. (ed.), *Unemployment as a World-Problem*, University of Chicago Press, Chicago, pp. 1–42; reprinted in Keynes, *Collected Writings*, ed. Robinson, E. A. G. and Moggridge, D. E., Vol. XIII, Cambridge University Press for Royal Economic Society, Cambridge, pp. 343–67.

Keynes, J. M. (1936). *The General Theory of Employment, Interest and Money*, Macmillan, London.

Keynes, J. M. (1980). *The Collected Writings of J. M. Keynes*, ed. Robinson, E. A. G. and Moggridge, D. E., Vol. XXVII, Cambridge University Press for Royal Economic Society, Cambridge.

Patinkin, D. (1982). *Anticipations of the General Theory? and Other Essays on Keynes*, University of Chicago Press, Chicago.

Pigou, A. C. (1943). 'The Classical Stationary State', *Economic Journal*, Vol. LIII, No. 4, pp. 343–51.

Presley, J. R. (1986). 'J. M. Keynes and the Real Balance Effect', *The Manchester School*, Vol. LIV, No. 1, pp. 22–30.

Robertson, D. H. (1926). *Banking Policy and the Price Level*, Westminster, P. S. King and Son.

Tobin, J. (1980). *Asset Accumulation and Economic Activity*, University of Chicago Press, Chicago.

Name Index

Pioneers in Economics

Section I: The Forerunners of Classical Economics

1. The Historiography of Economics
2. Aristotle (384–322 B.C.)
3. St Thomas Aquinas (1225–1274)
4. The Early Mercantilists
   Thomas Mun (1571–1641), Edward Misselden (1608–1634), Gerard de Malynes (1586–1623)
5. The Later Mercantilists
   Josiah Child (1603–1699) and John Locke (1632–1704)
6. Pre-Classical Economists Volume I
   Charles Davenant (1656–1714) and William Petty (1623–1687)
7. Pre-Classical Economists Volume II
   Pierre le Pesant Boisguilbert (1645–1714), George Berkeley (1685–1753), Baron de Montesquieu (1689–1755), Ferdinando Galiani (1727–1787), James Anderson (1739–1808), Dugald Stewart (1753–1828)
8. Pre-Classical Economists Volume III
   John Law (1671–1729) and Bernard Mandeville (1660–1733)
9. Richard Cantillon (1680–1734) and Jacques Turgot (1727–1781)
10. François Quesnay (1694–1774) Volumes I and II
11. David Hume (1711–1776) and James Steuart (1712–1780)

Section II: The Golden Age of Classical Economics

12. Adam Smith (1723–1790) Volumes I and II
13. Henry Thornton (1760–1815), Jeremy Bentham (1748–1832), James Lauderdale (1759–1839), Simonde de Sismondi (1773–1842)
14. David Ricardo (1772–1823)
15. Jean-Baptiste Say (1776–1832)
16. Thomas Robert Malthus (1766–1834) and John Stuart Mill (1806–1873)
17. Ramsay McCulloch (1789–1864), Nassau Senior (1790–1864), Robert Torrens (1780–1864)
18. Thomas Tooke (1774–1858), Mountifort Longfield (1802–1884), Richard Jones (1790–1855)

19. William Whewell (1794–1866), Dionysius Lardner (1793–1859), Charles Babbage (1792–1871)
20. George Scrope (1797–1876), Thomas Attwood (1783–1856), Edwin Chadwick (1800–1890), John Cairnes (1823–1875)
21. James Mill (1773–1836), John Rae (1796–1872), Edward West (1782–1828), Thomas Joplin (1790–1847)
22. James Wilson (1805–1860), Issac Butt (1813–1879), T. E. Cliffe Leslie (1827–1882)
23. Karl Marx (1818–1883)

Section III: Neoclassical Economics and its Critics

24. Johann von Thünen (1783–1850), Augustin Cournot (1801–1877), Jules Dupuit (1804–1866)
25. Leon Walras (1834–1910)
26. Carl Menger (1840–1921)
27. Eugen von Böhm-Bawerk (1851–1914) and Friedrich von Wieser (1851–1926)
28. Knut Wicksell (1851–1926)
29. Alfred Marshall (1842–1924) and Francis Edgeworth (1845–1926)
30. Gustav Schmoller (1838–1917) and Werner Sombart (1863–1941)
31. Dissenters
    Charles Fourier (1772–1837), Henri de St Simon (1760–1825), Pierre-Joseph Proudhon (1809–1865), John A. Hobson (1858–1940)
32. Thorstein Veblen (1857–1929)
33. Wesley Mitchell (1874–1948), John Commons (1862–1945), Clarence Ayres (1891–1972)
34. Henry George (1839–1897)
35. Vilfredo Pareto (1848–1923)

Section IV: Twentieth Century Economics

36. Arthur Pigou (1877–1959)
37. Frank Knight (1885–1972), Henry Simons (1899–1946), Joseph Schumpeter (1883–1950)
38. Edward Chamberlin (1899–1967)

39. Michal Kalecki (1899–1970)

40. Harold Hotelling (1895–1973), Lionel Robbins (1898–1984), Clark Warburton (1896–1979), John Bates Clark (1847–1938), Ludwig von Mises (1881–1973)

41. Irving Fisher (1867–1947), Arthur Hadley (1856–1930), Ragnar Frisch (1895–1973), Friedrich von Hayek (1899–1992), Allyn Young (1876–1929), Ugo Mazzola (1863–1899)

42. Harry Johnson (1923–1977)

43. Bertil Ohlin (1899–1979)

44. Piero Sraffa (1898–1983)

45. Joan Robinson (1903–1983) and George Shackle (1903–1992)

46. John Maynard Keynes (1883–1946) Volumes I and II